With the
compliments
of the
Canada Council

Avec les
hommages
du Conseil des
Arts du Canada

ANNE FRANCIS

An Autobiography

ANNE FRANCIS

An Autobiography by

FLORENCE BIRD

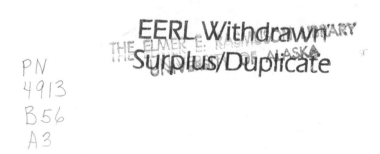
Clarke, Irwin & Company Limited, Toronto, Vancouver

For J. B.

ACKNOWLEDGEMENTS

Writing these reminiscences has been a valuable experience; it has added to my self-knowledge. I am grateful to Floyd Chalmers who persuaded me to write them, to Lise Rowntree who patiently and efficiently typed my illegible copy, to Ruth Gordon who read the galley proofs with professional expertise, and above all, to John Bird who always shared in the living and the writing.

CONTENTS

ANNE FRANCIS

An Autobiography

Prologue

The telephone rang and I answered it. I heard a crisp, secretarial voice.

"Mrs. Bird, this is the Prime Minister's office. The Prime Minister would like to speak to you. Please hold the line a minute."

For weeks I had been trying to get an interview with "Mike" Pearson for an article I was writing on Commonwealth relations, and was being given the run-around by his appointments' secretary. I was taken aback to hear that the P.M. wanted to speak to me himself. I thought that he was going to turn me down and wanted to make the blow as gentle as possible by doing it in person.

"Mrs. Bird, here is the Prime Minister on the line now."

I heard that unmistakable lisp.

"You think I'm phoning you about that interview you've been trying to get, but I'm not. I want you to be chairman of a Royal Commission on the Status of Women."

"Oh God," I said.

The Prime Minister laughed. I recovered myself and said, "Do you really think I can do it?"

"I wouldn't have asked you if I didn't think so. I'd like an answer as soon as possible because I want to make the announcement in the House right away. Come down to the office tomorrow morning and look at the terms of reference and tell me if you think you can carry them out. See you tomorrow. Good-bye."

A friend had come for tea that afternoon and when I went back to the living room she said, "You look awful. Has anything terrible happened?"

"I've had a shock," I said.

I was in two minds about accepting the appointment. I was enjoying life greatly. By coincidence, earlier that same afternoon I had received a telegram from a CBC program organizer saying that my outlines for two radio documentaries had been approved. That meant I could look forward to interesting research and trips to the United States and to Sweden when spring came.

Several of my friends had been chairmen of royal commissions, and I knew how exhausting, demanding and endless their work had been. My mind boggled at the thought of taking on a job charged with so much emotional dynamite. Selfishly I didn't want to take on a responsibility that would be bound to interfere with my personal life and that of my husband, J.B., John Bird, the Parliamentary columnist for *The Financial Post*.

On the other hand, for twenty years I had been writing with concern and dismay about what is happening to women, about the way women feel about themselves, and the way they are being treated in our society. In recent broadcasts I had supported the demands of Laura Sabia, that redoubtable champion of women's rights, who had threatened to lead a march of two million women on Parliament Hill if the government failed to set up a royal commission. I knew that inside the Cabinet Judy LaMarsh had been fighting a valiant campaign for a commission. (Canadian women owe a great deal to Judy for her stubborn insistence.)

For years I had also written and lectured about the need for women to stop being shrinking violets and not only to accept responsibility when it came their way, but to seek it out. I had long inveighed against the women who were unwilling to accept promotions because of "family obligations," meaning home, husband and children, since most men also have family obligations and yet are prepared to sacrifice evenings and weekends to the demands of public life.

Now my bluff had been called; it was up to me to put up or to shut up forever after.

I also knew that if I refused to serve on the commission I would be guilt-ridden, haunted all my remaining years by the faces of the women who over the years had helped to give me some understanding of their lives—so different from my own.

I thought of the women who had cleaned our houses and cooked for us in New York, Montreal and Winnipeg: of Kate Cox, with bent shoulders and gray hair, grown old while yet young, from too much child-bearing. Of Chrissy Wyatt, thin, pale, with crumbling teeth at the age of twenty. Of Maud Whiteley, with her Cockney cheer and humour, working, working, so proud of her clean, beautiful children. Of the girl from Barbados, heavy with unwanted child, singing a sad little tune as she lurched around the kitchen.

I thought of the girl who had committed an abortion on herself and who had cried out to me for help in the night. And I saw again, with nightmare memory, her pain-racked body and the blood-soaked towels and sheets in her bedroom, and wondered again, as I had then, how it was possible for one small body to lose so much blood and yet live.

I thought of the women of the 1930's lining up for the baskets of food we handed out to them in the basement of the church in Montreal. Of the courage, generosity, and unselfish team-work of the women volunteers in Winnipeg during the war. Of all the women in Canada relegated to badly paid, dull jobs, requiring only a fraction of their brains and abilities. Of the intelligent, conscientious women passed over again and again when men are promoted over them.

I felt I had an obligation to help such women. On the other hand I did not want to give up my delightful, interesting life as a broadcaster with frequent assignments in Europe.

After I was alone I paced up and down the apartment. I was torn by conflicting feelings.

I had often quoted my friend Elmer Davis, the American broadcaster, who had written that there is an obligation for older people to be courageous, to fight for the things they believe in, because they haven't much time left, and also because they have fewer personal commitments, fewer hostages to fortune, than young people. For most of my life I had written and lectured in defence of human rights and especially the rights of women, but now that I had the opportunity to do more than write and talk I was tempted to dig myself in.

That morning a Cabinet minister's wife had telephoned to ask J.B. and me to a small dinner—organized, she said, at the last minute. When J.B. came home late, I sat on the end of his bed while he changed his clothes, and recited the arguments, pro and con, which I had been debating in my mind that afternoon.

"What do you think I should do?" I finally asked.

"It's a decision you'll have to make yourself," he said.

I began to ask a stream of questions which he did not answer as he tied his tie and brushed his hair. Would it be fair to him if I took on such a demanding job that would require me to be away from home a great deal? Did he think my health was up to the strain? Was I too old? Would I be a good chairman? Wouldn't someone else do a better job? Wasn't I more useful as a commentator?

After awhile he said, "There is just one question you should be putting to yourself. If the Prime Minister of Canada asks you to take on a tremendous, difficult job to help half the people in the country, can you say no to him?"

It was a loaded question. He did influence me and he knew it. But then I had known all along while I argued against myself that I could not say no.

That night I found myself seated between two Cabinet ministers, and realized that the small party had been planned in order to give them a chance to persuade me to accept the appointment.

Both men wanted me to take on the job. But one of them was concerned that I might wreck my career as a writer and broadcaster on national and international affairs if I spent three or four years devoted entirely to the rights of women. I knew that I could not keep on broadcasting while I chaired the Commission, but I had not fully realized that when the report was completed I might no longer be in demand as a news commentator.

I was not worried by the possibility, however. I felt, intuitively, that there would be something else that I would want to try to do when the Commission's work was completed. I have always believed that it is unwise to attempt to go back in life, that it is important to keep on growing and to take on new ventures at different stages of a career. I had no idea what path I would follow later on but I was confident I would find it when the time came.

Having reached a decision, I was excited and hopeful about the reforms the Commission might be able to bring about. I was already at work asking questions—this time positive questions—in order to find out what was expected of me as chairman and how best to zoom in on the new job.

The next morning I went up to the Prime Minister's office in the Centre Block of the Parliament Buildings and Mary MacDonald, his invaluable executive assistant, showed me the terms of reference. While I was reading them, Pearson, in hat and coat, looked around the door and said, "Well, have you made up your mind?"

"Yes," I said. "I'll do it."

"Good. I'll announce it this week."

He shook hands with me and was gone.

And so it happened. At eleven o'clock on Friday morning, February

3, 1967—the Prime Minister announced to the House of Commons that the government was setting up the Royal Commission on the Status of Women in Canada with me as chairman, the other six members to be announced later.

I was at home writing when, at a quarter past eleven, the telephone began to ring. It continued to ring all day as reporters called from Parliament Hill, Quebec City, Montreal, Toronto, London, Ontario, and points west. Within half an hour French and English television teams arrived at our door and came rushing in with cameras, lights and rolls of cables. They pushed me and the furniture around, and in due course I was interviewed by a succession of reporters. Most of the women asked serious questions. Some of the men were also sincerely interested, but others were ill-informed and self-consciously flippant. As the morning wore on, radio broadcasters burst in with tape-recorders. A Canadian Press photographer began flashing lights all over the place. All sorts of people telephoned with congratulations, with advice, with ridicule, with warnings. Life in the apartment was totally disrupted. By bedtime I was speechless, my throat dry and constricted, my mind repeating itself like a phonograph record when the needle has become stuck in a groove, from having said the same things over and over again in two languages.

At six the next morning the telephone rang. J.B. answered it. A very drunk, very angry truck driver was on the other end of the line demanding that something be done about the rights of men. The telephone attacks went on for about ten days and then tapered off as the Commission slipped out of the headlines, but there were always a great many calls either from women asking for help, or from women who, because they themselves were comfortable and satisfied, maintained that there was no need for any change in the status of women.

One woman was a regular cocktail-hour caller, probably because that was the time when she downed her fourth drink. She kept telling me how normal she was, how normal her husband was, how normal her children were. And then she would end her recitation by saying, "Drop dead! Ha-ha. You won't be able to trace this call. Drop dead!" She was a nuisance because she would call several times in an evening. J.B. finally shut her up by pretending he was deaf, and saying at least half a dozen times, "Please, speak louder, I can't hear you. Please speak louder," until, in spite of being sozzled, she was permanently silenced by the sound of her own voice shouting inanities and insults louder and louder, over and over again.

During the first few days after the announcement reactions to the Commission were front-page stuff and the subject of leading editorials. The *Globe and Mail,* the *Toronto Star,* the *Toronto Telegram,* the *Montreal Star,* the *Winnipeg Tribune* and the *Winnipeg Free Press* took the Commission seriously, but with reservations, hoping sceptically that it might perhaps do some good. However, there was a general consensus in editorials across the country that the report would be pigeon-holed and forgotten. It also was often suggested that the Commission was a political gimmick to allow women to let off steam and to appease Judy LaMarsh and Laura Sabia's cohorts—a suspicion which was probably based on some truth.

It was evident that many newspapermen regarded women as garrulous fools incapable of agreeing about anything or bringing out a sensible report. Some columnists obviously saw women chiefly as sex objects. Others believed that the place of women was in the kitchen. Several seized the occasion to try to be funny at the expense of "the ladies."

A *Winnipeg Free Press* writer, F.S. Manor, wrote, "I believe that the Royal Commission is ill-conceived, superfluous and may have ominous results. It should be disbanded before a lot of bossy, ugly women spoil our lovely world."

Frank Tumpane, a *Toronto Telegram* columnist, wrote, "Now let's sit back, fellas, and see if they can agree on just what it is they do want."

Charles Lynch, of the Southam News Services, managed to be funny while showing a sympathetic, intelligent understanding of the situation. In his syndicated column he wrote:

> Forge on girls, victory is in our grasp,
> Hail to Judy LaMarsh,
> All praise to Lester B. Pearson,
> And strength to the good right arm of Anne Francis, otherwise known as Florence Bird, Chairman of the Royal Commission on the Status of Women.

> Now women can switch on their brains and prepare to take their rightful place in our society—all aspects of our society including politics, labour, business and the professions.

> For generations women have been letting their minds go to seed during prime years, accepting the back seat in the land of stag parties and being bulldozed by men of limited wit, limited energy, limited horizons, limited ambitions.

> Brilliant in youth, our women have permitted themselves to be put out to pasture in the prime years, only to be revived later in life

when they outlive men and inherit their holdings, whereupon they accept male advice on how those holdings should be administered.

They need have nothing to fear but other women. If they can get over the mistrust, if not loathing that they feel for one another, our national life will be enriched beyond measure.

I thought that last paragraph was poppycock, and still do. I know from personal experience about the generosity, kindness and loyalty of many women toward other women. I saw the way women worked together as teams in Winnipeg during the war. Personally I have received great affection, support and lasting friendship from a number of women. My life has been greatly enriched by my women friends—as much so as it has been by the men who have been my friends.

The *Ottawa Journal* made one of those shallow street surveys which I should not have taken seriously but which did depress me. The front-page article about it began as follows:

"Amazing."
"Incredible."
"A waste of money."
"Won't change my wife's status."
More than 70% of those polled in a *Journal* survey said they felt the problem would accomplish little.
"It's a good idea," was the cry of the minority, and not surprisingly most of them were women.
"I don't believe it. It's not the kind of thing I'd expect to hear."
"It's ridiculous, expensive and a waste of my money."

A number of prominent women pooh-poohed the Commission. Charlotte Whitton said, "It's the most fantastically inexcusable thing I've ever heard. I've been opposed to it from the beginning. The door is open to women if they weren't sissy-prissies making sandwiches for political meetings." (Yet, when the Commission's report came out, Charlotte did not attack it. She even made me feel that she was rather proud of it, and she asked me to autograph a copy, which she sent to the library of Smith College, one of the many universities that have given her an honorary degree.)

The President of the Vancouver Council of Women was quoted as saying, "Women have been around for a long time, and if they haven't managed to establish themselves by now, I can't see the point of energy being expended on the Royal Commission."

Many of the TV and radio broadcasters were either condescending or saw the Commission as a great joke.

It was not a heartening reception. But as time went on, I reached the conclusion that the lack of understanding and the strangely outdated attitudes expressed by so many people only indicated that the Commission was needed much more than I had at first realized.

To balance the picture, my colleagues in both the English and French press gave me, personally, more-than-generous treatment, and endorsed my appointment as chairman even when they had doubts about the need for the Commission. That personal encouragement was the greatest help to me.

In the months that followed—indeed all during the long grind of the Commission's work—I often thought how strange it was that I should find myself tackling a task concerned with the future of all women. And I frequently said to myself, "You've come a long way from Pine Street in Philadelphia."

The House

It was a "good address"—1732 Pine Street, Philadelphia.

Soon after my mother and father were married in 1900, they bought the house. All four of their children were born in the second-floor front bedroom and my father died in the same room twenty-five years later.

It was a large red brick house, one in a row of houses as alike as a line of Grenadier Guards. It was twenty-five feet wide, ninety feet deep, four stories high, and was divided into seventeen rooms. The front windows looked across Pine Street at a mansion belonging to Gifford Pinchot, sometime Governor of Pennsylvania. The rear windows looked out across the alley at a row of small, dilapidated houses, former slave quarters still inhabited by blacks.

My father, John H.W. Rhein, was a doctor, a neuro-psychiatrist, and three of the ground-floor rooms were given over to his offices. There was a waiting room, a consulting room, and a laboratory.

In back of the offices, the dining room, pantry and kitchen stretched out in a row. The dining room, which was big enough to seat fourteen people, was so dark that electric lights were needed all day. The pantry, the size of a big kitchen in a modern apartment, was the nightly habitat of an army of cockroaches which scuttled into retreat when you turned on the light. They were attracted by the grease which had permeated the cracks in the wooden counters, and though Mother detested them, there seemed to be no way of getting rid of them. All the old houses in that part of Philadelphia were infested with cockroaches.

The large combination laundry-servants'-dining-room-kitchen was painted mustard brown but had turned greyish with soot. It was totally devoid of labour-saving devices. At one side there were two stationary wash tubs, one of which held a large corrugated washboard, and there the ritualistic scrubbing of clothes took place on Mondays. At other times the tubs were covered with a board to make a table where a deep pan of dough, covered with a white cloth, might be set to rise, or where shallow pans of milk might be left overnight.

In the daytime, the huge black coal stove, on which food for a daily minimum of nine people was cooked, was a raging inferno. It also heated the hot water tank beside it, and on ironing day rows of irons were lined up at the back like cars in a parking lot. After dinner it was banked, and then it gave forth only enough heat to cook the breakfast oatmeal which simmered away in a double boiler overnight. (We all ate oatmeal religiously, my father with salt in the Scottish way, the rest of us with brown sugar and cream.) The stove could not have given out much heat at night because the kitchen was always chilly when we crept down to raid the icebox. I remember walking into the kitchen once and finding Agnes, the waitress, and one of her male followers sitting with their feet in the oven.

The front and back parlours were on the second floor back. The former was a music room housing the Steinway baby grand piano, my father's pride and joy, a music cabinet, and a great many tables and chairs. Little ornaments stood on every available surface.

When we were alone, the family sat in the small connecting back parlour—usually beside a wood fire since the coal furnace in the cellar never seemed to be able to force much heat upstairs. The children's bedrooms were on the third floor, so that even though we wore long-sleeved long-legged, scratchy woollen underwear from October to May, we were always chilly.

The first two flights of stairs of "1732" and the hall to my parents' room were covered with green wall-to-wall carpeting, but after that the stairs and halls were bare right on up to the attic, which was divided into a store room and two maids' rooms. It was cold up there in winter and breathlessly hot in summer. A few scraps of rag carpet covered the floor, and there were no curtains, only a torn green pull shade. We children were forbidden to go into the maids' rooms, for the same reason we were forbidden to go into the kitchen when the servants were sitting down to meals: because, Mother explained, they had a right to their privacy. On one or two occasion I did go up to the attic when Mother was making an inspection tour, and was revolted by the smell of unmade beds, stale sweat and chamberpots. (We all used white china chamberpots—"potties"—which the maids emptied and washed every morning; there was only one bathroom, a big converted bedroom, on the third floor.)

I once said to Mother, after an expedition to the attic, that I thought it was wrong that the maids had to live in such a horrid place. She replied that the attic bedrooms were a luxury for "bog trotters" brought up in the thatched cottages of Ireland. "They belong to a different walk of life," she said, "they don't mind."

I was not convinced. And I wondered why the maids didn't envy and hate us instead of waiting on us with cheerful obedience.

At night the house was battened down like a tramp steamer in a heavy sea. The maids closed and barred the heavy wooden shutters on the ground floor and put up the chain on the door leading from the vestibule to the street. We also bolted our bedroom doors at night. A couple of policemen, one black and one white, patrolled Pine Street, their deliberate, heavy steps making a comforting echo. Mother used to tell us that she remembered race riots, far-off, unhappy things which belonged to an intolerant past and would never be repeated. Although the streets were well patrolled there were frequent burglaries, and from time to time policemen ran along the flat roofs of our row of houses flashing lights, blowing whistles and trying trapdoors.

After everyone was in bed at night, we could hear the house; it creaked so that it was hard not to believe burglars and ghosts were climbing the stairs or walking down the halls. Mother kept telling us that old houses always creaked, and that there are no such things as ghosts. And anyway no child of hers ever gave in to fear. It was a good idea, she said, to be aware of real dangers, such as diving into shallow water or jumping onto a pitch fork buried in the hay loft. It was quite normal to be frightened by a bucking horse or a bull coming at you in a pasture. But brave people did not give in to fear or lose their heads. To lose one's head was regarded by all the family as a grave fault of character.

Although we took Mother's word as gospel, our hearts often beat faster as we lay in bed at night and heard stealthy footsteps coming up the stairs and down the hall outside our doors. And when we felt sick in the night it took courage to dash downstairs and bang on our parents' door. We often did it, though; at such times we always went straight to Mother and Father even when we still slept in the same room with a nurse or governess.

It was the house itself I feared; Father had cured me of being afraid of the dark by taking me into the parlour, letting me turn off the lights myself and holding my hand as I touched familiar chairs and tables until I knew that everything was still the same. He believed that if a child was nervous at night it needed to be comforted, not disciplined. Often—sometimes several times a night—he would climb upstairs and sit on the edge of my bed to answer patiently the innumerable questions designed to keep him there "just one more minute." As a final curtain he would sing Brahm's *Wiegenlied* and an American Indian lullaby.

Though fear of the house haunted our childhood, I can only remember one occasion on which I actually gave way to terror. Mother and Father had gone out one evening, and as I was then in my teens and free of the supervision of a governess, I took advantage of the opportunity to stay up late and read. I stretched out on the Madame Recamier sofa in the back parlour and picked up a copy of *Dr. Jekyll and Mr. Hyde*. It was an unfortunate choice. When finally I heard the sound of a key in the lock I was too paralyzed by fear to switch off the light and sneak upstairs, as I usually did on such occasions, and remained tearful and shaking on the sofa.

Years later, Mother told me that my habits were well known because the electric light bulb in the reading lamp would still be hot when they got upstairs. Father would say, "Florence has been reading again. Well, it won't hurt her."

The Family

When memory begins for me there were five other members of the family living in the house: Father, Mother, Aunt Florence Kane (Aunt Folly, or Aunt Fol), after whom I was named, my brother John, five and a half years older than I, and my baby brother Francis (Shan), seven years younger to the day. (My older sister, Mabel, Mother's daughter by an earlier unhappy marriage, was married when I was five, and so I never really knew her until I was grown up. And my sister Cornelia, who had been physically handicapped from birth, was living in a home for similarly afflicted people.) The household also included my German governess, Emma Louisa Kaeker, whom I called Kaekey, and three young Irish maids. We children were extremely fortunate in our upbringing. My father, a pioneer in the field of neuro-psychiatry, was ahead of his time in many ways. For one thing, he had advanced ideas about child psychology. He did not, for example, believe in spanking. Mother, on the other hand, said that there were times when a quick slap on the behind ("never, never on the face or head since you might deafen a child") was a necessity after extreme provocation to make clear to the child that "it had gone too far." But she was incapable of spanking us in cold blood as punishment after the event. When John and I fought each other to the point of physical harm, which we often did, or when I had a tantrum, we were sent to our rooms "to get hold" of ourselves.

I had a bad temper and was often sent upstairs as being unfit for association with other people. When he came home in the evening, Father would come up to my room and talk to me until I had recovered from my anger and could discuss the matter in the light of reason. I was soon ready to apologize and be forgiven. Apologies were

15

always accepted. "Forgive and forget," my mother would say if John showed natural signs of being unforgiving after having suffered indignities at the hands of a younger sister whom he would not hit because he was a male and older and stronger.

Though Father was infinitely patient, he did not condone uncontrolled behaviour. He conditioned us to believe in the importance of self-control—*empire sur vous même* as he called it—and taught us by example. Mother said that he had had a violent temper when young and had disciplined himself to curb and control it. I found this comforting, since it proved that it could be done, but was awed by his complete self-mastery; he never lost his temper or raised his voice. He was gentle and remarkably permissive, yet I respected his authority. It would not have occurred to me to disobey him.

Father was not only the one person who could help me work through my frustration tantrums but also the only one who could quiet my mind when I asked such questions as "Why do people have to die?" or "What happens when we die?" or "Why did Cornelia have to be born that way?"

The birth of Cornelia was a tragedy in the life of my parents. Mother had run an unidentified fever while she was pregnant, which may have accounted for the baby having been physically malformed, cruelly and grotesquely malformed, so that she could never live a normal life among ordinary people.

Cornelia survived until well on in her forties in a home for the handicapped. She had a generous, loving and responsible nature, and was much loved by the staff of the institution. She helped with the younger children, and though without hands except for a tiny thumb on each stump, learned to do beautiful crochet work in which she took justifiable pride. She understood why she could not live at home, but grieved that she had to be apart from her family.

It was difficult for my parents to make me understand why such a terrible thing could have happened to Cornelia, because they themselves found her birth so agonizing, so utterly devastating. Mother could never forgive her obstetrician for letting the poor infant breathe, even though intellectually she realized that he had interpreted his duty as a physician.

Father had wept when the child was born. When we talked about her he became silent and withdrawn; he was depressed for days after he took us to see her. But his professional experience enabled him to make my confusion bearable. My questions were unanswerable, but he helped me to face up to and accept the things in life which no one can change.

The fact of Cornelia affected my life in several ways. Mother was not well when she was carrying me; she haemorrhaged constantly and was required to spend six months in bed in order to keep the foetus. During that time she wrote half a dozen children's stories for one of the Philadelphia newspapers, and was paid $1,000 for them, a big sum in those days. She always said she was sure that my determination at the age of seven to be a writer was due to her occupation while I was in her womb.

However that may be, I certainly was affected by my parents' attitude toward me, which was coloured by their terrible grief over the condition of my sister. Often, when I was a child, Mother told me how her heart swelled with relief and joy to hear Father say, after my first cry, "Bessy, it's a perfect little girl."

Mother also often told me how I had brought joy to their lives, how much they had wanted me, and how glad they were that I was there. "You're my sunshine child," she would say, and I believed her.

The prenatal acceptance and the complete lack of rejection I received during the important early years of life have given me a sense of security and a feeling of being loved, so that I myself have been able to love deeply.

My father not only knew how to reassure a questioning intelligence, but also looked after me frequently during the night when I had attacks of vomiting. When I had whooping cough, Mother moved into the room with the baby, Shan, who also had the disease, and I slept in her bed. I'm quite sure Father's patience, tenderness and strong arms lifting me up and holding my racked head during those hot summer nights, influenced my attitude toward men in later years. He was at all times loving and encouraging, and never made me feel that he looked down on me in any way because I was a girl.

Thanks to my upbringing, I have never regretted being a woman—at least not since I became an adult. As a child and as a pre-adolescent, I was always a boy in my fantasies. That was probably because John treated me as a boy; he called me Bill, and does so to this day. Together we did all the interesting things that boys do: riding, swimming, sailing and fishing. Before I went to sleep at night, I would tell myself stories in which I was the hero, a young man of eighteen, a world traveller who had exciting adventures in many countries.

After I began to menstruate at the age of thirteen, Mother said I should be proud and happy because I was a woman and not a child anymore. It did not take me long to realize what it meant to be a woman and to rejoice in it. From that time, in my daydreams I was a beautiful, daring adventuress, brilliant writer and a world traveller whose knowledge of languages gave her entrée to every milieu in every country.

I have always loved the outdoor life and the life of achievement, and I have had great pleasure out of the love or the friendship of men, but have never identified myself with them or wanted to be anything else but a woman.

Mother, born in 1870, was a Victorian, but she was not a typical Victorian. She was not a typical anything. She had a kaleidoscopic personality. She was of the world and yet not worldly. In some ways she was a spoiled brat, and yet she was wise, and her advice, based on experience and a sensitive understanding of life, was usually sound.

She was one of the most beautiful women I have ever known, and stayed that way into her sixties because of her fine bones and tightly drawn skin. Her dark blue eyes, under curved, dark brows, were sad, although she was full of Irish humour and had a great sense of the ridiculous. Her hair was a curly mane of shining red gold which turned completely white by the time she was forty. Tall, with small, slender feet and long-fingered hands, she loved clothes, and wore mauves, pinks and blues which set off her high colouring. She always smelled deliciously of perfume.

Mother's beauty brought her much adulation and gave her a feeling of power. She prized beauty not only in herself but in others, tending to dismiss people as being uninteresting because they had "no looks." It was devastating for her when, due to illness, her face suddenly became an ugly, wrinkled mask when she was in her seventies. The loss of her beauty was much harder for her than it would have been for a woman who had taken less pride in her appearance. Her suffering at that time taught me a valuable lesson.

Though Mother was vain, her vanity did not destroy her, because she had so many fine qualities. For one thing, she had great physical courage and presence of mind. One morning, when we were living on our farm, she took me to West Chester with her in the little, open runabout. It was drawn by Colonel, Father's faithful old horse which had taken him on his rounds when he was a young physician. When we reached the outskirts of the town, Colonel began to shake all over and then fell down, upsetting the wagon. Mother yanked me to safety at the side of the road and then sat on Colonel's head to keep him from getting up and bolting or putting a shaft through his belly.

She shouted for help and after a while a drover came along and helped to get Colonel to his feet. He stayed with the horse while Mother telephoned my uncle and asked him to take me home in his car. She said she did not want anyone but herself to take the risk of driving the shaky horse, and drove Colonel the seven miles back to our farm, keeping him at a walk all the way. Several times she thought he was going to fall again when he began to weave back and forth on the road, but she spoke to him encouragingly and he kept going. Later the veterinarian said he was not safe to drive again, so he was put out to pasture in honourable retirement. For a brief time he renewed his youth, galloping with streaming tail and mane flying, across the meadows, until one day he dropped dead.

Mother was proud of John's courage and ability to endure pain without a whimper, and expected me to emulate his stoicism. She had a no-nonsense attitude toward her children. Once, when I was seven or eight, John cut himself badly with a knife. I stood watching her clean the wound in the bathroom washstand. The blood kept flowing out into the water and I kept looking at it, feeling queerer and queerer. As I slumped down in a faint, I heard Mother say to Kaekey, "Just roll her into a corner and pay no attention to her until I get this bandaged."

"Florence was just trying to draw attention to herself as usual," Mother announced to the world later. "No child of mine faints at the sight of blood." And I never have, since then.

Mother not only expected her children to be brave but also to be truthful. Lying was for her a major offence. She often said she had no use for a child who was afraid to take the blame when it had been naughty, and she could not abide a tattle-tale.

She read a great deal and, like all of her family, was intellectually involved in politics and international affairs. She had many liberal ideas. She supported the League of Nations and never ceased to deplore the fact that the United States had not joined it; she felt that justice had not been done to Sacco and Vanzetti; voted for Franklin Roosevelt; believed in birth control and sterilization for poor women who wanted it; thought capital punishment should be abolished; and abominated the way blacks were treated in the southern parts of the United States.

She took politics seriously because, on her mother's side, she was a Bayard. The Bayards had been involved in public life since the first of the family had settled in Delaware in 1649. Five of his descendants had been senators from Delaware—Democrats all. One of them had been a signatory to the Treaty of Ghent which ended the War of 1812, and one of them had been Secretary of State under Cleveland and subsequently the first American ambassador to the Court of St. James's.

Father, on the other hand, was a staunch Republican. After women got the franchise, Mother and Father always went to the polling booth together to cancel each other's vote. When I once asked why they bothered to go, Mother was indignant, saying it was the duty of every citizen to vote and essential for women to exercise the franchise because they had been so long denied their rights as citizens. She believed that blacks should have the same rights as other Americans, but she found it incredible that black men—at that time with little or no education— were given the vote in 1870, while even educated women could not vote or hold public office for another fifty years.

Mother was proud of her Bayard ancestry and often boasted about it. She was equally proud of her father's people, the Kanes, who were Yankees. John Kane, a graduate of Trinity College, Dublin, came to the New World ten or fifteen years before the American Revolution. He was a United Empire Loyalist and after the defeat of the British he moved to Halifax and then to England. Eventually he returned to New York and with his seven sons set up trading posts throughout the state. His grandson, my mother's grandfather, became a judge. A man of Roman rectitude, he sentenced his son to prison for sheltering runaway slaves on the family estate even though he himself did not believe in slavery. The most famous member of the family was Elisha Kent Kane, the Arctic explorer, who headed the second Grinnell expedition in search of Sir John Franklin.

Unlike Mother, Father never boasted about his family, but he seemed quite proud of his Rhein grandfather who had come from Germany in 1804 and his Early grandfather who had come from Ireland at about the same time. They had settled in Reading, Pennsylvania, which Mother regarded as socially less acceptable than Boston, New York, Philadelphia, Baltimore, Richmond or Charleston. She was surprised and delighted to discover, when the dark old portraits of Father's Early grandparents were cleaned, that they had been painted by the fashionable Sully, who had made portraits of her own ancestors.

My Father's father had been a physician, but for some reason, the family was not well off. Father had put himself through medical school by working in a pharmacy at night. When he began to earn money as a physician, he had supported one of his two older brothers while he studied law and the other while he studied medicine.

As a girl I used to be angry at Mother because I thought she was a social snob. I think now that she boasted about the achievements of her family in order to make her children carry on what she regarded as a great tradition. It was also a form of self-inflation to compensate for the fact that she had been practically ostracized by Philadelphia society after her divorce. She had married in 1891, and when my half-sister, Mabel, was nine years old, had divorced her husband. A year later she had married my father, at that time an assistant to Dr. G. Weir Mitchell, a distinguished neurologist. Father's connection with Dr. Mitchell, who belonged to an old Philadelphia family, was severed as a result of his marriage and he went into practice on his own, as a neuro-psychiatrist, becoming in time a highly successful, much-sought-after specialist in what was then a new field of medicine.

Mother became bitter about the way some of her friends treated her after her divorce. She was "dropped" by many and no longer invited to their houses. Some of them would cross the street rather than have to speak to her. Others cut her dead. In Philadelphia in the 1900's, gentlewomen did not divorce their husbands, no matter how unhappy the marriage; they carried on "for the sake of the children" or "for the sake of appearances." Divorce was not only socially unacceptable but, for the majority of women, it was also out of the question because of their financial dependence on a husband for bed and board. Unless they had inherited money, there was no other way open to them. The education given most "upper class" girls did not fit them to earn the kind of living to which they were accustomed, and the few jobs open to women were badly paid.

Mother was comparatively poor after her divorce and was determined to make a career for herself. She won a scholarship at the School of Industrial Design in Philadelphia and planned to become an interior decorator. She would probably have made a success of it, too, since she was a good draughtsman and an amateur artist with an admirable colour sense, but her financial problems were solved when she married my father.

My parents were very much in love when they married and they stayed in love until parted by death. Mother adored her children and was fiercely possessive of them, but I think she would have seen us all immersed in boiling oil if it became a question of that or being parted from Father.

She was, remarkably, in no way a Victorian in her attitude toward sex, which she believed was a great and powerful mystic force. She thought it was dirty and indecent for men to consort with prostitutes, or for a man and a woman to marry if they did not love each other, because both acts were a violation of sex. On the other hand, she thought that the sexual act between a husband and wife who loved each other was the fulfilment of their relationship and called it the "fullness of life." She told me she knew what she was talking about because she had experienced the "fullness of life" with Father. She did not approve of necking or petting because she thought it was nasty to rouse passions that could not be satisfied legitimately. She had a great scorn for teasers.

Unlike most mothers of the period, she explained the mechanism of sex and reproduction to me when I asked the usual questions, and never lied to me. Consequently I was amazed by the ignorance of my school friends. Many of them wouldn't have dared to ask their parents any questions about their bodies. Some of them were terrified when they started menstruating, thinking they were bleeding to death. Several had only the vaguest idea of how a child was born, being under the impression that it came out of its mother's navel. I couldn't understand why they giggled and covered their faces when they talked about matters which were discussed quite naturally in our family.

Father undoubtedly influenced Mother's ideas in this respect, since I remember her once shocking a group of friends by saying, "Jack says that people have done great harm to little boys by their attitude toward masturbation. He says it's quite normal and natural at a certain age and a child should not be made ashamed of doing it."

When we were in our teens, our parents' attitude toward prohibition infuriated John and me because it was so different from that of anyone else we knew. Neither of them approved of prohibition, regarding it as an infringement of human rights, but they refused to break the law, and no alcohol was served in the house from the time the Volstead Act came into force until it was repealed. "I can't ask my children to respect the law if I don't respect it myself," Mother said.

My parents had strong opinions and they expected their children to have opinions. In our family the children were heard as well as seen. We were encouraged to say what we thought and to defend our ideas with intelligent, factual arguments. Mother delighted in argument, and wanted to hear her children's ideas, but she drew the line at gossip about personalities.

"Talk about things and ideas, but not about people at meals," she would say—an admonition that was not always strictly obeyed.

Aunt Folly, my mother's sister, stayed with us in the winters. Although they did not look alike, they were very much alike in temperament, and despite the fact that they loved each other deeply they fought vigorously. It was probably a good way for them to relieve tensions, but it was hard on us, since we felt compelled, out of loyalty, to take Mother's side whether we agreed with her or not. When I was in my teens, I swore a mighty oath that I would not behave like that. For years I had to hypnotize myself into defiance of heredity, by saying over and over again, "You are not your mother. You are not your aunt. You are yourself. You are you, and you don't have to be like them."

Over the years Aunt Folly opened magic casements for me. Next to Mother and Father she was the person who had the greatest influence on me as a child and young woman. As built-in educational entertainment she beat television all hollow. I admired her immensely.

Aunt Fol, when I first remember her, was rather fat, putty-faced and dowdy. Her grey hair was thin and determinedly straight in spite of being put up every night in curlers made of little strips of cloth. She supplemented her bun with a "switch," a hank of matching hair which she washed every week and hung in her bedroom window to dry. She was not amused the time John grabbed it and rushed downstairs emitting war whoops and shouting, "I've scalped Aunt Folly. I've scalped Aunt Folly."

She never married, which was a pity, because she was warmly affectionate and generous, loved children, and had the capacity to delight and stimulate them. She had been engaged to be married when she was in her early twenties, but her fiancé had been drowned in a sailing accident off Newport, Rhode Island. Other men had been attentive to her, but being extremely sentimental she could not forget her lost love. As time went on she became more and more opiniated and eccentric—a typical old maid blue-stocking.

She shared many of Mother's liberal ideas but was more intellectual and more sophisticated in her judgments than her younger sister. She read *The Nation* and *The New Republic,* and belonged to the Contemporary Club, a forum for distinguished lecturers from all over the world. When I was in my late teens she used to take me with her to hear people like S.K. Ratcliffe and Norman Angel. Those evenings were nerve-wracking and humiliating for me because occasionally she would go to sleep and snore.

Aunt Fol had graduated from library school and was for a short time the librarian for Bryn Mawr College. Later she dreamed up and organized the travelling motor library for the State of Delaware which is still going strong. From time to time, when she needed money, she organized the papers or re-arranged the libraries of friends, including that of Owen Wister, the novelist.

Nevertheless she never put her mind to a steady career, preferring a gypsy-like existence, staying with friends and family and travelling when the wanderlust struck her, which was often. She did not need to work for money because her mother had left her an adequate annuity. Every other year or so she went to Europe, North Africa, the Middle East, Mexico or South America for months on end. In those days a three-week holiday in Europe was unheard of; it took about a week to cross the Atlantic, so people usually stayed on the other side for three or four months.

Aunt Fol spoke French, German and Italian and knew interesting people in many parts of Europe. She loved paintings, sculpture and architecture, and saw them with a discerning as well as a Baedeker eye. She was an inspired shopper, with a talent for finding just the right present for each member of her family, and she always had to buy an extra suitcase or two to bring home all the gifts. I am still using some of the cashmere shawls and chair covers she gave me nearly half a century ago.

Travel for her was adventure. When she was in her fifties she swam the Hellespont, saying afterwards it wasn't nearly as dramatic an effort as Byron made it out to be. In 1908 she was in Taormina when Mount Etna erupted.

She was asleep when the first earthquake shock took place, and was thrown from her bed. When she saw great cracks widening in the walls of her room, her immediate thought was to take the curlers out of her hair so that the family would not be disgraced by her being found dead with her head covered with little cotton bows. Afterwards, like the other tourists, she packed and went through the rubble-filled streets to the railroad station. When she arrived she saw hundreds of distraught people crowded on the platforms. Most of them were homeless. Many were injured or ill from shock and exhaustion.

"What am I doing here, trying to run away?" she said to herself, and went back to her hotel and unpacked her bags.

During the next few weeks she worked as a volunteer in a refugee centre. Later, after she had gone to Rome to stay with friends, she was astonished to be informed that King Victor Emmanuel had honoured her for her service to his country. She was proud of the medal and often showed it to us.

The courageous, adventurous side of Aunt Folly impressed me as a child and as a young girl. I greatly admired her erudition, her gift for languages and familiarity with foreign countries and people. I believed somehow that because I was named after her I would be like her in the respects that I admired. But I was also determined that I would not fight with people, blow my top or make scenes the way she often did.

I hoped that when I grew up I would be like Father, who did not raise his voice or fight with people. He was usually able to locate himself in the eye of the household hurricane and to remain calm and seemingly undisturbed by the high winds and rain which whirled around him. When Mother and Aunt Folly had an argument, and he found himself in danger of being swept into taking sides, he usually retreated into his laboratory as if it were a cyclone cellar, and did mysterious things with a Bunsen burner. Or else he would go upstairs and play the piano and sing.

During the winters when we were at "1732," we followed a disciplined routine. On weekdays we went to school in the mornings and in the afternoons we were turfed out to get fresh air and exercise by roller skating in Rittenhouse Square, a few blocks away. Drunk with power and speed, we raced on our four-wheelers around the outside walks and played crack-the-whip with screams of joyful terror.

Sunday was a dull day for us because Philadelphia "blue laws" forbade skating in public places on the Sabbath. After the eleven o'clock service, proper Philadelphia families, wearing their Sunday clothes, walked sedately in the Square. I only joined the parade occasionally when my Aunt Bessy Rhein, my father's sister, took me to church as a rebuke to my parents who only went to church for weddings and funerals.

I did not enjoy the Square on Sundays because I did not have any Sunday clothes; Mother disapproved of them as being a needless expense and a form of the wrong kind of snobbery. "People who dress up just to be seen in church are going there for the wrong reason," she often said.

We were not sent to Sunday School either, but Mother gave us brief religious instruction on Sunday evenings. "Your father says Christianity is your heritage," she said, "and you must know about it in order to be an educated person, just as you have to know history."

She read the New Testament to us and made us learn the Ten Commandments and the Twenty-third Psalm by heart, and showed us "holy pictures" by the great masters in a scrap book she had made in her youth. She said that many of the stories in the Old Testament were allegories and were not to be taken literally.

When I was twelve I asked to be confirmed.

"Do you want to join the church because you believe in its doctrine or because all your friends are being confirmed?" she asked.

When I admitted that I wanted to join because all my friends were preparing to join a church and I felt out of things, she said, "Religion is much too serious a matter to be undertaken for merely social reasons, because you want to be in the swim. When, after serious thought and study, you know what you believe, then decide what you want to do. No child of mine makes important decisions for the wrong reasons."

I never have been confirmed, but this does not mean I am without religious experience.

Father was an agnostic because his training as a scientist and his experience as a doctor had made him a man with an open mind. Once I asked him about the pile of books on spiritualism which for a week or so had appeared on his bedside table. "Do you believe in spiritualism?" I asked him.

"I don't believe in it and I don't not believe in it," he replied. "I've come across so many strange things in my study of the human consciousness that nothing would surprise me. 'There are more things in heaven and earth, Horatio. . . .' I have to go on searching for the truth and not let myself be blinded by preconceived ideas."

Father extended his passion for truth to his children. He did not approve of censorship, so we were allowed to read everything in the parlour library. He asked us not to read the medical books in his office, however, until we were sufficiently well informed to understand them—a reasonable request, which I accepted.

Books were then, and still are, my greatest source of interest, diversion, stimulation and pleasure. The Five-Foot Shelf of Classics compiled by President Eliot of Harvard—"essential reading for an educated person"—stretched at eye-height beside the sofa. I was determined to be an educated person, and had read most of them by the time I was sixteen, with varying degrees of understanding and interest.

Our taste for reading had been whetted early on because Mother or Aunt Fol read aloud to us almost every day. And, fortunately for us, they didn't like the same books.

Over the years Aunt Fol read us much of Kipling, Stevenson, Mark Twain, Dickens and Sir Walter Scott, skipping the dull descriptive passages in the Waverley novels in a masterly way. She was a dramatic reader, imitating male and female voices, and obviously taking delight in her own histrionic ability.

Mother read us the usual children's classics such as *The Water Babies, Hans Brinker and the Silver Skates* and *The Secret Garden.* When I was in my early teens she read us, among others, a number of the novels of Jane Austen, George Eliot, the Brontes and Thomas Hardy. Of them all, my favourites were *Jane Eyre* and *Lorna Doone,* because the heroines were so brave.

We also read a great many of Shakespeare's plays and went to see them whenever repertory companies came to town. We would read the plays aloud before we went to the theatre, each of us taking a part and delivering lines such as "Hark! Who knocks without?" in piping treble voices.

Reading was fun but the moments of intoxicating excitement came when we were in our seats admiring the gorgeous gold trim on the boxes and sniffing the lovely dusty theatre smell. It was a great moment when the red velvet curtain draped itself up to the ceiling and we could study the asbestos undercurtain and see eyes at the peep-holes. But the greatest moment of all was when the lights dimmed and the play began. For us the play was the thing. Even today, when I go to the theatre my blood pressure goes up a bit, and with some sort of sensitive, invisible antennae I seem to catch the tension of the actors waiting in the wings or taking their places on the set behind the curtain.

After seeing a play, John and I often put on our own productions. We would fasten a sheet across one end of his big bedroom and set out rows of chairs for Mother, Father, Aunt Folly and Kaekey. They were an appreciative audience and applauded in all the right places—though sometimes they laughed in the wrong places when we pulled a particularly funny boner.

All this made us quite theatre conscious, and at clan gatherings— Christmas and Thanksgiving—we entertained not only our immediate family but uncles and aunts and cousins with recitals of poetry. It must have been horribly boring to all but our doting parents, but it was no doubt good for us; it cured us of stage fright early in life, satisfied our childish need to show off, and helped to sharpen our memories.

Many of the poems and songs we recited in German or French. My father, a generation before Wilder Penfield, had come to the same conclusion as the world-renowned neurologist: that languages learned as a child are never lost but are stored by the brain, ready for recall when the right stimulus occurs. Father spoke German and French himself and wanted us to be at home in both languages. Consequently he insisted that Kaekey converse with us in German only. And when she left us I was sent to a French school.

Father also taught us to play chess at an early age, probably because he wanted to be sure of having someone to give him a game. He was one of those people who could concentrate on a problem to the exclusion of all else, and could also relax quickly by taking a catnap for five minutes or by playing games. He loved duplicate bridge, and Mother dutifully learned to play, though she had no natural inclination in that direction.

Music was Father's greatest source of relaxation and delight, however. He played the piano well for an amateur, had a gift for reading music, and could play a difficult score at first sight. He also had a true, if light, baritone singing voice. He sang lieder and arias from Italian operas in the bathroom in the mornings as he stropped his razor, and practised scales as he walked down the long halls or went up and down stairs. Almost invariably he went to the piano as soon as he came home in the evening, and played and sang for an hour or so until dinner-time. If the mood was on him he would play after dinner as well. Aunt Folly used to complain that the children would be kept awake and develop neuroses, but he would reply, "Nonsense. The sound of music never hurt anyone."

The house was not only full of music but also full of people. Father and Mother frequently had formal dinner parties, and friends were always dropping in for "potluck" meals, which meant they were served meat, potatoes, vegetable and dessert for lunch, and four courses for dinner. Most days, when I came home from school, one of Mother's sisters or nieces was sitting with her while she mended clothes, darned stockings or sewed on a dress she was making for me. The conversation was always boiling over with excitement, punctuated with laughter or expressions of indignation, and sometimes by tears. All the Bayards and Kanes are temperamental. They blow easily, indulge in frightful scenes, and forgive as quickly, enjoying the reconciliation as much as the fight.

Life for a child at 1732 Pine Street was not as confining as city life is for most children today because the house was big enough for us to have some privacy and also to have our friends for the night and for meals. We were never lonely or bored because of the security and companionship supplied by an old-fashioned, extended family made up of dynamic, interesting and interested adults. But I did not feel that I belonged in the city as I did in the country—at our summer place beside the sea in Rhode Island, or on the farm in Chester County, Pennsylvania.

The Farm

The farm, "Valhalla," was about twenty-five miles from Philadelphia—a hundred acres of woods, meadows and fields. For a child it had everything which the soul could yearn for, and it is for me a golden memory because there we were allowed a great deal of freedom and there was always something interesting to do.

There was a huge red barn with a hay loft full of sweet-smelling, resilient hay into which you could jump from wide beams or from the ropes suspended from the roof. There was a stable, on a lower level, where the horses lived in box stalls and the cows were lined up in iron collars while they were milked. There was a tack room which smelt deliciously of leather, and a carriage house where Father's big touring car was parked side by side with the buggy, the runabout and the general-purpose cart. At the side of the barn there was a pig pen, a large chicken yard with houses, and a duck pen. The turkeys and guinea-hens just roosted at night in the trees around the chicken yard. They had very poor ideas about the way to raise their young, and took off into the long grass to hide, where they fell prey to weasels or foxes.

There were a number of farm dogs—mongrel collies. And there were at least half a dozen barn cats, usually pregnant, which hung around at milking time until their individual feeding pans were filled with milk as a reward for keeping the rats down.

Shan was a baby during the years on the farm, so John had to make do with me for company. I followed his lead wherever he went and did my level best to keep up with him. It wasn't always easy, however; he didn't know the meaning of fear and would strain his strength to the limit to prove that he was not delicate in spite of a succession of illnesses and accidents. Tall, thin, intense, with large dark-circled, sad, hazel eyes and rebellious dark hair, he looked like the young saints in Raphael's paintings. I adored him and regarded him as the fount of all wisdom, though I sometimes fought with him violently.

John had an adventurous, imaginative mind; when we played together on the farm we led a glorious secret life of make-believe. We made trails through the bushland encircling the cow pastures, always alert and mindful of every telltale broken twig or flattened piece of grass. Sometimes we were mountain goats moving fast over rocks or jumping from crag to crag. Sometimes we were beavers, and built a dam to make a pond in the stream which wound through the meadows. We built houses of branches and reeds which were sometimes tepees and sometimes settlers' forts to be defended against the Redskins. Once we killed a bullfrog and cooked its legs over a wood fire, but we were not happy about that and did not repeat the experiment. Another time, to my dismay, John shot a chipmunk with a B.B. gun and then skinned, cooked and ate it. He said that the flesh, what there was of it, tasted like aromatic berries. On summer mornings, while the dew was still white and heavy on the grass, we picked mushrooms in the cow pasture, where they had sprouted overnight among the cowpats.

In late summer we picked wild grapes from the vines high up on the trees around a swamp. (The smell of sun-warmed wild grapes and the aroma of jelly cooking is delicious in memory.) One year John fell out of the tree he had climbed to get "the high-up ripe ones." His arm was broken but he insisted upon waiting, white with pain, while I picked up the grapes he had spilled. To cry or flinch from pain was against his Spartan code.

We also brought home baskets full of hickory nuts, walnuts and chestnuts and laid out the green-coated walnuts to dry in a room in the barn. (Once John painted his face and hands with walnut juice, so that he would look more like an Indian, and remained stained for some time afterwards, though we scrubbed and scrubbed him.) Chestnuts were our favourites; we roasted them in a cornpoper over the open fire in the parlour. At that time the blight was slowly killing off all the chestnut trees in Pennsylvania, but a few noble pasture shade trees still stood, defiant of death though partly withered, like old men after a stroke.

For me the horses were the best of the many good things about the farm. John and I knew how to ride, because the winter I was eight we were given riding lessons at the Riding Academy, as well as swimming lessons at Mr. Asher's Natatorium. Father believed that girls as well as boys should be able to enjoy outdoor sports, and that playing games and swimming and riding properly gave self-confidence as well as lasting enjoyment. He wanted us to be all-round people.

Kaekey, an experienced governess, taught me how to sew, knit, crochet and embroider, since they were considered essential accomplishments for a woman. I have found it useful to be able to sew on buttons, turn a hem or make curtains, but the experience on the farm and in Rhode Island has given a lasting dimension to my life, a source of deep enjoyment shared with my husband who loves country things as I do.

We children were not aware that the farm was a form of education. Like most children, we were full of curiosity and interested in everything, and the farm provided us with a rich and stimulating curriculum. The farmhouse parlour was lined with books, many of them concerned with birds, flowers, reptiles, fungi and insects. Mother knew a great deal about natural history; she kept bird lists and made watercolour sketches of flowers, or pressed them where they belonged in the flower book after she had identified them. We seldom went on a walk without bringing her a flower or fern, and we all took part in the game of tracking down the rare one she could not recognize at a glance. Later, during the First World War when Father was in France for eighteen months, he sent her pressed flowers in his daily letter. She identified them and put them into a scrap book.

Mother told us about the habits of bees, gleaned from her reading of Maeterlinck, and helped us to collect and mount butterflies and moths, which we killed with the traditional bottle of chloroform. We put caterpillars in an old shoebox, punctured the top with airholes, and fed them with leaves until they formed a chrysalis, then watched as they emerged transformed. Magic. Father gave us one of his microscopes and what it showed us was also magic.

My mother ran the farm, which meant she was the overseer and administrator. The farmer lived with his family in a small red frame house on the acres and the hired man slept in a room in the barn.

Mother used the back parlour as a farm office. There she did the accounts and read U.S. Department of Agriculture pamphlets on milk marketing, raising hens, the rotation of crops, fertilizers and the like. She also did a considerable amount of manual work. She made butter and picked huge masses of asparagus, sweet corn, peas and beans.

The farm did not pay, but Mother and Father figured that it paid us something more important than dollars and cents; it provided us with happy, educational summers as well as good food all the year round.

When the dog-days came around in August, and the heat of Pennsylvania descended in miasmal mist on the farm, the family moved to another heaven—Saunderstown, Rhode Island—for a month. There again we led the free life, swimming in the buoyant cold water, sailing in a variety of small boats suited to our age and ability, fishing for anything we could catch off the end of the dock, and picnicking on the rocks or on the long, lonely sands of Wesquag Beach where the Atlantic rollers thundered upon the land. We became sunbaked to a dark brown, our skins crusted with a powder of dried salt, our stomachs distended with steamed clams, lobster, soft-shelled crabs, sweet corn, and blueberry pie made with berries we had picked ourselves. We fell asleep each night exhausted by the many happy things we had done all day.

War

In August 1914 the family was on the Colonial Express on the way to Saunderstown, Rhode Island when a newsboy put his head in the door of the compartment and shouted, "Extra! Extra! War declared! Read all about it!" Father bought a paper and read out that Britain had declared war on Germany. Kaekey burst into tears, but Father said, "Don't worry, Miss Kaeker, it will be all over in three months."

I was only six at the time but I remember that day very well because I was so upset. It is always frightening for a child when an adult in authority behaves like a child, particularly if it is an adult one loves, and I loved Kaekey. She was not at all the prototype of a Prussian, being a tiny woman with dark bright eyes and dyed black hair worn in a pompadour. Her face seemed old and wrinkled, but anyone over thirty looks old to a child. She had been governess to my New York cousins, the Lockwood girls, and had come to me when I was five years old after Minnie Doyle, my Irish nurse, left.

Kaekey used to take John and me on walks and could climb a fence as well as we. She loved music and poetry and would sing German songs and ballads when she felt cheerful. Her seven brothers were foresters on one of the Kaiser's estates in Prussia, and soon after the outbreak of war she received word that they were in the army and had been sent into the trenches. I knitted socks and scarves for them and worried with Kaekey about their being wounded or killed.

During the next two years I was constantly upset when I overheard half-understood conversations about atrocities committed by the Uhlans in Belgium, and saw cartoons in the papers showing German soldiers with babies impaled on their bayonets. I was confused and horrified when I heard all the talk about the martyrdom of Edith Cavell.

When the United States entered the war in 1917, I was torn by conflicting loyalties because Germans became "the enemy," and I was, of course, a loyal American. My brother John disliked Kaekey, probably because he was at an age when he resented authority of any kind and especially that of a woman and a foreigner. He kept saying that she was a German spy and quite generally made her life miserable. Visitors to the house also made remarks which wounded her. I used to lie awake at night, quiet and tense, and listen to her weeping in the dark after she went to bed.

What was particularly confusing for me was that everyone said that *all* Germans were cruel and wicked and had to be beaten. Yet I knew that *one* German at least was neither cruel nor wicked, and the awareness of her tortured innocence gave me a lasting hatred of war.

I was unhappy about Kaekey, but I was much more unhappy when, in 1917, Father put on uniform and went away. A major in the Medical Reserve Corps, he had applied for active service as soon as the United States declared war on Germany, and in spite of the fact that he had Bright's disease he had managed to pass the medical. In August he was given orders to report to Fort Sam Houston, near San Antonio, Texas.

Though I was old enough to understand that his leaving had nothing to do with his feelings about me, and did not feel rejected, I was bereft. I missed him so much that I had, young as I was, a sympathetic understanding of Mother's grief at parting from him, because I knew how much she also loved and needed him. I felt very close to her. She was always able to pour forth her feelings in words, so I shared her sense of loss and her worry. She faced the responsibility of running "1732" and the farm, and carrying on with less money, since a major's pay was not nearly as much as that of a successful neuro-psychiatrist.

A few months ago my brother sent me a letter which he had found in a trunk full of Father's papers. It was addressed to General Somebody, Fort Sam Houston, Texas, and read as follows:

Dear General:
    Please send my father, Major John H.W. Rhein, to somewhere near Pennsylvania. Texas is too far away.
Your new Friend,
Florence Bayard Kane Rhein

My first attempt at lobbying was not successful. Six months later, in January 1918, Father was promoted to the rank of lieutenant-colonel and sent overseas as head consultant in neuro-psychiatry for the 2nd Army of the American Expeditionary Force. He was in France for eighteen months.

Soon after he went away, Kaekey left us to go and live with her married sister in North Philadelphia. She found it impossible to work for us or anyone else, since she felt an outcast. I did not want her to go, and felt she was being treated badly. I ached for her, but never wrote to her or she to me. Only Aunt Fol kept in touch with her. I saw her only once again, when Aunt Fol arranged for her to come to my wedding ten years later.

During the two years that Father was away, I lived in a matriarchal society dominated by my mother with assists from Aunt Fol. I was with Mother a great deal and she talked to me as if I were another adult, so that after a while I began to call her Bessy. All the elders in the family were horrified by my impertinence, but Mother, always the non-conformist, laughed and said she liked it, and thank you very much, but she didn't want anyone to interfere with her relationship with her daughter.

After Father was sent overseas Mother sold the farm. John and I were heartbroken by being evicted from "Valhalla" but took heart when Mother rented a fisherman's cottage at Saunderstown, Rhode Island for the summers. It had an outdoor privy, and we washed in a papier mâché bathtub which the maids filled with pitchers of water carried up from the kitchen. Delia, the cook, and Agnes, the waitress, did double duty as nurses for Shan, walking him up and down the lane in the afternoons or taking him to the pebbly beach. Often in the evenings they stepped out with soldiers from nearby Fort Kearney, and after I want to bed, I could hear young men singing, "K-K-K-Katie, beautiful Katie, You're the only g-g-g-girl that I adore. When the moon shines over the cowshed, I'll be waiting at the k-k-k-kitchen door."

John was sixteen and now regarded me as an incubus. All day long he was off and away with our cousins, the La Farge boys—swimming; sailing in their sloop, the *Golly,* (short for *Golliwog*); riding their polo ponies; playing "little wars" with lead soldiers in their garage; fishing in Narragansett Bay; or catching crabs off the bridge of the Narrow River, a tidal stream running from brackish Buckie Pond into the Atlantic. The La Farge cousins ignored the existence of a ten-year-old girl. It was not until I was in my teens that they discovered me and took me sailing or to shoot yellow-legs in the marshes at dawn. Then I became a close friend of Oliver, the anthropologist and novelist, and later of his older brother Christopher, the poet and novelist.

That summer of 1918 there were no other children of my age to play with, so that I became, more than ever, Mother's constant companion. With her usual energy and enthusiasm, she plunged into war work. She was in charge of recreation for the soldiers at Fort Kearney and put on dances for them on Saturday nights, recruiting partners from all levels of society. Young officers came to see her about arrangements, and invited her for a drive or an outing in a motorboat. When she occasionally accepted, she took me along as chaperone. She preferred men to women, and feasted on their compliments, but she was strictly a one-man woman and was not prepared to risk emotional involvement with anyone but her husband.

She tried to be both mother and father to her children while Father was away, and with me she succeeded very well. She restored the sense of security endangered when Kaekey and Father suddenly went out of my life. She talked about Father constantly, which somehow made him seem not so far away.

Aunt Folly did her best to take the place of Kaekey, whom I missed greatly. By that time I no longer needed a governess; I had been sent to Le Cours Français, a small, select school run by a couple of mothers who wanted their daughters to speak French fluently, since they thought, as my father did, that a well educated person should be able to communicate in more than one language.

All the lessons at Le Cours were in French except English literature and grammar, and mathematics. The French teachers were imported from France. The English-speaking teachers were Americans of impeccable social background, spinster gentlewomen with no money and no man to support them, who needed a job. They were uniformly middle-aged and nervous, and found it hard to maintain discipline because their pupils could feel their insecurity and took advantage of it. Only one of them, the mathematics teacher, was young. She held our hearts in thrall after her fiancé was killed in the war; she read us *In Flanders Fields* and *Rhymes of a Red Cross Man* while we wept because it was all so sad and so beautiful.

There were no organized sports, but two or three times a week a busty and wheezy woman came to the school and gave us callisthenics. For further exercise, we walked up and down DeLancey Street at recess, and in the afternoons, since school ended for the day at half past twelve, we walked around Rittenhouse Square; we were too old for roller skates.

While Father was overseas I wrote to him in French and sent back English translations of the letters which he had written in French. I also began to read French for my own pleasure.

I became a great admirer of the American doughboys and set great store by Le Maréchal Foch. There was a map of Europe pinned to the door of Mother's room, and we stuck coloured pins where the front line of the trenches were supposed to be and moved them back and forth as the newspapers reported advances or retreats. I rolled bandages for the Red Cross. And I boasted when Father was promoted to the rank of colonel. I was ardently anti-German and pro-ally.

Peace

Father remained in France for six months after the armistice was signed but the pressure was off my worry. When he came home we all rejoiced and life returned to normal, at least on the surface. There was a French-speaking Italian nurse for Shan, an upstairs maid again, and when the car was taken out of storage, a chauffeur.

In the years that followed, Father's health began to break. A "whiff of gas," as he called it, had left him with a chronic cough augmented by inveterate chain smoking. His kidney disease was still with him, and he developed high blood pressure. Still he was determined to rebuild his practice and to make up the money he had lost during the time he was on active service. Remembering the poverty of his youth, he wanted money in order to be absolutely sure that his children would have the best possible education. Fiercely ambitious for his children, he sent us to expensive private schools and made plans for us to go to university. He expected his sons to have a profession. I had decided to be a poet or a novelist so he gave me books about writing, a rhyming dictionary and *Roget's Thesaurus,* and talked to me often about poetry and writing.

He worked hard, compulsively, carrying the responsibility of his own private hospital, long office hours and work in public clinics, as well as lecturing at the University of Pennsylvania Medical School where he had been a professor for years. Somehow he also found time to write medical papers; in his lifetime he wrote a hundred published papers based on research and clinical experience. He became an authority on drug addiction. Years ahead of his time, he maintained that drugs are a crutch for maladjusted people and that addicts should be treated as sick people. Over thirty years later a member of the RCMP Narcotics Branch, testifying before the Canadian Senate Committee on Drugs, said that no one had understood the nature of addiction better than Dr. John H.W. Rhein.

During the early 1920's, when I was in my teens, Mother was greatly concerned about my father's health. She used to go with him when he went on his rounds to see his patients, and would sit in the back of the open car, shivering under a lap rug, while he paid a call. "It's a comfort for both of us to be together," she said when I asked her why she spent her afternoons in such an uncomfortable way.

As far as I was concerned Father seemed just the same as ever. My life was busy and interesting and I was full of myself. I was happy at Le Cours Français. I liked my schoolmates and they liked me. I enjoyed French and loved learning poems by heart and having a part in the Molière play at the closing exercises. The school work was easy for me, so that I was usually head of the class and sat at the top of the long wooden table which served as a desk for the eight of us. I was docile, eager to please, conceited and confident of success in anything I wanted to do.

Once a week, in the afternoons, we went to a "sculpture class" where we dabbled in clay. Once a week we went to dancing class. All proper Philadelphia children began their coeducational social life by going to the Thursday afternoon dancing class where they were given the one-two-three routine and danced cotillions. In due course they went to the Friday afternoon dancing class and then to the Saturday Evenings where the boys wore tuxedos and the girls wore modest chiffon evening dresses and silver slippers. The next year the girls came out and as debutantes danced with the same boys they had danced with year after year, from the time they were seven. After that they paired off to marry, settle on the Main Line, and bring up their children the way they themselves had been brought up. It was a cosy, safe society. People knew where they belonged and what was expected of them and did what was expected. I was the only one of my classmates at Le Cours Français who eventually broke away from this secure, preordained pattern of existence.

I graduated from Le Cours when I was thirteen years old and was then sent to Miss Irwin's School in Philadelphia. There, to my chagrin, I found myself two classes ahead of my former classmates at Le Cours. I walked with them at recess and in the afternoons, and went to their houses constantly and they to mine. I never became a close friend of any of the girls in my own class; they were so much older than I that we seemed to have very little in common.

I was never again head of my class, though always close to the top, and I had to work harder than before. In those days Bryn Mawr College, where I had been entered years before, required more subjects than other colleges and had its own examinations which could be taken over a period of three years. I passed the entrance examination in French and Algebra when I was fourteen, completed my senior matriculation with an average of 85 by the time I was sixteen, and was accepted by Bryn Mawr.

The summers when I was fourteen and fifteen I spent at Pinelands Camp on Lake Squam in New Hampshire, one of the first camps for girls in the country. I liked everything about Pinelands, the view of the mountains in the distance, the great "Whittier Pine" beside the bungalow in whose shade the poet used to sit and write, the overnight hikes in the White Mountains, the companionship and team competitions with other girls. I rowed on the second crew and won the second prize for swimming. I was never first in sports but at least won a gold pin for neatness and deportment.

Some of the girls stayed in bed during the first day or two when they were menstruating and most of them were off sports for four or five days, as was customary at that time. But not I. Before I went to camp, Miss Dalton, the director, had visited Mother to find out what I was to do during my "periods."

"I want her to carry on as usual, but not to go in swimming in cold water," Mother said. "Her father says there would be fewer neurotic women if they ignored a perfectly normal bodily function instead of feeling sorry for themselves. Many women, he says, use menstruation as an excuse for shirking their duty or as a means of intimidating their husbands."

During my second summer at camp two Boston girls and I, tent mates, became an inseparable trio. We were always together. We sat together at meals, laughing and talking among ourselves. We walked together through the woods to the lake for rowing practice or swimming lessons. We made no effort to mingle with the other girls whom we considered dull clods.

One morning Miss Dalton called the three of us to her office. "I've decided to separate you and put you in different tents," she said.

We were appalled. "What have we done?"

"That's just it," Miss Dalton said, "you haven't done anything. You haven't helped any of the younger girls who are homesick. You haven't helped to organize games on rainy days. You haven't helped the swimming counsellors with the girls who are having trouble learning to swim. You haven't taken an interest in anybody but yourselves. All you do is swagger around with your noses in the air. I'm ashamed of you."

We were overcome with surprise and guilt, and felt utterly deflated. We promised faithfully that if she spared us the humiliation of separating us we would mend our ways. She agreed to give us another chance.

We withdrew to the deep woods where we wept and made plans to show Miss Dalton what we could do. Afterwards it was a surprise to find that some of the girls we had thought dull were not dull, only homesick or shy, and that they were very likeable. And also, to our surprise, we actually enjoyed helping the younger girls who were having trouble fitting in.

The summer I was sixteen I spent with the family at Saunderstown. There, beside Narragansett Bay, we had a big shingled cottage, which had been built after the war with the money that came from selling the farm. At that time the summer colony was for us a family reunion: there were sixty-three uncles, aunts and cousins living within a distance of three miles. Nine of the cousins were young men a few years older than I. They called me Bill, since they were John's contemporaries and had picked up the nickname from him, and they treated me as a sort of mascot, taking pride in teaching me to dance, sail, dive, shoot and play poker and vingt-et-un. Oliver La Farge, in particular, became a close friend until his death: he lent me books which we talked about by the hour over tea on our front porch or while sailing in the *Golly*. Although he was seven years older than I, he never made me feel young or inexperienced and I was able to talk to him more freely than to anyone else.

Our family and his close friends called Oliver by the nickname Inky, which he had given to himself when he was a small boy; he had always alluded to himself in the third person as Indianman which he pronounced Inkyman. Mother maintained that the La Farges have Indian blood through the wife of Oliver Hazard Perry, one of their ancestors. Certainly Inky looked like an Indian, as did his older brother Christopher, the poet and novelist. He had high cheek bones, a beige skin, and straight, black hair. As a boy and young man he dressed for the part when he was at Saunderstown, wearing a hunting knife in a sheath on a belt around his waist, and moccasins and khaki trousers and shirt at a time when all the other males in the family wore sneakers, dark blue sailor pants, and middy tops purchased from the U.S. Navy surplus store in Newport.

After he became an anthropologist Inky developed into a recognized authority on Indian culture in the southwest of the United States, Mexico and Guatemala. He learned to speak some of the Indian languages and was often able to pass as an Indian. The Hopi Indians took him for a Navajo and the Navajos took him for a Hopi.

When Oliver's first novel, *Laughing Boy,* won the Pulitzer Prize and became a best seller, he gave up anthropology, to the distress of museum people, who said he was one of the most brilliant men in the field, and devoted himself to writing. He went to live in Santa Fe, and his empathy with Indians made him an ardent exponent of their cause. He spent the rest of his life writing about their problems and working on their behalf with the Bureau of Indian Affairs. We wrote long letters to each other once or twice a year until his death in the 1960's. In one of them he wrote, "My heart bleeds for the Indians. I write about them and feel guilty because I make money out of it."

In later years, when time had shrunk the difference in our ages, Christopher La Farge also became a close and valued friend, but in my teens Inky played a more important part in my life than any of my other contemporaries. An intellectual, he nevertheless had a tremendous feeling for the out-of-doors, for the woods and for the sea. He was regarded as an odd ball by many of his conventional Groton and Harvard peers, and Mother always made fun of him, saying he was a mass of affectations and a play actor. But I loved him dearly.

Cousin Flos La Farge, the mother of Oliver and Christopher, took an interest in me and invited me to her "readings"—a coveted honour. Cousin Flos was Florence Bayard La Farge. (When in doubt our family named the girls Florence Bayard, so there were seven of us, five living at that time.) A dozen of her friends and relations met at the La Farge house at 3:30 every Thursday afternoon in summer. They sat on the verandah and knitted or sewed while Cousin Flos read aloud. At five o'clock, tea (in a large silver pot covered with a tea cosy) was put on the table beside a curate holding toast with homemade jam, thin bread and butter, and fruitcake. During tea there was discussion of what had been read.

Cousin Flos usually chose articles from the *Atlantic Monthly, Harper's* Magazine and *Blackwood's Magazine.* The discussion often became loud, hot and heavy, and there was much shouting, since so many Bayards and Kanes were together at the same time. The readings often broke up in confusion, with someone loudly proclaiming that she would never, never come again. But everyone always came; the members of the chosen group wouldn't have missed the fun for anything.

That autumn, when I was still sixteen, I went to Bryn Mawr College. I roomed with Polly Pettit who had been in the class ahead of me at Le Cours Français. The old residence halls of Bryn Mawr, designed by the architect, Walter Cope, the father of my Cope cousins, were built of grey stone in the academic tradition of the old world, and inside the woodwork was painted dark brown. Polly and I each had a small, unheated bedroom and shared a good-sized study with an open fireplace. A large window, above a deep window seat, looked out over trees, lawns and grey stone buildings.

I loved the atmosphere of the place. The professors, aloof and impressive in their academic gowns, treated us as adults, and their lectures were stimulating, even exciting after the routine learning at school. In particular I loved the college library. It had cloisters built around a fountain in the centre of the quadrangle, and there were deep armchairs in front of the fireplace in the big high-ceilinged reading room. It was a wonderful place to read and for a girl to dream when she lifted her eyes from her book to look into the flames.

I majored in English, worked hard on my compositions and received good marks in spite of my bad spelling. Polly was taking a pre-medical course and found science easy, which I did not, so she helped me with biology and psychology and I helped her with her English papers.

That year Bryn Mawr was a great adventure. It was fun to make new friends from other parts of the country, fun to be on my own and not to be told when to work, or to play, or to go to bed. Like all of the other freshmen, I revelled in being able to stay up late talking about life, love and philosophy.

Though Bryn Mawr was fine during the week, I always went home for the week-ends, since Philadelphia is only half an hour away. And I was not the only inveterate week-ender. There was a great exodus every Friday when the girls, who had worn shabby sweaters and grubby tweed skirts under their black academic gowns all week, suddenly blossomed out with carefully curled hair and well pressed dresses. We all departed on the famous "Paoli Local" on our way to Philadelphia and points east as soon as our last class was over, and were not seen again until Sunday night. "The train man," carrying a lantern, always met the trains after dark and walked the mile with us along country roads to make sure we were safely delivered to the residences.

Bryn Mawr was considered very *avant garde* that year because the students held a mass rally in the gymnasium and all but four of us voted in favour of lifting the ban on smoking on campus. The newspapers carried headlines, and there were editorials expressing horror at the depravity of the young—and the dangerously permissive attitude of the old—when the Board of Governors (most of them Quaker gentlemen) gave us permission to smoke tobacco in the sitting rooms. The day after the ban was lifted I made myself embarrassingly sick by smoking a pipe during a bridge game.

Our morals were supposed to be protected by a self-governing student body—known as "self-gove"—that operated on the honour system. The rules they were required to enforce were in the best boarding-school tradition. We were forbidden "to motor unchaperoned after dark with a person of the opposite sex," and if we wanted to go to the theatre or a concert in Philadelphia we had to sign in The Book in the Hall Warden's office. A graduate student would stay up and let us in, since the hall doors were locked at 10:30. Drinking in the halls was forbidden. I cannot remember that drug-taking was even mentioned; in those days drugs were not a problem.

Carey Thomas, the famous president of Bryn Mawr between 1894 and 1908, was an impassioned feminist, and her spirit was still strong on the campus when I was a freshman. We were all supposed to be the sort of women that the extreme Women's Lib girls want to be now. I took it for granted that women should be emancipated and independent, but I thought the feminism angle was being carried too far. At our college dances we put on our best evening dresses and danced with one another, a practice that I considered unhealthy at the time, as I do now. When a man was daring enough to come to a hall to take us on a date he was subjected to jealous scrutiny by students who, giggling and fluttering at the mere sight of a male, peeked at him around the edges of the velvet curtains in front of the ground floor reception room. It was rather like being incarcerated in a nunnery without having the dedication of a nun.

When, recently, I went to a college reunion I couldn't help but think that if the ghost of Carey Thomas were to come back now she would hardly recognize the place. "The train man" still meets the evening locals, but now he transports the late comers in a station wagon. The new buildings are unashamedly modern, with a solid, metallic elegance. Two of the halls (one of them Radnor Hall where Polly and I lived) are now the residences of both men and women. There are men, wearing blue jeans like the girls, all over the campus and in the class-rooms. And the new president is a man.

I think the changes are, on the whole, for the better since, as one of the students put it, "We know we are going to have to work and live with men for the rest of our lives, so we had better get used to being with them while we are at college." However I wish that a woman could have been given the presidency when Katherine McBride retired because there are in the United States, as in Canada, so many qualified women, scholars and good administrators who have long been passed over in favour of men. I think the alumnae should have made an effort to carry on the tradition established by the three fine women who have been presidents of Bryn Mawr. I think it was particularly important to do that now that the college has become co-educational, since men must become accustomed to the idea that women can—and should—hold positions of responsibility and authority.

The summer after my freshman year at Bryn Mawr, Miss Dalton asked me to come back to Pinelands as a counsellor. It seemed fabulous to be paid for doing all the outdoor things I enjoyed most in a place I loved. I took my first job seriously, and was thrilled by Miss Dalton's confidence in me when she asked me to drive the milk truck after the regular driver became ill. I had to pass the examination for a pro-fessional chauffeur's licence, of course, but Father had taught me to drive John's old Model T. Ford when I was fourteen, and I had received my driver's licence on the day I was sixteen, so there was no problem.

I felt grown up and independent when I drove the heavy truck up and down the steep New Hampshire hills to the dairy every morning, stopping on the way to pick up the mail bag at the Center Town Post Office.

At the end of August I tasted the heady wine of financial in-dependence when I was paid a hundred dollars and opened my own checking account. However, my earnings dwindled away rapidly when I went back to college. Mother gave me only $5 a week as an allowance and I blew it all on chocolate sundaes, waffles with maple syrup, fifty-cent theatre tickets in the gods, and train tickets to Philadelphia or to New York to stay with friends.

When I returned to Saunderstown from camp that summer I was frightened when I realized that Father was ill. A blood vessel had broken behind one of his eyes so that he had to wear dark glasses and could not read. I suddenly saw that his hair was thin and white and that he stumbled often when he walked. It was strange not to see his wide-set, compelling blue eyes that seemed to draw the truth out of a person. Although he was only fifty-six he looked like an old man.

During the next few weeks I read Ibsen aloud to him in the mornings. We talked about the plays and often disagreed with each other about them. When we discussed *A Doll's House,* I was all for Norah, and thought she was right to leave her husband in order to find herself. Father agreed that she had to find herself, but thought she had an obligation to stay and help her children to escape from their father's pernicious ideas. By his approach to Norah's problem he helped me to understand the difficulties involved in making decisions. At first, when we discussed *Ghosts* and *The Master Builder* I said they were sinister and depressing but changed my mind when Father, having a professional interest in them, explained to me that they are profound commentaries on society as well as dramas about sick individuals.

I also read him the proofs of the last medical paper he ever wrote. It was about suicide. His thesis was that a person who decides to take his own life is mentally ill, because the will to survive is the deepest instinct, and any healthy animal must obey it. He believed that suicide should not be a criminal offence, and that people who try to kill themselves should be given psychiatric treatment.

One day when we were taking a walk, Father, who was holding my arm, told me that he was in despair because his physician had advised him to retire. "He told me to live like a cabbage," Father said, "and I can't live like a cabbage."

I shared his despair. When I was a child I had been taken to see his older brother who had had a stroke, and I could not bear to think that Father might become paralyzed and helpless, neither alive nor dead, the way Uncle Will had been. I prayed nightly that he would die rather than have that happen to him.

The autumn of my sophomore year at Bryn Mawr started happily. Polly Pettit and I, opposites in temperament and interests, liked each other and got along so well that we had decided to room together for another year. As far as work was concerned, I was in my element. We were studying Shakespeare in the course on English literature and were required to read ten plays and write a long thesis on some aspect of them. I had both read and seen nine of them, had discussed them with the family for years, and so was delighted to have a chance to put down in writing what I thought about them.

I was also lucky enough to make the select list of students who were allowed by the Dean to take Dr. Georgiana Goddard King's course in Italian Renaissance painting, the most popular course at Bryn Mawr at that time. "G.G." had the gift of teaching, as well as great erudition, a probing, iconoclastic mind, and a deep love of the Quatrocento in Italy. She believed that no one could understand Renaissance painting without knowing about the roots of the Renaissance and what it meant. Her reading list for the course included not only the expected Berenson and Vasari, but also Petrarch, Boccaccio, St. Francis of Assisi, and scholarly books about the Medici, the Popes and the history of Florence. I loved the slides of the paintings she showed, and was fascinated by her analysis of them and by her scintillating remarks about life and the way men's minds worked at the time.

I also took a course in medieval architecture by a lesser professor, an inhibited young man from Princeton. He was not stimulating but I am grateful to him because he introduced me to Henry Adams' *Mont Saint-Michel and Chartres,* which opened magic casements for me.

One night in the autumn I went to bed around eleven o'clock after working on a long paper entitled *Her Infinite Variety,* about the women in Shakespeare's plays. At 12:30, when I was fast asleep, Polly came into my room.

"Wake up," she said. "Your mother wants to speak to you on the phone."

I put on my dressing gown and went downstairs to the phone booth in the front hall. Mother's voice was quiet but strong. And she was brief. "Florence," she said, "your father is very ill. I want you to come home. John is on his way out to get you. Get dressed and be ready when he arrives."

I said, "Yes, Mother," and hung up.

While I dressed, Polly went to tell the Warden what had happened. When she came back we played Double Canfield until the Warden appeared at the study door in her dressing gown and invited us to have a cup of coffee in her sitting room.

The three of us sat drinking coffee, talking little, for what seemed like a long time. Then the doorbell rang. I went out to John who was waiting on the doorstep in the pouring rain.

One of his fraternity brothers was in the driver's seat of his battered old Model T. Ford. We climbed in the back and John put his arm around me. "Bill, you'll have to be brave," he said. "Daddy is dead."

Disintegration

The day before Father's funeral I was taken shopping by someone. I can't remember who took me because I was in a sort of cataleptic state from shock. But I do remember the agony of trying on an endless succession of black shoes in an effort to find a pair comfortable enough to wear on campus, yet which didn't look like the horrors our old school teachers used to wear. And I remember how I resented the sympathy of the salesman. I didn't want to exhibit my grief. I was tearless, but there was no courage inside me.

That day we also bought a black woollen dress, a black skirt and sweater, black cotton stockings and white handkerchiefs with black borders. One of Mother's friends sent me an old, black, fur-trimmed coat. It was too long but nobody ever got around to shortening it.

The house was full of people. Relations came and sat with Mother in her bedroom and talked about Father. Someone, perhaps Aunt Fol, brought boxes of black dresses on approval, and a milliner arrived with hats and long veils for the widow to try on. Black bands were sewn around the sleeves of my brothers' coats and they were made to wear black ties. Ten-year-old Shan, with his black armband, drifted silently around the house, outside of all the bustle—the saddest of little boys.

Black-edged notepaper and visiting cards were ordered from the stationery store for Mother and me.

Father's body was laid out in the front office, and strangers—his patients—came to say good-bye. From time to time, when no one was around, I went and looked at what was there. It was not Father.

Mother insisted that I go back to college two days after the funeral. I felt conspicuous in my mourning, and my insides seemed to be made of lead, but I was still tearless. My friends told me I was very brave, and it was impossible for me to tell them how I really felt.

Every weekend I went home to a house of gloom. The doors of Father's office opened into empty rooms. No one sang in the halls or to the rhythm of a razor being stropped. No one played the piano; it was closed and all the sheets and books of music had been shut away in the music cabinet.

Mother became a different person. When Father had been away during the war, they had written to each other every day, so there was always communication. Then she had been buoyed up by hope and by pride in her ability to show Father how well she could manage. Now there were no letters, no hope; and no one cared whether she managed well or not. So Mother poured all her love on to her children.

She gave them love but she could not give them security, because she was insecure herself. She was worried about finances, even though her financial adviser assured her there was no cause for concern if she would just sell the house and live more simply. She was also pathetically possessive of her children; she felt we were all that was left to her in life—and this at a time when two of us were in the inevitable process of leaving her.

John, who was in his senior year at university, had fallen in love with a friend of mine and wanted to get married. He also wanted to do post-graduate work in geology. Mother was horrified that he would dream of marrying so soon after Father's death—and before he could support a wife. No one had ever heard of a wife working while her husband completed his education. There were many bitter arguments which made the atmosphere of our home even more unhappy.

I, for my part, was sadly missing the gaiety and activity that had been part of our lives before Father's death: the young people coming and going, the parties, the singing, the arguments and repartee at meals, the ringing of the phone. But Mother, who was Victorian in this one respect at least, insisted on strict observance of mourning. She refused to accept invitations or to ask people to our house. She forbade me to go to parties.

After three months, realizing I was forlorn, Mother relented some-what. She made me a black taffeta evening dress so I could go to the houses of friends informally for dinner. She also made me a white crepe de Chine dress to wear for dinner at Bryn Mawr when spring came. After six months she allowed me to go into lavender, but she herself wore unrelieved black for three years, only putting on coloured clothes when her children said they were so depressed by the sight of her that they could not bear it any longer.

Mother was deperately lonely since she withdrew from all her friends except her immediate family. She hugged her grief to herself, feeling that it was disloyal to Father to forget him for a minute or not to mourn for what she had lost. Her self-pity was destructive. She knew that, but became so engulfed by it that she could not shake it off. She was sure she would soon die of a broken heart and spent a good deal of time pasting the names of her children inside bureau drawers and under tables and desks, to simplify the work of the executors of her will and in the hope of reducing the inheritance tax. I still have jewel boxes on which are written in her writing, "I gave this to my darling daughter Florence, in 1925."

Early in the spring she sold the big house and rented a small one two blocks away on Pine Street. It was as if "1732" had eaten a piece of cake like the one Alice ate in Wonderland, and had shrunk all over. When the Steinway baby-grand and the big furniture were put into it, the tiny rooms, three of them on each of the three floors, seemed to contract even more, so that we were always moving on narrow circuitous routes around big chunks of mahogany.

There were no servants' rooms, but that did not matter because the only help we had then were Ben Bush, the man of all work, and the cook. And they lived out.

For me, going home for the weekends was like entering a battle ground. John had been so upset by Father's death and by the arguments over his future that he had failed two of his final examinations and Mother refused to finance his education further unless he postponed his marriage.

The upshot of it all was that John gave up the idea of getting a degree and took a factory job. A year later he married his fiancée, a girl of sterling character. They have had a happy married life but because their parents did not have the foresight to back John in his ambitions, he was denied the opportunity of fulfilling himself in a profession for which he was admirably suited.

While the bitter arguments were going on I was torn with sympathy and love for Mother. I longed to be able to help her, yet could not. I was furious at John for hurting and upsetting her; I had never been seriously in love myself, and was incapable of understanding the extent of his urge to realize his manhood. I found myself embroiled in emotional scenes which left me exhausted and frustrated, swinging like a weather vane blown by divided loyalties. As time went on I became increasingly frantic. More and more I wanted to do something entirely different. Death seemed all about me and I wanted to live, live, live, while there was time.

College was no longer the interesting, satisfying place it had been the year before. Except for the course in Renaissance painting, the lectures left me intellectually dry. I enjoyed the reading for the philosophy course but soon found the professor wanted his own ideas, rehashed, instead of *my* ideas about what I had read. The upper classmen explained that no one was such an idiot as to read Plato and Aristotle when all one needed to do was to take copious notes during the professor's lecture, learn them by heart and put them on the examination paper.

I craved physical activity to relieve pent-up feelings, and gave myself a rapid heart by smoking incessantly and playing centre forward on the water-polo team. Consequently I was taken off sports for three months and made to rest for an hour three times a week on the roof of the gymnasium.

Having gone for years without missing a day at school, I suddenly had a succession of colds. Then, three days before the mid-year examinations, my eyelids swelled up in yellow, dribbling puffs so that I could barely see. I went to the infirmary and the college doctor gave me a thorough going-over. She had been an intern when father was chief of Psychiatry at the Pennsylvania Hospital and had admired him greatly. So she was partial to me and took more than an ordinary interest.

"I can find nothing whatsoever wrong with your eyes or anything else," she said. "Your heart seems to be normal again. All I can think is that you are tired and upset by your father's death. Stay here. Rest today, and tomorrow start working for your exams. I'll get your roommate to bring your notes and books."

"Do you think my eyes will be well enough for me to take the exams?" I asked.

"I think you should go ahead and take exams even if they remain the way they are now."

I took the first of the examinations with my eyelids puffy and drooling. As usual when faced with questions on a paper, all sorts of information and ideas I didn't know I possessed poured into my mind. I always enjoyed examinations because of the euphoria induced by this inrush of recall. I forgot my eyes, and was only concerned with writing, in some sort of readable form, the answers which came to me with such exciting force.

When the examination was over the swelling of the eyelids had gone down, leaving purple welts as if I were recovering from a black eye. By the next day they were back to normal, and gave me no more trouble during the other examinations. I passed them all with good marks. The same thing happened again before the final examinations.

Up till then I had been a healthy, satisfactory, precocious child who had lived up to everyone's expectations at school and camp. I could be depended on to do the right thing after an outburst of temper and the remorse which would follow it. So Mother was naturally dumbfounded when I arrived home one weekend in the spring and said, "I've decided to leave Byrn Mawr. I'm going to come out next year."

My former classmates in Le Cours Français, who were two years behind me academically, were graduating from high school that spring. They were all going to take part in the old-fashioned ritual of coming out into society, and had been urging me to be a debutante with them. Moreover, one of my best friends at Bryn Mawr was leaving to come out. I was tired of mourning, of studying all the time. I wanted to have fun. I was obsessed with the fear that I would die young without ever having really lived at all.

My ambition to write, to have a career, to graduate from college and then travel had melted away.

"You must be out of your mind," Mother said. "I can't afford to buy you the clothes you will need to make a suitable debut and I refuse to entertain for you, so you won't be asked to many parties."

"I want to have fun," I said.

"This coming-out business," she said, "is really saying to the world 'I have a daughter here who is ready for marriage.' A debutante is like a girl in an oriental slave market. She's dressed up and strutted around at teas and dinners to catch the highest bidder. It never occurred to me that you wanted to be just another Main Line matron, but that's what will happen to you."

When the word got around, older members of the family took me aside and told me I was selfish even to suggest spending money on such foolishness. It was my duty to stay in college, and I was behaving badly—worrying my mother when she had so many other things to upset her. My father, they said, would have been very disappointed in me if he had known. I listened unhappily but I couldn't explain what was making me feel so desperate. I remained obstinate.

After weeks of battle Mother gave in and agreed to let me do what I wanted. She made it clear, however, that she regarded coming out as a stupid, useless performance. She kept telling me I had brains and should use them, not waste a year being a social butterfly. I was as much a disappointment to her as John.

When the autumn came Aunt Fol and my aunt Sarah Kane gave me the usual coming-out tea at a hotel. Mother refused to go to it because she was still in mourning. A cousin gave a theatre party for me, with supper afterwards at the Ritz. No one else entertained for me. But though I could not return their hospitality, my friends loyally asked me to dinners, dances and balls.

Most of my dresses were made-over hand-me-downs from my half-sister Mabel, although Mother did buy me a new coming-out dress, a pale blue taffeta *robe de style* with pink facings, and the mother of a friend treated me to a green velvet by Henri Bendel.

At first I revelled in the late dinner parties and in the dances. There were seven or eight balls that season, and at all of them I danced and danced until breakfast was served around six o'clock in the morning. My energy was unlimited when it came to dancing. I knew a great many young men who had gone to dancing school with me, and they and John's fraternity brothers conspired to make sure I would never get stuck, so there was usually someone to cut in as my partner passed the stag line.

When a ball was over, the chaperone, Mrs. Stanton, would take me home in a taxi, along with three other debutantes. We must have been almost the last girls in North America to have a professional chaperone.

Mrs. Stanton was a small, perky Cockney with bright, dark eyes and a pointed nose. She always wore the same greenish-black dress, coat and hat, and seemed to have a perpetual cold in the head. She was proud of her scrapbook of newspaper clipping and photographs of her "young ladies" and conscientious in the performance of her duties. She was always waiting for us in the dressing room when we arrived from a dinner party, and gave us the once-over before we went into the ballroom, buttoning our long kid gloves and making sure our skirts hung properly.

"You look sweet, dear. Have a good time," she would say to each of us.

If any one of us got stuck with a partner for too long, or failed to get a supper partner, she would flee, fighting back tears, to the dressing room. Whereupon Mrs. Stanton would take her home and then return to wait for the others. I never needed to be taken home early because I was having a good time. For me dancing was living, and I kept Mrs. Stanton waiting until the orchestra had played "Good Night Ladies" and gone home.

Although Mother insisted that I be chaperoned at balls she allowed me to go out for dinner or to dance at night clubs with young men. But she made me promise to take a dollar in my purse—"mad money"— in case I needed to take a taxi home, and I had to take my driver's licence as well.

"Don't let any boy drive you if he has had too much to drink. Insist on taking the car keys and driving yourself."

During prohibition in the United States people talked about drinking very much the way we talk about drugs today. Even the most reliable bootleggers had been known to sell lethal booze to their customers. Everyone knew of someone who had been blinded, made seriously ill, or even killed by wood alcohol. Everyone deplored the fact that "nobody knew how to drink like a gentleman any more." The hip flask was as ubiquitous as the wrist watch, and it was fashionable to drink in parked cars even if the contents of the flask tasted like hair-tonic flavoured with juniper drops. I had promised Mother not to take even a glass of sherry that winter, and I kept my promise. I felt guilty about the whole coming-out business and wanted to please her about something.

As the winter wore on, a change began to come over me. I began to wonder if this trivial round was all there was to living. I began to worry about all the food that went to waste. Night after night, we would sit down around 8:30 to a five- or six-course dinner. Philadelphia hostesses prided themselves on their good food, so we eighteen-year-olds and the somewhat older young men we were supposed to catch were regaled with raw oysters or caviar; green turtle soup or consommé with sherry, shad roe or terrapin or lobster Newburg; squabs or filet de boeuf; green salad with cheese; and rich ice cream. On Friday nights we would go on from a dinner party to a ball at 10:30. And around midnight we would be served a three-course supper with much the same food. As a rule our plates would be taken away half full since no matter how much we danced we couldn't possibly eat that much. I knew there were poor people in Philadelphia and I wondered if it was right for us to live this way. Once I asked a waiter what happened to all the food which went out.

"It gets thrown out in the garbage," he said in a voice which—understandably, I thought—was critical, even vindictive.

As time went on, I began to understand why Mother felt the way she did about society. In later years I shared the view of my family that I was selfish and stupid to leave university in order to spend a winter dressing up and whirling from party to party.

Now I am more forgiving of myself. At that time everyone expected me to behave like an adult because I was academically precocious, while in fact I was still emotionally immature, an adolescent with all the doubts, insecurities and introspections that adolescence is heir to. Moreover, I was suffering horribly from grief and a terrible sense of loss and disorientation. I was selfish, certainly, as most young people are selfish, but I was also confused; I had lost my way on the path of life as a result of Father's death and Mother's desperate reaction to her own grief.

Today, looking back on that year from the vantage point of nearly half a century, I am not sure that it was utterly wasted. It has given me understanding of the anxiety and confusion of the adolescents of today who are looking for their own paths as individuals in the insecure, materialistic world in which they find themselves. I can identify my eighteen-year-old self with the university drop-outs of recent years and sympathize with their feeling that they must do their own thing and pack adult experience into their lives. I do not despair of them as they work their way toward maturity.

That debutante winter also worked something out of my system. It's probable that if I had not come out, I might have felt all my life that a lovely world of glamour had passed me by. Instead, the experience cured me of any remote yearnings to be part of the social set. It taught me what sort of person I did *not* want to be, although I did not yet know what sort of person I *did* want to be.

Recuperation

When Lent came around, bringing the debutante season to an end, many people we knew went south to escape the winds and rain of March. Mother and I could not afford to go south, but that did not worry me, as I still had a full social life. There were half a dozen men who took me to the theatre, dinner or dancing regularly, and came for tea on Sunday afternoons.

A red-haired boy, Manson Radford, who had been my best beau since I was fifteen and whose photograph always stood on my desk, was at Annapolis at that time. Though I only saw him now and then, I was happy when I was with him. We talked about everything under the sun, read poetry to each other, and were amused by the same things. I had great affection for him but I was not in love with him.

Another young man, a lawyer, who was considerably older than I, also took me out frequently. Bob Oliphant was well bred and well established. Though we disagreed about almost everything and bickered continually, I thought I was in love with him. Yet when he asked me to marry him I said, "No. It won't work. It won't last. I'm not going to see you any more." But I kept on going out with him just the same. I don't think he loved me or really wanted to marry me, but after we had parted in anger or bleak mutual frustration he would come back, and I would be pleased, and excited by the thought of seeing him again. It was one of those chemical, explosive relationships which keep the divorce rate up. We both knew it, but we couldn't stay apart.

At that time I was beginning to worry about what was happening to my brain.

I signed up for courses in French and the history of art, and went to

57

lectures at the University of Pennsylvania. I began to write short stories, which collected rejection slips. I wrote to the Philadelphia Art Gallery asking for a job, and was rejected.

When summer came and we went to Saunderstown, I continued writing, working every morning in a little studio in the woods behind our house. But I only succeeded in adding to my collection of rejection slips.

The Friday before the Labour Day weekend, Inky La Farge asked me to go sailing with him. It was one of those glorious New England days when the air is clear and sparkling. There was a strong southeast wind, a choppy sea. We tacked, close-hauled, down the bay, sitting with our wet behinds in the tilted scuppers, our feet braced on the wooden casing for the centreboard. I had the tiller, which fought like a spirited horse as we took the spray of white-capped waves. It was wonderfully exhilarating.

"I'm going cruising tomorrow," Inky said. "Three of the men who were in my class at Harvard are coming up from New York on the Colonial tonight. We've cruised together every Labour Day for five years. The weather forecasts are for bright and clear."

We talked for a while about cruising, about the anchorage at Block Island and the best things to cook in a small galley kitchen.

Suddenly there was a loud, cracking sound. The mast broke off short and fell into the water. The mainsail lay flat, a crumpled heap of canvas, half in and half out of the water. The *Golly,* a minute before alive and full of creaking, slapping sounds, became absolutely quiet. The back stays had pulled out. She was an old boat, and the mahogany deck had rotted around the screws.

Somehow we pulled the mast and sail on board and lashed them with the main sheet. Then Inky made a jury rig out of a boat hook and the jib and we sailed home.

"Well," said Inky, "there goes the cruise. We'll have to take her up to Wickford tomorrow and see what Allie Saunders can do about making her a new stick."

I was cold and very wet, my back hurt from heaving up the mast, and I felt ashamed because I had been at the helm.

"I'm terribly, terribly sorry," I said. "I feel awful about it."

"Forget it, Bill," he said. "I should have taken a reef. I'm the skipper and it was my responsibility. Forget it."

"I'm sort of a hoodoo," I lamented.

"That makes three," said Inky. "So now we're home free."

What he meant was that for the third time I had done the wrong thing when I was with him. When I was fourteen I had fainted, my form of sea sickness, when I had been sailing with him. When I was sixteen I had shot myself in the foot with a .22 while we were shooting at a floating target. Now, at the age of nineteen, I had dismasted his beloved sloop.

The next day when I went down at noon to swim from the La Farges' dock, Inky introduced me to three young men, the disconsolate guests whose cruise I had ruined.

"This is the kid cousin who took the stick out of the *Golly,*" he said.

They were polite about the misfortune, but I felt sure they loathed the sight of me. I thought all three were attractive, but one of them, John Bird, a tall, thin man with a moustache and an English accent, was particularly so. He was also very daring. He climbed to the top of the cupola roof of the dock and did a competent high dive, something nobody had ever done from there before.

I clasped my hands as he climbed up and said, "Oh, Mr. Bird, Mr. Bird, please be careful."

That afternoon, Inky's married sister phoned me and said, "I'm having a dinner party for Inky's friends, now that they can't go sailing. Come in after dinner around nine. We're going to play games, charades or something."

I dressed carefully for the occasion, putting on a bright red, sleeveless silk dress with a wide fringe starting a few inches below the waist and ending at the daringly high hemline just below the knee. When I arrived at the party, dinner was not yet over and I heard roars of laughter as the maid ushered me into the dining room and pulled up a chair for me. Mr. Bird was in the midst of telling a fantastic story about the adventures of a friend of his, Hilary Belloc, who for a time had earned a precarious living by showing the vintage film *The Birth of a Nation* to the natives of Tahiti. The way he embroidered the tale and made it wildly funny reminded me of my Kane relations. It was only much later that I found that he also had a liberal dose of Irish in him.

After dinner I sat on a small sofa beside my cousin Henry Wharton. I was surprised and delighted when Mr. Bird came over to us, said, "Do you mind if I barge in?" and, without waiting for a reply, sat down between us. Being so close to him I became aware of his unusually large dark-blue eyes and his long, slender hands. I was also aware of an indefinable chemistry taking place between us. After we began to play an intellectual pencil game I began to feel that we were the only people in the room.

I was impressed as I watched his pencil flying across the paper, and even more so when he won the game. No one had ever defeated the talented, versatile La Farge men at a word game before.

After the game was over Mr. Bird and I talked to each other quietly in low voices. The chemistry between us grew stronger. The other people in the room receded to a great distance, and their voices and laughter blew over and around our quiet little island. Later, my cousin Florence Lockwood said she had never believed in love at first sight until she saw it happening in front of her eyes that night. It was not love, not yet, but certainly there was a strong mutual attraction.

When the party broke up, Oliver La Farge and his three guests walked me home the quarter mile or so down The Waterway.

It was dark going through the woods which bordered the lane and the going was rough, so I tottered in my high heels. Mr. Bird lent me his arm, and as we all strolled along, talking and laughing, I could feel the chemistry between the two of us growing stronger.

Our house looked out from a wide lawn toward the mouth of Naragansett Bay. Beaver Tail Light House blinked at us across the riffled water and a planet hung bright and red in the star-studded sky.

"That's Mars," Mr. Bird said.

It was the first time I had met a young man who was interested in stars, and I was impressed because my father had thought it was important for a person to know the constellations.

Somebody suggested the planet might be Saturn.

"I doubt it," Mr. Bird said, "but if it is and we had a telescope we should be able to see the rings around it."

I went in the house and brought out Father's army field-glasses, and we took turns lying on a huge, flat rock below the terrace while we scanned the skies above. We did not see any rings but we made a great deal of noise which Mother commented on unfavourably when I went up to bed.

The next morning Flos La Farge came down to talk to Mother, who said to me afterwards, "Your cousin Flos says Inky thinks you ought to know that you mustn't imagine you've made a conquest just because John Bird was so attentive to you last night. He's famous for being a misogynist. He's very brilliant; came from Oxford to Harvard on a scholarship, and now he's working for the British Foreign Office in New York— at the British Library of Information."

"I've never met anyone like him before," I said. "He's the most attractive man I've ever met."

I was not cheered to hear Inky's message but I thought that Mr. Bird had also felt the chemistry and might not ignore it.

I had hoped to see Mr. Bird again during the weekend, but the next day Inky and his guests went into the "back country" to fish for trout. I made up my mind that I would probably never see John Bird again, and that was that. But on Labour Day morning, Inky's guests were on the La Farge's dock when I went there to swim. We all took turns going off the diving board and then raced out to the *Golly"s* empty mooring. (I should have felt guilty at the sight but now did not, because I was secretly glad that Inky and his friends did not go cruising that year.)

Afterward, sitting on the dock, conversation was general, and Mr. Bird did not pay any special attention to me, or I to him. But, as I was walking home, he came dashing after me across the croquet court. He was wearing an enormous long white dressing-gown over his bathing-trunks and had tied a towel around his head. I thought he looked very dramatic, like an Arab, except that he had a huge sandy moustache.

"Wait a mo', Miss Rhein," he said. "It just occurred to me that I expect to be in Philadelphia in a few weeks' time. I wonder if you would have lunch or dinner with me?"

"That would be fine," I murmured.

"I'll telephone you," he promised, and dashed off across the lawn with a wave of the hand.

I thought about him a good deal after I went back to Philadelphia for the winter, but remembering Inky's message, I kept reminding myself that a clever, older man of twenty-five would have hardly more than a passing interest in a girl of nineteen who had wasted her brains in order to come out and was now at loose ends.

That autumn, although I was lunched, dined, and taken to night-clubs by a number of men, I saw more and more of Bob Oliphant. I told Mother I thought I was in love with him but had nevertheless refused to marry him. She could not understand my attitude, and kept saying that if I married I would settle down and "everything would be all right."

In those days marriage was regarded as the ultimate goal for every girl, as it still too often is today. Not to marry was to be a failure. In those days I didn't know any career women—only dreary old maids who were by definition unattractive or they would have found a man to marry them. Even Aunt Fol, whose brains and spirit I admired, had obviously missed out on life because she had never married. Inevitably, social pressure and my own acceptance of the mores of the time were making me drift into marriage with Bob in spite of my conviction that it would be a fiasco.

In October Mr. Bird telephoned me from New York and invited me to the Penn-Harvard football game. When I told him I couldn't go with him because I had already agreed to go with Calvert, a student in the School of Architecture at the University of Pennsylvania, he invited me for dinner after the game. I accepted with pleasure—indeed with a great deal of pleasure.

A few days later Calvert told me he had taken it for granted that I was going with him to a dinner-dance at the Lilacs Boat Club after the game. I didn't want to stand him up, but I also did not want to miss seeing Mr. Bird again. When I told Mother I didn't know what to do, she said I had better write to John Bird explaining I had mixed up my dates and inviting him for tea on the Sunday after the game. Mother kept saying that she really didn't know anything about John Bird, and that "everybody" would be at the Lilacs Club.

I followed her advice and carefully composed a letter to Mr. Bird. I said I hoped he would not be offended and would come for tea.

A few days later I received a brief note written on a page of thin, Foreign Office stationery with the Lion and Unicorn crest embossed in white. It was a triumph of one-upmanship.

> Dear Miss Rhein:
>   Disappointed—yes. But offended, on so slight an acquaintance —never. As it happens I will be staying over in Philadelphia and accept with pleasure your invitation for tea.
>   Yours sincerely,
>   John Bird

I was at once squelched and encouraged.

John Bird did come for tea on the Sunday and to my amazement drank five cups of it. We both posed a little, trying to impress each other. We argued about the relative merits of Catullus and Horace. I had been enchanted by Catullus when I had read him at college at the age of sixteen, but had found Horace dull and stodgy. John Bird agreed that Catullus was a superb lyric poet who had written some of the greatest love poems of all time, but contended that Horace was not to be despised. I admitted that Horace's poems were much better than I had previously thought when J.B. recited one or two of them in a beautifully modulated voice and then translated them so that I could grasp the full flavour of the meaning as well as the rhythm of the metres.

We went on to talk about books and found, to our surprise and pleasure, that although J.B. had been born in South Africa and educated in Ireland and England before going to Harvard, we had been brought up on the same books: the animal stories of Ernest Seton Thompson, the Uncle Remus stories, and Robert Louis Stevenson. We found we both liked poetry, Mozart, sailing, walking in the woods, and identifying birds and wild flowers. We covered a lot of ground. Rather shyly we agreed to stop addressing each other as Mr. Bird and Miss Rhein.

J.B. did not pay me compliments about my appearance, but subtly, without my realizing it, he was making love to me by making me feel that he understood and respected my opinions. We seemed to agree about most things but when we disagreed we argued in a spirit of stimulating, intellectual exercise, as my family did around the dining-table, instead of angrily, as Bob and I did. That afternoon the chemistry was still very much there as far as I was concerned but I now was not sure if J.B. felt it.

After he had left I told Mother that he was the only man that I had ever wanted to marry.

"What nonsense," she said. "You've only seen him once or twice— at Saunderstown and now this afternoon—and you begin to talk about wanting to marry him. You can't really be so stupid as to think a man like that would ever think of marriage. . . ."

"On so slight an acquaintance," I finished, sadly remembering J.B.'s letter.

"Exactly," Mother said, and added, in her laying-down-the-law voice, "I think you're behaving very badly to Bob. You go everywhere with him and everybody expects you to announce your engagement, and now here you are mooning about this young foreigner you hardly know. I never heard of such nonsense."

Shortly before that Mother had received a windfall in the form of an extra stock dividend. She had been talking vaguely about spending it on a trip abroad, and now she decided definitely the time had come to take me on a grand tour of Europe. We would leave right after the New Year. An extended trip would soon cure me of my foolishness.

Mother and Aunt Folly began spending their evenings planning a four-month itinerary in Italy, France and England. I was excited by the idea of going abroad for the first time, and began reading books about the places we were going to see. I was particularly enthusiastic about seeing Italy because of the course I had taken at Bryn Mawr on the painting of the Italian Renaissance.

A few weeks after J.B. came for tea, he wrote inviting me to New York for dinner and the theatre. I accepted after Mother had telephoned Cousin Flos La Farge to make sure it would be convenient for me to use the guest-room in the little house on 23rd Street, near Gramercy Park.

It turned out to be a hectic few days—typical of the roaring twenties. The night before I was to leave I danced until two o'clock at a night-club. Nevertheless I got up early the next morning and went riding. My horse threw me, but it was not a bad fall, and after a hot bath I felt fit enough to take an early afternoon train for the two-hour trip to New York. There I went directly to Cousin Flos'.

In due course, J.B., looking very handsome in a tuxedo, arrived to pick me up for an early dinner. I was pleased that he had brought me a red rose to pin on my dress. But I was disappointed when he told me he had invited Arthur Ponsonby, a British colleague, and a girl whom I didn't know to go with us. I had expected the two of us would spend the evening together alone.

Nevertheless I managed to say, "Good. What fun!" quite enthusiastically.

We were to meet Ponsonby and the girl at J.B.'s favourite speakeasy. We arrived at the old brownstone house in the West Side Fifties, were scrutinized through the wire grille, gave the counter sign, and were admitted. While we waited for the others we drank Angels' Wings— cocktails made with crème de cacao, cream and cognac. When half an hour had gone by we gave up and started dinner. I kept hoping the other couple would never arrive, but when we were half-way through the meal, they came rushing up to our table, explaining that Ponsonby had forgotten the number of the speakeasy but not the block, so that they had been to three "speaks," stopping for a drink at each one, until they found us.

Somehow we managed to reach the theatre as the curtain went up on Sean O'Casey's *The Plough and the Stars*. J.B. had been at school in Ireland in 1916 and, when we went into the lobby for a cigarette between acts, he told us anecdotes about the days of the "trouble."

After the play was over we went to Child's and ate cornflakes. Then we took the girl home in a taxi. At that point J.B. suggested it might be fun to go dancing. Ponsonby said he thought it was a fine idea. So we went to the Hotel Roosevelt and I ate lobster Newburg and danced with the two men alternately.

Ponsonby came along in the taxi when we went back to the La Farges', but stayed in the cab while J.B. helped me unlock the door and made sure I was safely inside. When we were in the vestibule there was a new intimacy in the way we both giggled about Ponsonby's lack of tact. But I still wasn't sure if J.B. had wanted to be alone with me as much as I had wanted to be alone with him. He shook my hand very formally when we said good-night.

A day or two later I wrote J.B. a bread-and-butter letter thanking him for the dinner and theatre party and suggesting he come to Philadelphia for dinner with the family.

The dinner turned out to be trying. Shan was silently but visibly convulsed with laughter over J.B.'s accent, and Mother was furious at him. I felt gauche because Aunt Fol and J.B. carried on a lively, uninterruptable dialogue about literature, England, and European politics. But I was at the same time pleased because J.B. held his own against Aunt Fol and showed himself a master of conversational gamesmanship.

After dinner Mother and Aunt Fol were tactful enough to leave J.B. and me alone by the fire in the little upstairs sitting room. Shan, however, had every intention of settling down with us for the evening until Mother called him. To my embarrassment, we could hear him saying in tones of injured innocence that he couldn't see what was wrong about sitting quietly and talking to his own sister. He was twelve at that time and we loved each other and were good friends, but he had a wicked sense of humour and enjoyed teasing me whenever possible. After we were alone, J.B. and I talked about everything under the sun and it was a happy evening.

The next day Mother was unenthusiastic about J.B., saying he did not seem to know when to go home. Aunt Fol said she thought he was very clever and most amusing but added that in her opinion Bob was "more like us"; after all, he was an American.

I did not see J.B. again until I had tea with him in New York the day before sailing for Europe. The two hours we were together seemed like ten minutes because there was so much to talk about. He told me he was going to ask some of his friends in England and on the Continent to look me up, and said he hoped I would meet his mother when I got to London. Suddenly overcome by a curious shyness, we shook hands when we parted and promised to write.

That night I had dinner with Bob before going to the theatre and then went supper-dancing with him. We bickered as usual, and he kissed me good-night in the taxi on the way back to the hotel. I knew I was "two-timing," and felt depressed and miserable. I was like the girl in the old song:

> I know who I love
> But dear knows who I'll marry.

The next morning when we went aboard the *Conte Biancamano* I found a book, *South Wind,* by Norman Douglas, and a note from J.B.:

> Since you are going to Naples I thought you might be amused by this. Arthur Balfour once said that if the devil were to write a book, *South Wind* would be it.
> Bon Voyage.
> J.B.

Europe

When the *Conte Biancamano* docked at Naples, after stopping at
Gibraltar for a day and at Algiers for a couple of days, we were met
at the wharf by a chauffeur, Angelo, with a car Mother had rented—an
enormous, beige-coloured, seven-passenger Fiat, the kind with a glass
partition between the enclosed back seats and the open front seats.
Angelo was young, with the litheness of so many young Italian men.
He had enormous liquid brown eyes, the whitest of teeth, and high
colouring. If he had taken off his chauffeur's cap and uniform and
put on a velvet tuque, tights and a puffed-sleeve jerkin he could have
been the model for one of the elegant young men with falcons in the
fresco *The Journey of the Magi* by Benozzo Gozzoli.

When we had cleared customs Angelo piled our vast conglomeration
of hand luggage on top of the car and roped a tarpaulin over it, a chore
he repeated every time we moved, cheerfully and efficiently and without
fuss. Our trunks were always sent ahead by rail to the places where we
planned to stay for several weeks.

Often today when I pack for a trip abroad in one large and one
small suitcase I think with amusement of all the things we considered
essential for a journey. In 1928 I packed four evening dresses, a
costume for the fancy dress ball on board ship, an evening wrap, a
variety of cloche hats to match my daytime costumes, a supply of toilet
articles, a leather writing-case, and quantities of books.

As well as clothes, Mother took table covers and a few ornaments.
She had a way of making even the most impersonal, dreary hotel room
look cheerful and lived-in. We also took shawls and steamer rugs, for
the hotel rooms were chilly.

Angelo seemed to have the road-maps of Italy and France printed on his brain, since he seldom made a wrong turn during the three months he drove us. He lovingly coaxed the long, top-heavy car up the hairpin turns to Ravello and later navigated the curves of the Grande Corniche with calm assurance that we did not always share. Somehow he squeezed through narrow alleys or weaved his way through rush-hour traffic without making a dent or scratch on the unwieldy monster. He drove fast and free across the Campagna Romana, hand on horn, beaming with delight as peasants, donkeys, goats and chickens scattered before us.

In southern Italy we did the usual things that tourists do today, only more thoroughly, more conscientiously, since we had more time and the Grand Tour was supposed to educate Shan and me as well as help me to get over my "nonsense." Dutifully we tramped after guides in churches and museums, and went to Paestum, Pompeii, Herculaneum, Sorrento, Capri and Amalfi. We went up the funicular to the top of Vesuvius and looked down at the molten lava puffing up breaths of steam in the crater, and marvelled at the curious flaws in human intelligence which allowed people to build their homes in the path where burning, suffocating death has descended so often.

In those days tourists in January were treated with loving care because there were so few of them. But even at the height of the school-teacher invasion, Europe was very different from the Europe of today. There were no autostradas or autobahns, few automobiles and no scooters. We were among the fortunate few, like the Americans in a novel by Henry James, who had enough money and enough leisure to enjoy Europe in a relaxed, dilettante way.

In Philadelphia I had always thought of myself as being poor because all of my friends lived more luxuriously and seemed to have more money than we had. Mother used to say that we were neither rich nor poor but "comfortably off." But after Father died she also felt poor, though once in a while she would give way to sudden bursts of extravagance. Taking her children on the Grand Tour of Europe in a chauffeur-driven automobile was a typical spending spree, though she insisted that it was cheaper for four people to travel that way than by trains and taxis.

After "doing" the right places around Naples we piled into the Fiat and Angelo drove us to Rome. We spent a month there in a pension called Villa Margharita. In my diary I keep repeating day after day, "Cold places, these pensions." Mother didn't like the villa because the table napkins were rolled into rings with our names on them and only changed once a week, by which time they had become stiff with spaghetti sauce.

Aunt Fol didn't like it because it cost five lira to have a hot bath. That was an outrageous imposition in her opinion, so she took a daily sponge bath in the big china wash basin in the bedroom we shared. She undressed and washed behind a screen so that I would not see her naked. I thought this was ridiculous Victorian modesty and kept telling her that at camp and college I had become familiar with many examples of the female anatomy, all of which seemed remarkably similar to my own.

Aunt Fol not only covered herself, she covered books. She was shocked to find that I was reading *Les Faux-Monnayeurs* by André Gide. "What would people think if they saw you reading a book of that kind?" she said.

She covered the offending volume with brown paper and then, to my rather annoyed amusement, read it herself late into the night. She also covered the books by Dumas that Shan read while we were sightseeing. He used to sit on a bench in an art gallery and read, looking up and staring at a painting speculatively from time to time, to give the impression to our fellow tourists that he was absorbed in his Baedeker.

Although Mother, Aunt Fol and I were fascinated by the sightseeing, Shan was having an excruciatingly boring time. No one seemed to think that there was any harm in his missing half a year of school because the mystique of the Grand Tour was such that he was supposed to absorb a kind of education as valuable as any that could be learned at school. We were somewhat concerned about the fact that he had no one his own age to play with, however, and he, for his part, was becoming defiant of the "monstrous regiment of women." Mother and Aunt Fol were always telling him to sit straight, not to spill the carafe of water at meals, to wear his hat differently, to come and look at this or that wonderful painting or piece of sculpture. He found the long, late hotel dinners very tedious and suffered from lack of the right kind of exercise. (Exercise of a kind we had in plenty; we all got museum feet from trying to keep up with Aunt Fol who turned out to be indefatigable in her enthusiasm for the museum-art-gallery circuit.)

Shan's defiance took various forms. He irritated Aunt Fol because when he went out he wore his hat tilted over his nose, and she made fun of him when he removed it devoutly every time a funeral hearse, drawn by plumed black horses, went by. He spilt the water in the carafe whenever he filled his glass, and refused to let anyone else fill it for him.

He also amused himself by a series of practical jokes. He would ring all the bells in my bedroom and then absent himself, leaving me to cope with the maid, the valet and the porter in my elementary Italian.

Once, when we were in Pisa, I stepped out on the balcony in my dressing-gown to look at the crowds gathered to pay tribute to Mussolini who was speaking there that day. Shan locked the balcony door behind me and then leaned from the window and shouted, "Ah, La bella, la bella!" Any young female with long blond hair is regarded as "bella" in Italy, so there were cheers and applause from the street.

Fortunately Mother was in her adjacent bedroom, heard the noise and rescued me. She took us out for tea afterward, and when Aunt Fol ordered vermouth and soda I seized the siphon and squirted soda water across the table straight into Shan's face. Mother was furious, pointing out that anyone so immature and silly as I could hardly be expected to make a sensible decision about anything as serious as marriage.

Aunt Fol adored Rome and wanted us to savour every aspect of it. She knew the city well since she had stayed there frequently for months at a time with her great friend Etta Dunham of New York who had married the Marchese de Viti di Marco, an economist and former Minister of Finance.

The de Vitis invited us to their palazzo for lunch and dinner a number of times. We were impressed by the fine rooms furnished with handsome furniture, and greatly enjoyed the good food and wine served by menservants wearing white gloves. But we thought it odd that the brocade covering on the walls was beginning to strip off in shreds and that so many of the chair coverings were threadbare or worn through.

One day the Marchese told us what Mussolini had done to him and to Italy. We sat in the library while we talked, and from time to time our host—or our hostess—would get up quickly and open the door into the corridor to make sure that no servant was listening. De Viti said that his estates in southern Italy had been confiscated by Mussolini. As a result, his two daughters, having no dowry, would never make good marriages. He had no job and no hope of getting one, since no university or other institution dared employ him. He told us about the torture of the castor oil treatment and the beatings meted out to little people who dared to oppose the dictatorship, and the exile, to islands such as Lipari, of intellectuals and other influential men who might conceivably organize a revolt against tyranny.

He spoke bitterly of the constant petty heckling that made life miserable. Only a week before, he said, when Ferrero, the historian, had

My maternal great-grandmother, the first Anne Francis, wife of Senator James A. Bayard (1802-1864).

My mother, Elizabeth Kane Rhein

My father, Dr. John H.W. Rhein

4. *Age 6, on roller skates in Rittenhouse Square, Philadelphia*
5. *Age 10, in the library of 1732 Pine Street, 1918*
6. *A flapper, 1922*
7. *Age 20. Dragged off on "the grand tour." Aboard the Conte Biancamano en route for Naples, 1928*
8. *After a swim in the Rivière du Nord, Montreal, 1934*
9. *With a 4¾ pound bass caught in Clearwater Bay, Lake of the Woods, 1940*

10. *With newspapermen at SHAPE, Paris, 1955, before leaving on NATO tour of Greece and Turkey*

11

11. *Broadcasting on Capital Report, around 1950*

12. *At home under painting by John Lyman, Ottawa in the sixties*

13. *John Bird on a Rhine River ferry, Bonn, 1959*

14. Public Hearings of the Royal Commission on the Status of Women, Winnipeg, 1968. Left to Right: Commissioners Lola Lange, Jeanne Lapointe, John Humphrey, Florence Bird, Doris Ogilvie, Jacques Henripin, Elsie Gregory MacGill.

15. Surrounded by briefs, Ottawa, 1968

16. At work

7. *Receiving honorary degree from York University, 1971*

8. *Invested as Companion of the Order of Canada by Governor-General Roland
Michener, Rideau Hall, Ottawa, 1971*

19. *In Copenhagen preparing radio documentary on Denmark for Project 60 of the CBC*

20. *With J.B. at the Frogpond, 1973*

come for lunch, a uniformed man on a motorcycle kept circling the house until the constant noise made everyone jittery and rational conversation became impossible. Ferrero was under constant supervision of this kind.

We were naively shocked by these revelations. Our friends returning from Italy had fed us the clichés of the period about the trains running on time and the absence of beggars from the streets since Mussolini had come to power. I had been charmed by the sight of the carabinieri, with their green capes and plumed hats, who swaggered in pairs through the streets of Rome. Now I began to see them as the instrument of a government sustained by force. I can't remember having heard the term "police state" at that time but I realized then the concept of a police state. I found the régime of Mussolini frightening.

For me Cavour and Garibaldi were noble names, names to conjure with; I thought of the Risorgimento in the way I thought of the American Revolution, as the revolt of the downtrodden against unjust authority. I found it shocking that the dream of freedom for Italy should have come to this.

For me Rome was like a lump of lead on the mind; it was too much for me. It seemed austere and foreboding after the dramatic beauty and bright sunshine of southern Italy. For some reason the huge buildings and the extravagance of the Baroque architecture kept me from seeing the warm rose colour and time-mellowed ochre of the houses and the walls around them, which now give me such pleasure. I thought of Rome as a grey city.

The truth is, I think, that Rome is not a city for the young and inexperienced. The roads of life have led me back there half a dozen times since that first visit and always I find it more and more magnificent, more and more stimulating to the mind and deeply satisfying aesthetically in spite of the noise, the traffic, the Vespas, and the all-pervading smell of exhaust fumes which the industrialization of northern Italy and comparative affluence have brought to the city. Over the years I have come to enjoy the Baroque immensely. Perhaps an understanding and appreciation of a decadent period in art increases with age because age is itself a form of decadence. But that first year I yearned for the clean, uncluttered lines of Romanesque and Gothic architecture and the lovely, seeming simplicity of Trecento and Quatrocento painting.

It was a different matter when we settled into Florence for a few weeks. It was easy to get to know the heart of the city—Giotto's Tower, the Duomo and the Baptistry—because it was so small; and it was easy to love because it was so perfect. Day after day I went to the Uffizi and the Pitti. In both of the great museums I met the original paintings which G.G. King had shown us on slides during her mind-expanding lectures at Bryn Mawr. During the course she had made sure that we would be steeped in the art criticism of Bernard Berenson. Now the studying paid off because I not only knew that I liked Florentine painting but *why* I liked it. G.G.'s insistence that we understand the whole culture of the Renaissance now made Florence a multi-faceted delight. Moreover, I had recently read a great deal about the Medici and was enchanted to find myself at last in their home town.

Shan and I happily explored side streets and alleys, wandering aimlessly wherever an unexpected flight of steps led us up or down or where an archway opened onto a square or courtyard. This is still my favourite way of getting to know an old city. Over the years I must have walked hundreds of miles that way, with radio producers or my husband, not only in the daytime but at night when a city takes on a new dimension.

That winter in Florence I walked a great deal alone because I needed to think. And all the time we were working our way north to Paris by way of Genoa, Menton, Avignon and Auxerre, I was thinking about a decision I had to make. The future had become a reality, not just a distant, romantic dream.

Though the entries in my diary are chiefly concerned with descriptions of the places where we went and the people we met, from time to time there are revealing entries about how I felt. During the early weeks of the tour I missed Bob. I missed his "line," the extravagant flattery which men have always found to be so successful with women. In Naples I wrote, "I need my Bob to tell me that it doesn't matter if I am dumb as long as I am beautiful." But after a while, as letters from John Bird began to arrive regularly, there is less mention of Bob and more mention of J.B. in the diary: "John Bird says I have very good stuff in me. He thinks some day I can develop into a real person if I work on it." This was a new kind of compliment from a man and I found it more satisfying than the usual kind that Bob dished out mechanically.

Up until then I had been of two minds about compliments. I had felt that the automatic male-to-female compliments demanded by good manners were insincere. I had no great opinion of my appearance: I knew that I wasn't nearly as beautiful as Mother or my half-sister Mabel, and I was used to being told that the boys had inherited the good looks in the family. So I generally brushed off praise of that kind. On the other hand, I did like compliments about my clothes because they were a tribute to my taste and my own personal style.

Now I found I was thinking about what J.B. had written in his letters. Perhaps he was right and I had good stuff in me and had the power to mould it myself and to make myself into the sort of person I wanted to be. Gradually the idea took hold of me that a woman can be what she wants to be and can follow any path she wants to follow. It became a profound belief, a personal conviction that had nothing to do with any theories about free will. I still believe that.

In Paris I received a cable from J.B. which I knew required an answer. I had never let myself believe that he was in love with me but now I thought timidly, unbelievingly, that he was. And then the next minute I thought that maybe I had misunderstood or attached too much importance to his message—a line in Latin from Catullus. I knew by that time that I was in love with him but feared that he might not be serious or that I was making a fool of myself by thinking he was. I found it hard to believe that anyone so clever, well educated and witty could really want to marry me.

I put off answering his cable because I didn't know what to say. For three days running in my diary the same sentence appears in the midst of descriptions of shopping and sightseeing: "What am I going to do about John Bird?"

After four days I sent a cable and also wrote to J.B., trying to explain how I felt. A fortnight later I received a letter from him which made it clear that he really did love me although there was no mention of marriage.

During the four months we were abroad J.B. courted me by letter and cable but also organized a fifth column to press his cause. When we arrived in Genoa, a junior in the British Consulate turned up at the hotel with flowers and a note of introduction from J.B. He spent the evening telling Mother and me that J.B. was an Oxford Blue, something which meant nothing at all to us, an Isis Idol, something which meant even less, and the first Davison Scholar from Oxford to Harvard, which was impressive.

When we arrived in London, J.B.'s Oxford friends came to call, with invitations. One of them took me to Oxford. At lunch I said I had never had enough caviar in my life and he ordered a pound of it. We ate it and drank sidecars, a popular concoction, and then went and looked at the room J.B. had when he was at Trinity College. Another day he took me to Simpson's-in-the-Strand for lunch. I embarrassed him and threw the waiter into confusion by ordering tea—for lunch.

Another one of J.B.'s Oxford friends took me dancing, to the theatre, to dinner and to spend the weekend with his family in a country house. In my diary I describe a typical long dinner of the period. It ended with port and walnuts. "It was the best port I have ever tasted," I wrote. I am sure that it was also the first I had ever tasted.

During our stay in London Mother began to be worried about the way J.B. was exerting remote control over my emotions. She began finding all sorts of reasons why he was not a suitable person for me to marry. She kept saying that she didn't know anything about him or his family although a succession of obviously respectable Englishmen had been telling her about them for days on end.

"J.B. has just put them up to it," she said. "I want to meet his mother."

I also wanted to meet his mother. So we were both glad when she wrote inviting us for tea and saying that Donald Wood, an American friend of J.B.'s, had offered to accompany us on the train and show us the way to her house in Radlett, a small village near St. Albans in Hertfordshire.

I was terrified by the thought of the confrontation between the two mothers. But I began to feel better when, on the train, Mother discovered that Donald Wood was a distant cousin. Since he was a kinsman and an American, Mother showed signs of believing him when he said he thought highly of J.B. and his family.

As far as I was concerned, the afternoon was a great success. Mother and Mrs. Bird, an elderly widow, liked and understood each other in spite of their very different backgrounds. They both loved flowers and left Don Wood and me by the fire while they walked around the garden examining the herbaceous borders, and no doubt talking about J.B. and me.

"They are the same kind of people that we are," Mother said on the way home.

She was, however, not pleased that J.B. had no financial prospects. The cottage at Radlett was charming but small and unpretentious, and Mrs. Bird had made it clear that J.B. would not inherit any money or property.

(J.B. is, by birth, a fourth-generation South African. His father, for many years head of the Natal Civil Service, had been presented with a

C.M.G. by a grateful government, but his widow received only a modest pension since in those days civil servants in South Africa were poorly paid. When J.B. was two years old Mrs. Bird had taken the eight children to England to be educated. They were an intelligent, talented brood. Three of the boys had gone to university and two into the army by way of Sandhurst and Woolwich. The eldest of the three girls, Marie, had studied Jacques Dalcroze eurythmics in Geneva and was at that time one of the premier teachers of the dance in London. Later she created the B.B.C. television serial *Andy Pandy,* a puppet show for four-year-olds which became famous and ran for years and years.)

We sailed for New York on the *Minnewaska,* a broad-bottomed cabin-class steamer. All of us had dripping colds in the head, gifts of the English spring, but I was determined to be free of a pink nose and bleary eyes by the time we reached home. So I spent most of the voyage in the upper berth of the cabin alternately dreaming about J.B. and reading *Lawrence of Arabia* by Lowell Thomas.

On one of those bright exhilarating mornings which New York does so well, the *Minnewaska* was nosed into dock by little tugs pulling away like piglets at the dugs of a fat sow. Mother and I stood side by side leaning over the rail, looking down on the waving, shouting people on the end of the wharf.

"Do you see what I see?" she asked.

"Yes," I said. "I kind of thought he might be here."

A tall, thin figure in a long, dark grey ulster and a broad-brimmed felt hat was pacing up and down at the side of the wharf away from the crowd.

"Are you going to come to Philadelphia with us this afternoon?"

"No," I said. "I'm going to spend the night in New York."

"Well, please, as a favour to me, stay in the Plaza. Mrs. Waln is going to be there tonight and if anyone asks I can say you were chaperoned."

Mrs. Waln, one of my mother's Philadelphia friends, had been with us on the trip in a semi-detached way, staying at the same hotels but travelling in her own car in the company of a friend, with whom she fought continually, and a black maid whom she ordered around one day and treated as friend and confidante the next. I didn't catch sight of her while I was at the Plaza but the fact that she was there meant that the proprieties had been observed.

That night, as if we had known it for always, J.B. and I, on our sixth meeting, agreed that we were going to marry each other. He spent the following weekend with us in Philadelphia and after much argument, we persuaded Mother to announce our engagement.

She was not happy about it. J.B. was earning an adequate if modest salary but showed no interest in becoming rich and had no prospects of ever inheriting any money. When Mother objected to our marriage on financial grounds J.B. suggested a four-year engagement so that he could become established as a newspaperman.

The fact was that J.B. by then had printer's ink under his fingernails. He had worked in Kansas on William Allen White's paper, *The Emporia Gazette,* for a year after leaving Harvard and had become imbued with a vast admiration for White and a burning ambition to emulate him. He had lived with the Whites while he was cutting his eye-teeth as a cub reporter and had come to know well the famous editor whose wisdom, wit, grass-root perception and unashamed sentimentality had given his paper a national reputation and remarkable political influence.

After a year in Kansas, J.B. had returned to England and taken a job on Fleet Street, but had given it up when the Foreign Office suggested he go to New York as the officer responsible for analyzing the American press. He had been in New York for four years and enjoyed the work but did not want to be a bureaucrat for the rest of his life. He wanted to get back to newspaper work.

Mother was outraged when J.B. kept insisting that he did not intend to stay in the Foreign Service. She had a low opinion of newspapermen with the exception of Walter Lippmann. And J.B.'s suggestion of a long engagement dismayed her.

"I never heard anything so fantastic in my life," she said "Nobody ever heard of a four-year engagement."

"It's quite a common practice in England," said J.B.

I spoke up. "I couldn't possibly wait for four years, and I don't mind being poor."

"You don't know what you're talking about," Mother said. "You're spoiled rotten and have very expensive tastes."

Finally we compromised by agreeing to a six-month engagement so J.B. and I could "get to know each other," as Mother put it. Since we had only seen each other six times before getting engaged, that seemed a reasonable solution as far as I was concerned. I didn't want to upset Mother any more than I already had since Father's death.

During the half year of waiting, J.B. put me through what amounted to an immersion course in the British Commonwealth, an institution I suspected of being my chief rival in his affections. I read books by Trevelyan and Zimmern with interest but also with some difficulty. Bryn Mawr required only American and ancient history for entrance so that the bare knowledge I had of my British birthright as an American came from the elementary books Mother had read to me when I was a child.

I worked hard on the reading that summer, as if I were preparing for an examination. I had plenty of motivation. Having been conceited about being better read than most of my contemporaries, I was stimulated to sharpen my mind and widen my knowledge when I found that I did not understand many of J.B.'s literary, historical and political allusions, and that I was often out of my depth when I was talking with him. I did not even understand some of his jokes because they were based on the assumption that I knew things I didn't know.

Remembering Nora in *A Doll's House,* I was determined that our marriage would be a partnership between intellectual equals sharing the same interests. J.B. was of the same mind. His mother was a woman of intelligence, ability and force. He found it deplorable that her life had been entirely confined to housework, childbearing and childrearing. He did not want that to happen to me, and he encouraged me by saying, "You've got a first-class brain. In ten years' time you'll be ahead of me."

J.B. also sent me, among other books, Turner's *The Frontier in American History* and Frank Kent's *The Great Game of Politics.* I was deplorably ignorant of the workings of machine politics in the United States. My grasp of American history was also pretty sketchy, although I had studied it continuously year after year from the early grades in school until I passed my senior matriculation. But the courses had become stuck like a needle on a phonograph record, repeating the same thing over and over again. Each year we had started anew with Christopher Columbus and stopped with Lincoln's assassination. As far as I was concerned, all that happened after that was vague, even though in my senior year at school I had, in a few last hectic weeks of cramming, raced as far as the second election of Woodrow Wilson in 1916 in order to be prepared for the college entrance examination.

To help me to understand him better J.B. also sent me Thoreau's *Walden* and *The Education of Henry Adams.* He said, "These two books brought me to North America." *Walden* I did not appreciate for

another twenty years, not until we found our own Walden pond in
Canada. But *The Education of Henry Adams* made as great an impression on me as *Mont Saint-Michel and Chartres* had done while I was
at college. Many years later, when I happened to mention that I had
read *The Education* a couple of times, Max Freedman, the brilliant
Washington correspondent of the *Manchester Guardian,* told me that
he re-read the last three or four chapters every two years when there
was an American election. He found it fascinating that the hostility of
Congress toward the Secretary of State is today much as it was when
Adams described it in 1905.

When Cousin Flos La Farge offered us, as a wedding present, the
choice between a sofa or Henry Adams' two great classics, we chose
the books because Adams had influenced us both so much. Mother
thought we were being utterly impractical since we had hardly any
furniture and were planning to spend J.B.'s savings on a honeymoon
abroad. But we were adamant, so Cousin Flos had the volumes bound
in red leather, embossed in gold with fleurs-de-lis. They have gone with
us to many dwellings in five cities and stand in the bookcase beside me
as I write.

J.B. and I wanted a simple wedding, with only close family and close
friends. We planned to be married in the late summer in the little white
clapboard church at South Ferry, near Saunderstown. (We chose Rhode
Island because we had met there. And we had a romantic feeling about
the church which stood high on a hill looking out toward the Atlantic—a
landmark for sailing vessels since Colonial days.) However, J.B. was
not able to save enough money for a honeymoon in England until
November, by which time the summer cottage was closed.

The little house in Philadelphia was too small for even a minimal
gathering of the clan, so we were married in a small, beautiful church
at Mountchanin, Delaware, and a large reception was held in the huge
house of a very generous cousin who offered it for the occasion.

"A wedding is a tribal ritual," J.B. said when I moaned because I
thought we were being treated as puppets and made to do not what we
wanted but what the family thought was right and suitable. But as time
went on we were carried away by the loving kindness of my family and
the interest and enthusiasm of our friends. There were many parties and
we enjoyed them. It was exciting to open all the presents and it was
fun to have a dinner dance the night before the wedding, with guests
from New York, Boston and Kansas as well as Philadelphia. None of
J.B.'s family were able to come but many of his friends were there; they

had come from far and wide to fill his side of the church and give him moral support.

That night after the party was over Mother came into my room and sat on the end of my bed. "There's something I want to say to you," she said. "I want you to promise to try to be generous to Mrs. Bird. J.B. is her youngest son. She's old and sick, so let him be alone with her once in a while. Don't hog him. Let her wash his socks if she wants to and let her fuss over him. Try to remember you'll have him all your life and she'll never have him again."

"I promise," I said.

Mother kissed me good night. At the door she stopped and turned back to me. "Are you sure you want to go through with it to-morrow? If you have any doubts it's better to stop now."

"I have no doubts," I said.

We thought it was a gorgeous wedding and were happy about it. It was, of course, very traditional. I wore white satin and a long veil. The groom and the ushers wore striped trousers, cutaway coats, spats, ascot ties and silk hats. The bridesmaids wore tulle the colour of yellow chrysanthemums.

That morning J.B., who had been billetted with friends, had wakened early and gone for a walk in the garden. There he came upon a sundial on which were inscribed the words: "Grow old along with me. The best is yet to be." When he told me about it that evening, we laughed, thinking it corny and yet somehow nice. It turned out to be a prophecy.

England Again

J.B. had three months' leave coming to him, so after the wedding we went abroad to stay with his family and friends. We also planned to visit Guernsey, where J.B. had lived with his mother while he went to Oxford.

Before we embarked, however, we spent a night in New York so that we could see "The Front Page," a play which gave me an erroneous, rather daunting conception of the career my husband proposed to follow as soon as he could get the right job.

Our first crossing of the Atlantic together, on the *Lancastria,* a small Cunarder, was a test of nerve and stomach, which we weathered with zest, walking the heaving deck and eating kippers for breakfast. We were delighted to find that we shared a love of the sea and were both good sailors.

As we approached the shores of Britain we ran into heavy seas in a full gale, and a day before we were due to dock we were called off our course by an SOS from the *Pommern,* a German naval training barque that was being washed toward the Casket Rocks off Alderney. The passengers on the *Lancastria,* the few not in a prone position in their cabins, were locked into the main saloon to keep them out of the way while the crew launched a lifeboat.

J.B. and I leaned out of the window and watched the manned boat being lowered past us from the top deck. Every time the steamer rocked, the boat slammed against her side with such shattering force that we were sure the boat timbers would be turned into matchsticks. A young woman, very pregnant and very seasick, leaned beside us. She was an admiral's daughter and kept shouting, "Three cheers for our brave British tars" until, like characters in *H.M.S. Pinafore,* we all gave forth a feeble "Hip-hip-hurrah!"—whereupon she rushed away to be sick in the nearest lavatory.

When the lifeboat was launched, we could see it wallowing, one moment out of sight, the next appearing precariously on the lip of a monstrous wave. It had only gone a short distance toward the schooner when its sea-anchor was carried away; it could no longer make headway, and barely managed to get back to the *Lancastria*. We kept wondering what would have happened if it had been our own ship that was in trouble. Could lifeboats full of frightened passengers ever have been lowered, let alone have survived the seas? We were also concerned for the safety of the young men on board the *Pommern*. Two other liners, having poured oil to no avail, were standing by. After a while, as the lighthouse on the Caskets began to flash closer and closer in the failing light of evening, a salvage tug came out of Cherbourg, shot a breech line to the doomed vessel and took off all the cadets.

When we reached England we stayed with Mrs. Bird in Hertfordshire. I kept the promise I had made to Mother on the night before the wedding, and there was no mother-in-law trouble on our honeymoon. Mrs. Bird and I became fond of each other and before I left she told me she felt very happy that I had married her son. I was glad there had been no friction or even tension between us to cloud the happiness of those first months of marriage. I was even more glad about that six months later when she died, because death magnifies both happy and unhappy memories.

Mrs. Bird looked like the portraits of Queen Victoria in her old age. She was down-to-earth, firm, essentially tough, and yet a warm human being. The daughter of a rural doctor, she had been brought up in the country of the Drakensburg Mountains of Natal, and had lived a pioneer life before her marriage, often riding horseback thirty miles to a dance and back again with the dawn. She had not the slightest idea of what my life in Philadelphia had been like and imagined that my background was much the same as her own. She had acquired this illusion from Owen Wister's book, *The Virginian*. J.B., who had met Wister at the La Farges', had given her an autographed copy of the book long before he met me. Mrs. Bird knew Owen Wister was a close family friend and took it for granted that my way of life had been the same as the one he described in *The Virginian*. We did not disillusion her.

It was typical November weather, damp and rainy, but that did not keep J.B. and me from walking miles across the country every day. The lovely smell of wet earth always reminds me of England, the joy of those walks and our shared excitement in discovering each other.

J.B.'s brothers and sisters came to visit and made me feel at ease. No one mentioned my accent or my North American table manners. I also met a number of J.B.'s Oxford friends. We went up to London to have lunch with one of them, John Sutro, who lived in Hampstead. Before lunch Sutro showed me over his house, a large mansion full of modern paintings, *avant garde* sculpture and *objets d'art* in glass cabinets. In the roaring twenties bright young people were supposed to talk flippantly, cynically, in short, throw-away sentences. At that time I thought of myself as a bright young person so I followed Sutro around, making what I considered sophisticated comments on his collection. After discussing a portrait of his uncle, Alfred Sutro, the dramatist, we came to a strange piece of sculpture which looked like someone's head.

"And this, I suppose," I said, "is a portrait of you in your youth."

"No," said Sutro morosely, "that is a frog by Epstein."

At lunch there were three more of J.B.'s Oxford contemporaries, Evelyn Waugh, and Harold and Willy Acton, grandsons of Lord Acton (the Roman Catholic historian and political philosopher who is famous for his "power corrupts" statement and whose ideas have so greatly influenced the thinking of Pierre Elliott Trudeau).

Evelyn Waugh, a blond young man with pink-rimmed eyes, reminded me of the chestnut worms my brother and I used to race when we were children on the farm. At that time he was married to a young woman also named Evelyn, who wore her black hair in an Eton crop. The first of Waugh's brilliant, satirical novels, *Decline and Fall,* had just been published and was enjoying a great success. He was feeling inflated by all the acclaim, but J.B. made him shrink, because J.B., twice his size and a beef-eating athlete, had once intimidated him at the Hypocrites' Club to which they both belonged. All through lunch Waugh kept swelling with intellectual pride and making bright, cryptic remarks in a high-pitched voice, only to relapse into nervous silence, as if fearing a physical assault, when J.B. cleared his throat and came back at him.

Willy Acton, a handsome, dark-haired, pink-cheeked young man sat opposite me. I kept staring at him, fascinated; I had never before seen a man wear a monocle except in comedies about silly-ass Englishmen of the Bertie Wooster type. I thought it a contortionist's feat that he could eat, drink and carry on a lively conversation without having his eyeglass drop into the soup.

I was seated beside one of the Isaacs family, a brother of Lord Reading, a kindly middle-aged man who made me feel less wet behind the ears than the Oxford contingent. Harold Acton, a string-bean type of Englishman with a weak jaw, was on my other side. At first he and I got along very well. He had just been to the West Indies and told me, in a drawling, affected voice, a long story about swizzle sticks.

"Rum is all very well in the West Indies," he concluded, "but I am a Pernod man myself."

"Just like Enoch Soames," said I, remembering an absinthe-drinking poet in *Seven Men,* a book by Max Beerbohm that J.B. had lent me as a relief from so much history reading the previous summer.

Acton did not reply, but instead looked at me coldly, turned his back and talked to the woman on his right for the rest of the meal. I had no idea what I had said to offend him, but later J.B. explained that Acton thought I was deliberately insulting him because his first slim volume of poems, only just published, had received poor reviews. The allusion to Enoch Soames had, in fact, been all too apposite; Beerbohm's poet had sold his soul to the devil in return for being projected a hundred years into the future in order to find out how posterity had judged his poems. The devil paid his part of the bargain. But when Soames visited the British Museum in 1992, he discovered that his name appeared only as a fictitious character mentioned in a humorous story by Max Beerbohm. What is more, the story was written as an illustration of how seriously young men of the 1890's took themselves.

I did not have to sit in silence for long after Harold Acton's back was turned toward me, however, for with the champagne and dessert the conversation became general. It was dominated by a violinist who had just returned from a concert tour in the United States during which he had played at a number of universities in the Middle West.

"It was really most trying," he said. "All the students kept necking like mad while I was playing. They tell me that on the mornings after my concerts, the campus grounds were simply carpeted with French Letters."

In a loyal small voice I ventured that Bryn Mawr was not like that, but nobody listened. The talk shifted to Judge Ben Lindsey, whose recent book, *Companionate Marriage,* had caused shocked head-shakings in the more conventional circles but had met with the approval of the Oxford graduates. All those present seemed to feel that Lindsey was a compassionate man, well ahead of his time.

That memorable lunch at John Sutro's was followed by a weekend equally memorable in another way. It was spent at Oxford with J.B.'s old tutor, H.A. Pritchard of Trinity, White's Professor of Moral Philosophy. In November Oxford is cold, and as soggy as a sponge with evening dews and dampness. "Pritch's" house was full of mould, mildew and must. The halls were unheated, and there was only a small coal fire to warm the living room, which was preserved from "fug" by a half-open window that let in blasts of icy mist.

There was a dinner party on the Saturday night, and since it was a black-tie affair, I wore a sleeveless, low-cut dinner dress over the lace-trimmed voile underwear I had made myself the previous summer. No one had told me that Englishwomen wear woolly vests and knickers under their dresses in winter, and I marvelled that the wives of the Oxford dons that night seemed impervious to the awful chill. I was reminded of Socrates' description of his sensations after drinking the potion of hemlock; all feeling went out of my feet which turned to blocks of ice, but the rest of me was all too sentient. Some of the women covered their bare shoulders with a little fur cape, but I didn't even have a woollen shawl. So I grimly clenched my chattering teeth and froze.

During dinner, Lionel Curtis, then editor of *The Round Table,* the English counterpart of *Foreign Affairs,* sat beside me. He persisted in treating me as a spokesman for the American government and kept asking me questions about American foreign policy while the table listened, waiting for the pundit to analyze my replies.

"Ah-hum, Mrs. Bird," he said, "what would you have done if Britain had scrapped her navy right after the war?"

I said I did not know.

The conversation turned to international affairs and I relapsed into silence, guzzling the overcooked beef and comforting Bordeaux in order to stimulate my circulation.

In 1928 there was still much discussion in Britain about the way Woodrow Wilson had sold the world the idea of the League of Nations only to have American adherence to the League vetoed by the Senate. Many people blamed the sabotage of Wilson's dream on the Constitution.

"Ah-hum, Mrs. Bird," said Lionel Curtis, "when do you intend to write a new Constitution?"

I had tremendous admiration for Wilson. When I was still at school I had gone to the memorial service for him held in Philadelphia after his death. I was also a strong supporter of the League, but regarded Henry Cabot Lodge as the villain of the débacle, not the system of government. I had been brought up to regard the American Constitution as sacrosanct, the ultimate, ideal expression of the principle of democratic government. I thought that Curtis was trying to be funny and gave what I thought was a bright-young-people reply in the spirit of the question.

"I'm planning to write one up on the boat on the way home," I said.

The silence which followed was as chilling as the room. No one laughed. I thought Lionel Curtis was a loathsome old man.

At the time I wondered if he were being intentionally cruel to an inexperienced twenty-year-old but now think it more likely that he was merely trying, in a ham-handed way, to bring me into the conversation; that he was merely trying to be polite.

I excused myself early after dinner, and leaving J.B. to carry on a conversation about the political significance of the South Orkney Islands in the Antarctic, a geographical area that was new to me, climbed into the huge double bed which felt as if the Columbia Glacier instead of a hot-water bottle had found its way between the sheets. I had put on a couple of sweaters and a pair of J.B.'s socks, and planned to read until he came upstairs. It was more than I could bear when I found that all the books in the guest-room bookshelf turned out to be written in Greek. Mrs. Pritchard was a Greek scholar. The only book in a language I knew was *Pickwick Papers,* which I read without enjoyment, feeling young, lonely and inadequate.

These days it is fashionable to talk about culture shock but at the time I just thought I was homesick.

New York

The honeymoon over, we settled into an apartment in New York City. We had a small bedroom, living room and kitchen, on East 29th Street between Lexington and Third Avenue. The narrow apartment house was crunched between a synagogue and a funeral parlour which had a huge electric sign that spelled out "Mortician" in red letters. (It gave our bedroom an eerie glow when we put the shades up at night.) The single window of the living room opened onto a narrow areaway and so did a window in the synagogue. As a result we were forced to take a detached part in the synagogue services. One of the two cantors had a superb voice, visceral and deeply emotional, that billowed into our rooms when spring came and windows were open. Having neither radio nor phonograph, we enjoyed the music and hoped the good cantor would be practising when our friends came for supper. At night, too, we could hear the el rushing down Third Avenue, but it did not shake the house, and soon we did not notice the periodic roar which blended into the low-pitched, incessant voice of the city.

To my surprise, I found I had considerable adjusting to do. New York itself I took in my stride. I had been there many times and had always found the great city exciting, a sort of absinthe cocktail for the mind and senses. Rows of houses flanking city streets made me feel at home and the clanking of trolley cars on Lexington Avenue reminded me of the cars on Pine Street in Philadelphia. But at first I felt hemmed in by the small boxlike rooms, and I had difficulty in getting used to being alone during the day, and also in learning to cook.

Always before there had been people around to talk to if I was bored, lonely or depressed. At college you needed only to stroll down the hall to find an animated discussion going on. At home Mother's bedroom had been a centre of family conversation at all hours of the day. Now there was no one to talk to after J.B. went off to work in the morning. The housework was soon done and then the long day stretched ahead until he came home at 6:30. I never spoke to any of the other tenants or they to me, as is the way in big cities where people are afraid of becoming involved with their neighbours.

I did have arguments every other day with the iceman, a hefty character with bulging muscles who smoked a bad five-cent cigar and spoke with a Brooklyn accent. The drill was for him to put a block of ice in the service dumb-waiter and then come upstairs and lift it into the ice-box. He agreed that I couldn't handle a fifty pound block but thought I should be able to deal with a twenty-five pounder myself, even if I was dressed in my best. I didn't agree with him, but he won the argument when he said, "A great big strapping creature like you ought to be ashamed of yourself!" After that I flexed my muscles and heaved the smaller blocks of ice.

I had a slight acquaintance with two or three young women of my own age who were living in New York. But when I had lunched with each of them and they in turn with me, my winter's daytime social life was over.

Once in a long while I would go up to Murray Hill to have tea with Cousin Flos LaFarge, and that was always a stimulating and happy interlude. Dressed in a green silk Japanese kimono, she would greet me with a shout, "Firenze, darling, come in, tell me all about yourself," and then she would pour strong black tea from the Kirk silver teapot, which brought back memories of happy summers at Saunderstown, and carry on a fascinating monologue about everything from Dante to Theodore Roosevelt. She was a witty, effervescent blue-stocking. I always thought that Bloomsbury was her spiritual home even though she was a confirmed New Yorker.

After a while, however, my loneliness wore off and my days fell into a satisfying routine. I read in the mornings (some history but more George Bernard Shaw, Aldous Huxley, and T.S. Eliot), and in the afternoons I walked, in rain or shine. I would go downtown and wander through the Bowery, the Tenderloin and the Village, or venture uptown to the Metropolitan Museum and the art galleries on 59th Street, or make my way across town to explore the West Side. After five-thirty I would go shopping in the Sicilian street market in the next block between 3rd and 2nd Avenues. I had discovered that at the end of the day the price of vegetables was reduced to a few pennies in order to clear the barrows. The fat, talkative Italian women were friendly and pleased when I told them how much I loved their beautiful native land and when I admired their big-eyed babies. I was glad to have someone to talk to and would take my time, walking the length of the block and filling my shopping bag bit by bit.

As the winter wore on I began to write. I persuaded the editor of *The Saturday Review of Literature* to send me children's books to review. After a time I was also sent run-of-the-mill books for adults, so I had the pleasure of seeing my name in print for the first time as well as receiving small cheques. Determined to keep my identity as a writer, I used my maiden name, Florence Rhein.

Learning to cook and run the apartment required far greater adjustment than learning to be self-sufficient. My education in the art of housekeeping had been negligible. I had learned how to make a bed at camp but I had never done any housework at home. I had never cleaned an icebox or a stove, let alone scrubbed a floor. I knew how a table should be set, how food should taste and be served, and how to plan a dinner party menu, but I had never cooked a meal or even peeled a potato. As a girl I had been forbidden to go into the kitchen, because "bothering" the cook was regarded by Mother as a serious crime, the sort of thing which makes good cooks leave. On rainy Sundays when the maids were out, I had sometimes been allowed to make fudge or cinnamon toast for tea and I had often made scrambled eggs late at night after coming home from a party or a movie. But that was the extent of my cooking experience.

My friends had been brought up in the same way; we had always had servants to wait on us and it was taken for granted we always would.

My sister-in-law had gone to cooking-school during the year she was engaged because she knew she was going to be poor after she married. But though I knew that J.B. and I would also have a very limited income, I had taken his immersion course in the Commonwealth instead of going to cooking-school. I was confident that any intelligent person could learn how to prepare a meal with the help of a good cookbook.

Mother, Cousin Flos, and most of the family had kept saying: "You'll never be able to do all your own housework," but I didn't believe them. I was sure that I could do anything I wanted to do.

In New York my arrogance took a fall. The classic of the era, *The Boston Cooking School Cook Book,* as I soon found out, is not for the novice, or for that matter for anyone who wants to economize. It presupposes at least an elementary expertise, and expertise is what I didn't have. I didn't know the difference between boiling, simmering, parboiling, coddling, or braising.

When I confessed to Aunt Fol that I was like a comic-strip bride when it came to cooking, she sent me a cookbook called *What and How,* written for beginners, with a play-by-play description of how to prepare food as well as how to cook it. The kind German butcher on 3rd Avenue was also a great help. He explained the different cuts of meat to me and how to cook them.

But I had to learn by trial and error, the hard way, instead of by watching someone else cook, or by being supervised. I was shaken when I put milk in a saucepan and it boiled up and over the stove. Nobody had warned me about this. I had learned in physics that when water boils it turns to steam, but had not realized in a practical way that if you put vegetables on to boil and go and read a book, the water will boil away and the vegetables will burn. (That winter in New York I spent quite a lot of time scraping the bottom of pans, even after I understood that cream soups have to be stirred frequently or they will stick and have a horrible taste.) It was a surprise to discover that tears flow when you chop onions. The final humiliation was that I even had a terrible time opening cans; my fingers were always being cut because the lever-style opener kept slipping.

In due course J.B. became chief can-opener, onion-chopper and potato-peeler. He kept telling me that it rested him to use his hands after working at the office all day.

It was a shock to discover that vegetables and meats have an individuality of their own and can't be cooked exactly by the clock as the cookbooks so optimistically suggest. Roasting meat was a dicey affair that winter because the gas oven didn't have a thermostat and the thermometer didn't work. The cookbook said to test for the correct temperature by holding the hand in the oven for a few seconds. But as I didn't know what the correct temperature should feel like, that didn't help much.

Two outstandingly awful meals haunted me for years. One of them was a Sunday lunch for Oliver LaFarge who had just received an advance from the publisher for his Pulitzer prize-winning novel, *Laughing Boy.* He had been broke while writing it, and J.B. had lent him a hundred dollars to tide him over. The day he came to return the loan and to celebrate the great occasion with us, he had a hangover from too much celebration the night before. When J.B. cut into the blue and bleeding shoulder of lamb I brought in on the platter, Oliver turned green and left the table, to my shame and mortification.

The other meal was for Alf Landon, a Kansas friend. He and J.B. had sat in the backseat of the "Campaign Dodge" when William Allen White had come out against the Ku Klux Klan and was running for Governor during the Coolidge-versus-Davis presidential election in 1924. The beef I cooked that night was black on the outside and dark brown, stringy and tasteless all the way through. The roast potatoes, on the other hand, were not cooked through, and bounced across the plate when you tried to cut into them. I liked Alf Landon because he was so nice about trying to eat the food. He struck me as a pleasant, small-town politician, rather simple and somewhat corny. I was stunned eight years later when the Republicans nominated him to run against Franklin Roosevelt; it was like pitting a midget against a giant.

J.B. knew how to cook steaks and fry eggs and bacon, but that was the extent of his culinary skills. We were both starting from scratch, and since cooking became a collaboration, we shared responsibility for the occasional triumph and frequent failures. For a long time we had the greatest difficulty with what J.B. calls "synchronization"—the art of having meat, potatoes and green vegetables ready to be served at the same time. As a matter of course J.B. also lent a hand with the dish-washing so that we could both be free to go out together or read aloud to each other. We sang as we washed up—students' songbook things— and the chores were quickly done.

Every Thursday, J.B.'s former roommate in New York, Francis Howard, came to cook spaghetti for dinner. His mother belonged to an old Roman family and Francis had learned to cook spaghetti during one of his frequent visits to Italy.

He used to arrive with a package of socks to be mended by me, put on J.B.'s dressing gown as an apron to protect his clothes, and go to work in the kitchen. There was always a pot-bellied bottle of Chianti to drink with the feast and freshly grated Parmesan cheese to sprinkle over the Bolognese sauce. After dinner J.B. and Francis would take turns reading aloud from Chapman's Homer while I mended their socks, something I could do well thanks to Kaekey's training when I was a child. The Chapman was a first edition belonging to Francis Howard, and was treated with the greatest veneration. When each happy evening was over I would wrap the book carefully in newspaper and put it in a drawer in my desk to make sure that nobody spilled coffee or cigarette ashes on it.

Francis Howard, in his mid-twenties, was a tall, heavy-set man, very gentle and slow-moving. The children of mutual friends called him the Heffalump because of his elephantine presence. He was devastatingly handsome, with the curly dark hair and great liquid eyes of Italy and the clean features and high colouring of England. He loved poetry and music, particularly Bach, and had a bubbling, small-boy sense of humour which from time to time brought him down to earth from a distant, dreamy remoteness.

Francis was blissfully unaware of time, a quality which made him the despair of New York hostesses. He had a way of arriving in the middle of a dinner party, or floating into the Metropolitan Opera during the second act, or forgetting all about an invitation he had accepted. This behaviour did not prevent him from being showered with invitations, because he was the most eligible of eligible young men.

When J.B. and Francis Howard had roomed together J.B. also had been a much-sought-after "extra man." During the four years he had worked in New York he had been on the list for débutante parties. He did not enjoy débutantes as a rule and refused most of the invitations, but he did go out a great deal to dinners given by older women whom he found more amusing than gushing eighteen-year-olds. He had become a good friend of half a dozen rich, intelligent and witty married women in their thirties who collected artists, writers and intellectuals in the hope of becoming *neo-salonières*. They were well groomed, beautifully dressed women—very sure of themselves. When I first met them they made me feel gauche and about as elegant as a duck-billed platypus, but as the winter wore on I began to regain my self-confidence because they were nice to me. They asked us for dinner again and again, and we always had a good time. We could not afford taxis but used to find our way by subway or street car, wearing our full evening regalia. In those days J.B. always wore an opera hat when he was dressed in tails or a dinner jacket but no one ever insulted us or made us feel uncomfortable.

Two things which occurred while we were living in New York altered my outlook on life. During the winter I came down with a bad attack of influenza which left me very tired. Consequently J.B. persuaded me to try to find a cleaning woman for half a day a week to deal with the kitchen floor and the big dirt that had accumulated while I had been in bed. Cousin Flos suggested that I might persuade Kate Cox, her former parlour-maid, to lend me a hand. She gave me Kate's address, somewhere on the West Side.

Kate had no telephone, so I decided to go to see her rather than write. I found the place without difficulty; it was a tall brown tenement house in a noisy street where many children played. But I felt reluctant to go in and climb the long narrow staircase. As I stood plucking up my courage, a young man came down the stairs, looked at me curiously and then said, "What is a girl like you doing here?"

"I'm looking for a cleaning woman," I said. "She lives somewhere in this house."

"I'm an insurance agent," the young man said, "and I'm a Mason. See my ring? I don't think you should go up there. This is a tough part of New York."

That settled it, of course. I remembered suddenly how Mother had gone into a brothel—what she called a "house of ill-fame"—to rescue a maid who had disappeared while working for us. I could hear Mother saying, "No child of mine gives in to fear."

"I'm not afraid," I said untruthfully to the young man. "Don't worry about me. I'm going up."

"I'll wait here and if you don't come down in ten minutes I'm coming up after you," he said.

I climbed the canyon-like stairs. I could hear people talking behind closed doors but I didn't see anybody. Two flights up I found the apartment number Cousin Flos had given me and tapped on the door. After a second or two it was opened by a thin, hump-backed woman with straggly grey hair.

"I'm looking for Katherine Cox," I said.

"I'm Kate Cox."

I could hardly believe her. Only a few years before she had been a straight-backed young woman, always smart in her neat black uniform and crisp white apron.

"I'm Mrs. LaFarge's cousin," I said.

"I remember you well." She smiled, thereby showing several dark gaps in her teeth. "Come in."

She said she would be glad to work for me. "I need the money," she added.

Then she showed me over the apartment. There were two bedrooms, each only big enough to hold a double bed and a chair. There was a couch in the kitchen which was also the dining and living room. To my astonishment there was no bathroom.

"This is a cold-water flat," Kate explained. "We wash in the kitchen sink. There's a toilet at the end of the hall. There's two families, fourteen people on this floor, so sometimes it takes a bit of waiting to get in. There's seven of us here. The four kids sleep in the one room and my husband and me in the other, and the boarder sleeps in the kitchen."

Laundry was hanging in the kitchen and unwashed pots and pans stood on the table. Remembering the little white desk and bookcase in my bedroom at 1732 Pine Street, I wondered how the children could do their homework.

Every year when we had gone through New York on the way to Rhode Island, I had been shocked by the tenements along the railroad tracks. Bedclothes always hung out of the windows to air and sometimes frowsy-looking women and pallid children leaned out and watched the train go past. I had been touched often by the sight of geraniums and petunias in tin cans standing on the window sills or fire escapes because it showed that even people living in such run-down places had a yearning for colour and beauty or perhaps just for growing things. I had often looked into the bare rooms with wondering sadness as the train slowed down, but that morning when I went to see Kate was the first time I had ever understood the way that people have to live in tenements of that kind. I was revolted by the smell of the place, the sordidness of it all, and felt ashamed that I had ever thought of myself as poor.

When I went downstairs the Mason was striding up and down in front of the house.

"I was just about to come up and look for you," he said.

"It's awful, isn't it?"

"That's nothing. I've seen hundreds worse than that," he said, "and you ought to hear what it's like at night. Bedlam, that's what it is."

Kate turned out to be a great comfort to me. She found time in half a day to clean the apartment, polish the silver, wash my underwear and prepare a casserole for dinner. She was always efficient, good-natured, kind, full of unlikely stories and jokes. She found my ignorance of the fundamentals of housekeeping amusing, but she was also sympathetic and coached me by means of a hint here and a hint there so that in time I began to know my way around the kitchen. I developed the greatest respect for her. I couldn't understand how she could keep going, and remain so cheerful and unresentful when she was so tired and old before her time.

That visit to a New York tenement gave a sharp prod to my social conscience. It was J.B. who was responsible for the next time my warm puppy nose came up against the cold iron of reality. I had spend a couple of weeks in Rhode Island to get away from the suffocation of a New York August and had just returned when a heat wave rolled in from the south. Sleep that night was practically impossible as we lay naked in our beds, tossing, our bodies not only feeling like, but also looking like boiled lobsters because of the ruby glow from the undertaker's sign. No breath of air came through the windows. We sweated and the sheets under us felt like hot metal, bruising our damp flesh.

One Saturday evening, after supper, we walked over to Madison Square and sat on a bench, hoping for a breath of moving air which never came. I wore only a cotton dress and a pair of sandals. It was too hot for anyone to care about clothes.

I was in a bad temper, constantly harping on how a cool wind would be blowing off the sea into my old bedroom that overlooked Narragansett Bay. "Nobody," I said, "*nobody* stays in New York on a weekend in August."

J.B. didn't say anything then; only laughed and suggested a milkshake or an ice-cream soda. But the next day he said, "Come for a Sunday walk. I want to show you something."

Slowly, under the relentless hot sky, we walked downtown and then eastward through the Tenderloin to the river. There were people all around us. They sat on doorsteps, on chairs on the pavement, on iron fire escapes, on roof tops. They looked worn out, pale, drained, as if they had been stretched on a rack. Children played on the street, yelling at each other in strident voices. Sometimes too hot to yell, they just sat on the curb. We passed a group of children who ran, shouting with delight, in and out of the spray from a spouting fire hydrant. We sat on the end of a wharf on the East River and watched naked boys diving into the filthy, scum-covered water.

"Nobody," said J.B., "*nobody* spends a weekend in New York in August."

"It was a stupid thing to say," I said. "I'm sorry."

Washington,D.C.

In the autumn of 1929 we moved to Washington, D.C. because J.B. had taken a job as editor of a current events paper designed for classroom use in high schools. The pay was good, but what was more important, the move brought J.B. back into newspaper work and got him down in the political centre of the country. We both felt that it was a stepping-stone in the right direction.

On the day the moving van came to our little apartment in New York the stockmarket crashed. J.B. had stayed to supervise the movers while Ben Bush drove Mother and me to Washington so that I would be on hand when our goods and chattels arrived.

It was not a restful trip. When it was time for lunch, we were in the rolling hills of Maryland. Mother told Ben to stop at a nice-looking roadside restaurant. We went in and the proprietor ushered us to a table, but when Mother mentioned that Ben also wanted lunch, he said, "We don't serve niggers here."

Mother left at once, indignantly sweeping out of the restaurant like a cyclone. She had always inveighed against Jim Crow laws and had forbidden us to ever use the word "nigger." She always talked about "coloured people," and treated blacks as courteously as she treated other people.

That day in Maryland we stopped at four restaurants, and at each one it was the same story. Ben kept saying, "Please, Mrs. Rhein, I ain't hungry. You and Miss Florence just go ahead and eat."

And Mother kept saying, "If you can't eat, I won't eat. It wouldn't be right."

Eventually we found a shabby restaurant which allowed us to sit at a

table and Ben to sit at a counter with the truck drivers. This was still
Jim Crow, but at least Ben could eat.

We had dinner that night with J.B.'s new employer. It was not an
auspicious occasion. He had just built a $70,000 house and, three
weeks before the crash, had plunged deeply into the stock market on
margin. He was white, distraught, practically inarticulate all through
the unfortunate meal.

Mother was no help at all. For some reason she got on the subject of
chiropractors for which she had acquired the disdain of a physician's
wife. She was emphatic in her indictment of the whole tribe, and when
Mother was in full cry she was very emphatic. She was embarrassed,
though not as much as I, when our host remarked, when he could get
a word in, that his wife's eight brothers were all chiropractors. My rage
and indignation at Mother was far greater than any concern about the
stock market crash. J.B. and I had practically no money and no invest-
ments. Everyone I knew had jobs at that time, so it never occurred to
me that educated people like us would ever have any problem about
getting or holding a job. During the election campaign of the previous
year many people had said that it didn't really matter whether it was
Al Smith or Herbert Hoover who was elected because the country was
so prosperous that no administration could harm it. I had not the slightest
understanding of what was happening, not a clue.

During the following months, however, I began to be worried like
everyone else. I couldn't understand what had gone wrong with the
richest country in the world. After the first rash of suicides and failures
of brokerage firms, everyone kept echoing President Hoover's repeated
announcements that the United States was going through a temporary
recession, that all would soon be well. The oft-repeated bromide "Prosperity is just around the corner" failed entirely to keep up people's
courage as stocks went down and down, dividends were cut, and the
ranks of the unemployed grew daily larger.

In spite of the growing cloud of worry on the horizon, J.B. and I
enjoyed Washington. After the dark concrete canyons of New York, it
was wonderful to be in a city of wide streets, where there was so much
light and so many trees, and where Rock Creek Park was close at hand
for walks. We had found a four-room apartment on California Street,
near Connecticut Avenue, a quiet, tree-lined, bourgeois part of town.

I shopped at an A & P a few blocks away from the apartment. There
little black boys, in the best American free-enterprise tradition, waited
outside the door, offering their express wagons to carry home the

groceries for a fee of ten cents. I usually hired one, and he would trudge behind me as I led the way back to the apartment.

We used to park our Model A roadster on the street at night. Every evening at nightfall the elevator man of our apartment would nip out and hang a bicycle lamp on the rear axle. This was our way of conforming with a city by-law which specified that stationary cars must have a parking light of some kind.

That Model A Ford was a source of great pleasure, and a form of emancipation since it enabled us to get out into the country for walks and picnics. J.B. had given it to me as a surprise for a twenty-second birthday present. We named it Alberta—Albie for short—after the tubby little channel steamer which had taken us to Guernsey on our honeymoon. Albie cost $450, a great sum at that time, but we drove her for eight years without any problems. She never spent a night in a garage in her life except during the winter hibernation period. I'll admit it was a nuisance when it rained unexpectedly and we had to put up the top. We were always soaked by the time we had attached the isinglass side curtains, chiefly because, for some reason, we kept putting them on upside-down.

J.B. worked hard that winter in Washington, happy to be back in writing again and glad of the opportunity to learn the job of editing. The circulation of the paper went up and people began to talk about his lucid, informed articles. He realized that the recession was not going to end, and began to study economics seriously in the evening. The living room looked like a college room full of text books.

We also played a lot that winter. To my surprise, friends of the family called on me, leaving stacks of engraved cards which accumulated in a bowl on the hall table. They followed up their visits by asking us for dinner. We were also invited to parties given by the British diplomatic mission, since Sir Esme Howard, the father of our New York spaghetti cook, was the British Ambassador at that time.

The fact that I was old Mrs. Tom Bayard's great-niece gave us an additional entrée to the social merry-go-round. Widow of my great-uncle, the former Secretary of State who was also the first American Ambassador to the Court of St. James's, Mrs. Bayard was something of a legend in Washington where she was considered the last of the *grandes dames*.

Mother had insisted that I call on Aunt May, so J.B. and I went to pay our respects on a Saturday afternoon. The door was answered by an elderly black butler who threw open the drawing room doors and announced us as if we were visiting royalty. We were graciously received by a very petite *grande dame,* slim, wrinkled, straight-backed and imperious. She fascinated us with her small talk, which centred that day on the iniquities of the automobile.

"I still take a drive behind a good pair of horses," she said. "Gentle people do not own automobiles."

J.B. and I gave each other a long look which said, "Thank God we parked Albie around the corner out of sight."

"I ignore automobiles," said Aunt May. "When I walk across Connecticut Avenue, I just lift up my cane and the motorists stop. Sometimes they swear at me, but they stop."

She then launched into an anecdote often repeated in the family. "Some years ago people kept parking in front of the house, so that my carriage couldn't draw up to the front door. It was more than I could bear, so I wrote to the Secretary of State, complaining that the property in front of my house was being used as a stable for cars, which appear to be taking the place of horses. I told him I wanted No Parking signs put up. He wrote back saying that it was against the District's bylaws to put No Parking signs in front of a private dwelling. However, he added that cars are not allowed to park in front of a driveway, so in consideration of the great contribution made by my husband to his country, the government would build a driveway across the pavement at its own expense."

The pavement was quite narrow, so the driveway took up most of it. But at least no cars could be parked there, and the vacant stretch constituted a monument to the memory of Tom Bayard. We wondered if the matter had been taken to the Cabinet.

Aunt May had a strong sense of family, and she very kindly asked us to her rare parties. This was a mixed blessing as far as J.B. was concerned. She explained that her doctor had given her the same instructions he had given ex-President Taft. He had forbidden them to give evening parties, but did permit them to entertain during the day. As a result, she gave dinner parties at lunchtime. Sixteen people. Six courses of magnificent food.

Everything was conducted with the formality of the Victorian era. In the dressing room each female guest was presented with a card bearing the name of the man who was to take her into the dining room. Each male received a similar card with the name of the woman to whom he was to give his arm. Since Aunt May, half-blind and in her late eighties, wrote the cards herself, it was almost impossible to decipher the strange, squiggly scrawl. Over the sherry the men would edge around, showing their cards to the women surreptitiously. It reminded me of the men in Paris who used to sell dirty postcards to tourists. The game was to try to match cards without your hostess being aware of what was happening. I thought it wildly funny the first time a bishop, and a few minutes later an elderly senator, and then a judge of the Supreme Court nudged up to me, murmuring, "Do you think this could be your name?"

It was usually four o'clock before we rose from the table, sated with food, having eaten our way through turtle soup swimming in sherry, crisp devilled crabs, fried chicken and hominy, and bisque ice cream blanketed with brandy.

The men always had their coffee, port and cigars in the smoking room, because Aunt May did not permit smoking in the drawing room. As far as I can gather, this period was not taken up with a discussion of Weltpolitik or the economic problems of the nation, but was confined to a sort of drawing of lots to see who had the best right to creep away without saying good-bye. Only a few chosen ones could do that, because Aunt May would have noticed and been offended. J.B. was usually one of the early departers, since all the other men realized he was the youngest, the most harassed-looking and obviously the one most likely to get into trouble if he did not get back to the office until just on closing time.

While the unemployed were planning to march on Washington, the so-called society of the national capital was being rocked by the battle royal between Dolly Gann (the sister and official hostess of the Vice-President and Speaker of the Senate, Charles Curtis) and Alice Roosevelt Longworth (the wife of the Speaker of the House). Mrs. Longworth insisted that she should claim precedence over Mrs. Gann because a sister is not in the same league as a wife. Mrs. Gann stood by her rights as official hostess. The feud presented a great problem for those responsible for protocol, since the dowager not given precedence over the other at lunch or dinner would walk out rather than accept an inferior position at table.

J.B. and I thought it all utterly absurd. But we were entranced when we heard a story told by the wife of a member of the Canadian legation. She had seen, in a lingerie shop, some purple satin underwear embroidered with American eagles, and the salesgirl had told her that they had been made to order for Mrs. Gann. Soon after, at a legation party, the guests ended up singing,

> She has . . . purple underwear,
> I never cared for purple underwear,

> But she has purple underwear,
> And that's my weakness now.

to the tune of "She Has Eyes of Blue". I have it "from an informed
source" that the Canadian minister, Vincent Massey—later the very
model of a model Governor-General—joined in the song.

That winter in Washington I was busy writing book reviews and
reading text books on economics and political science, so that I could
keep up with J.B. and understand why there was so much suffering
and poverty everywhere. I also wrote, unpaid, a few articles for the
weekly paper my husband was editing. The publisher liked my stuff
and offered me a job as editor of a weekly newspaper used by Current
Events classes in junior high schools. I was not to begin work until the
school year started the following autumn.

Full of confidence and enthusiasm, I started to read with a serious
end in view, and also took typing lessons so that I could write directly
onto a typewriter. In time I became a fast typist, though a shockingly
inaccurate one, because my fingers never learned to keep up with my
ideas.

During the spring of 1930, J.B. became increasingly worried about
the future. Circulation of the weekly had gone shooting up under his
editorship and he was enjoying a mild *succès d'estime,* but revenues
were shrinking as the depression deepened. One day he came home and
told me that the publisher had made it clear that his job would probably
not be there the coming year. Furthermore publication of the weekly
Current Events paper for high schools was going to be suspended, so
that I was out of a job even before I had it.

We were both bitterly disappointed. J.B. reacted in typical British
fashion, with a stiff upper lip. I reacted vociferously, after the manner
of the Kane family. At such times J.B. is the one who suffers most,
because he bottles up his emotions. I am fortunate in being able to
express my feelings and so get rid of my tensions.

Our shock was somewhat softened by the fact that so many people
we knew were finding themselves out of a job or having their salaries
reduced. Mother, who was dependent upon dividends from her invest-
ments, was frantic. Now she wrote to say she had spent two hours with
her "man of business" who advised her to "try to live differently"
once again because her income had been so greatly reduced. She had
come out of the session close to tears, but had been forced to laugh by
Ben Bush, who had opened the car door for her with his usual flourish
and said, "Well, Mrs. Rhein, does we eat this summer?"

That spring we faced a crisis in our lives. Should J.B. stay on in his job in the hope that the publisher would weather the storm? Should he look for another job in the States? Should we go to England? Should we move to Canada? Neither of us, of course, would even consider going to South Africa; the attitude of the dominant whites toward the black majority ruled it out for us.

We talked about what we ought to do for hours, night after night, and long into the night. We walked in Rock Creek Park and talked and talked. We took long drives in Albie and talked and talked. We realized that we were at a crossroads and that the turn we took would decide the future course of our lives.

J.B. was confident he could get a job in the States. In fact he was offered a good job on the *New York Herald Tribune* by Stanley Walker, the city editor. But he knew he would never reach the top if he did not become an American citizen, and that was something he could not bring himself to do. He was also sure that he could get a job in England because of his reputation at Oxford. But I did not want to live in England; I am a North American.

For some time J.B. had talked about going to Canada. He had spent many holidays there visiting friends he had made at Oxford. Now we both talked about it.

The only part of Canada I knew was the Thousand Islands: we had spent two Labour Day weekends on Hickory Island with the parents of Donald Wood, the cousin who had taken Mother and me for tea with Mrs. Bird. I realized, of course, that the life there was not typical of the country. The Woods were rich Americans who lived in luxury, with three or four servants to run the huge house and two boatmen to look after the motor launches and sailing canoes. However, I had met several Canadians at a conference on international affairs at Williamstown, Massachussetts, the previous year—G.R. Parkin, Frank Underhill, Percy Corbett, Jake Viner and Wynne Plumptre. J.B. and I had sat with the Canadian group at meals and I was fascinated by the witty, iconoclastic conversation. I found those men exciting, very different from the men I knew in Philadelphia or met at parties in Washington. They didn't like what was happening in the world around them, and had strong ideas about what must be done to improve the quality of life in their country. I listened to them, saying little, and I must confess that I often didn't know what they were talking about. But I was very impressed.

Later I had met two more of J.B.'s Canadian friends—Frank Scott, a professor of law at McGill, and Brooke Claxton, a young Montreal lawyer. They had written to J.B. saying they were coming to Washington for a lawyers' convention and would get in touch with us when they arrived. On the day before the conference opened the telephone rang. It was Frank Scott saying that he and Brooke couldn't get into their rooms at the Mayflower Hotel until late in the day. I suggested they come up to the house for tea.

Around four o'clock the doorbell rang and I opened the front door to see a tall, broad-shouldered man with sandy hair and a bulbous nose. Although we were undergoing a typical Washington heat wave, he was wearing a heavy Harris tweed suit and thick, hand-knitted socks. Sweat was pouring out of his hair.

"I'm Brooke Claxton," he said. "I've just climbed to the top of the dome of the Capitol Building. The guide reported it was 120 degrees up there under the copper roof and I believe him."

Without even a how-do-you-do, I asked, "Would you like a bath?"

"More than anything else in the world," he replied fervently.

I showed him the bathroom and gave him one of J.B.'s clean shirts. It was the beginning of a lasting friendship, but I never could take Brooke entirely seriously, even after he became a federal Cabinet minister. The essential image of him in my mind was always that of an exhausted young man melting like a snowman on my doorstep.

I liked both Frank and Brooke immensely and was interested in their dreams for Canada. When the time for decision came I thought of them, and decided that if they were typical of the sort of people we would be associating with in Canada, there were distinct advantages in going to that country.

There was another strong argument in favour of going north. I believed that if, by mutual agreement, we went to a country where both of us were beginning a new life together we might avoid some of the problems inherent in an international marriage. J.B. would never, when angry or frustrated, be able to accuse me of having been responsible for his having become an expatriate, and I could never, in a moment of loneliness or irritability, turn to him and say, "I gave up my country for yours." There could never be any recrimination of that kind because we would both have made the same sacrifice. I was right about that, except that from the day we became landed immigrants we never regarded becoming Canadians as a sacrifice; for us it was a fulfilment.

We were also drawn by a sense of adventure. We felt we would be "seeking our fortune" in a country where we would be entirely on our own and free of the feeling that people were nice to us, or helped us to get a job, because of family connections or accident of birth. Moreover, we might be able to make more of an impact, have more influence on the society of a young country with a small population than we would in a huge country like the United States, or a tradition-bound country like England.

The truth is that both of us were individualists, determined to do our own thing. We felt that having no children we were free people. It never occurred to us to look for, or expect, "security," that word so popular even with the young today. It was a word we never used. I never thought about it in relation to ourselves, but years later J.B. told me *he* had worried about starting from scratch again.

And so it was that on a hot June day we saw our furniture put into storage and then, full of hope, turned Albie's nose northward.

Canada

We drove north through the Adirondacks. As Washington summer turned into northern spring, J.B. kept singing the praises of Canada. He was eloquent about the way the Mounted Police had preceded settlement in the West, so that law and order prevailed in a way unknown on the lawless, violent American frontier. He expounded on the virtues of British Parliamentary institutions. Above all, he looked forward with eager anticipation to having a legal drink in a "civilized" country whose citizens would never have considered such a ridiculous law as the Volstead Act. Weaned on bathtub gin and bootleg booze, I had visions of ruby-red wine in a thin-stemmed crystal glass such as we used to have on the table in England and on the Continent.

It was a Sunday afternoon when we arrived in Montreal. After finding a boarding-house on Dorchester Street we sallied forth to a nearby Italian restaurant called the Roma. J.B. ordered spaghetti bolognese and a bottle of Chianti. After a while the spaghetti arrived along with a coffee pot.

"We want our wine now and our coffee later," said J.B.

The waiter poured Chianti from the coffee pot into our coffee cups. "No wine allowed on Sunday," said he with a wink.

It was just like a New York speakeasy.

Shortly after our arrival, Brooke Claxton, then a member of the executive of the Association of Canadian Clubs, and Graham Spry, its secretary, suggested that J.B. go on a lecture tour to all the Canadian Clubs in the country.

On trips to Montreal before we were married, J.B. had spoken a few times to the Group, an informal public affairs club to which Claxton and

Spry belonged, so they knew he was an interesting and well-informed lecturer. They warned him that it would be a rugged trip and particularly exhausting in winter weather. It was such a rugged schedule, in fact, that Kenneth Lindsay, a British Labourite, had been obliged to give it up after delivering about seventy lectures. J.B. and I were not frightened off by their warnings. We thought it a wonderful idea, since it would enable us to see the country of our choice as well as help J.B. to find a newspaper job.

It was arranged that J.B. was to go on a Canadian Club tour from the Maritimes to Courtenay, B.C., and as far north as the Peace River district, all expenses paid, but no fee. We were determined that I should go along, as Canada was to be my country as well as his. We had saved a thousand dollars during our first year of marriage, so we felt justified in spending some of our capital on such an exciting adventure.

J.B. settled down in Brooke Claxton's beautiful old chalet-style house on Côte St. Antoine Road in Montreal—the old Decarie farm house where Brooke claimed the Montreal melon was first developed. There, during the summer, J.B. did the research and prepared the three speeches he was to offer to the Canadian Clubs, while I stayed in Rhode Island with my mother.

In September we took the train to St. Stephen, New Brunswick, where J.B. gave the first of the hundred speeches he was to deliver to a variety of audiences during the following five months.

I did not hear many of his talks because although the CNR had given me a newspaper pass, the CPR had refused to do so. (I think now that they were quite right, considering that I had no experience and no newspaper affiliation, but at the time I was indignant.) The Canadian Club tour itinerary, involving a succession of one-night stands, included many places not touched by the CNR, so that J.B. and I travelled separately for a great deal of the time. I became a railroad buff, an authority on time-tables, and spent hours figuring out how I could get to a place on some small CNR branch line in order to join my husband for even a few hours.

At that time, in 1930, Graham Spry was up to his neck in an effort to sell the government and the public on the importance of implementing the recommendations of the Aird Report on broadcasting by setting up a national broadcasting system like the BBC. Consequently, he and his secretary did not have the time to figure out my strange and complicated schedules. They did their best by notifying the big city clubs that I was accompanying my husband, but did not tell many of the smaller clubs in places where they thought I would not want to go. As a result, I often did not turn up when I was expected, to the fury of the presidents of the Women's Clubs who went to meet me at the train armed with a corsage and a carefully prepared schedule of entertainments. On the other hand, I sometimes arrived at places where no one knew of my existence. Since I often checked into a hotel hours before J.B. or late at night after he arrived, the executives of the clubs sometimes decided that I was a blonde hussy he had picked up on the train and refused to have anything to do with me. The rare brush-offs, however, were made up for by the people who decided we were on our honeymoon and gave us wedding presents.

In the 1930's the Canadian Clubs, like the Chatauqua circuit, performed a very important function, especially for Canadians living in rural districts. There was no CBC then, and anyway many people could not afford radios. Telephones were a rarity in the country. Few people could afford newspapers. When the snow came, people on farms were cut off from other human beings. For them, the Canadian Club speakers provided much needed contact with the outside world. People on the prairies would drive fifty miles to hear the speaker, and would make a night of it, often staying until just before dawn, when they had to get home to feed and water their animals. After the speech they wanted to ask questions and visit with one another.

We were frequently invited out for meals, and then *we* asked questions in order to learn as much as possible about Canada. It was a marvellous experience for both J.B. and me, since we heard what was on people's minds in every part of the land, in small towns as well as big cities, and began to understand some of the problems of this enormous country.

On this trip, as in Montreal, I was at first frustrated by the Canadian custom of conversational purdah. I had been accustomed to men and women, old and young, mixing and talking together. Not so in Canada. Invariably, at a party, the men would congregate in one corner of the living room, or stand around in the kitchen drinking beer and talking about unemployment, wheat, the B.N.A. Act, social welfare, the dust bowl in the Palliser Triangle, and—particularly in the Prairies—about international affairs, since they were so dependent on foreign markets. The women gathered together on the other side of the room and discussed babies, knitting and recipes, all necessary parts of life, but not the things which interested me. After a while, encouraged by J.B., I refused to be squeezed into this social pattern and boldly moved over and sat with the men. It seemed insane not to make the most of the opportunity to learn as much as I could.

During the Canadian Club tour, as I racketed across the continent, I was a source of curiosity to travelling salesmen in the Pullman smoking cars. They used to shake their heads and say, "What is a nice, pretty girl like you doing travelling all by herself on such uncomfortable, out-of-the-way trains?" Since I was lonely, it was nice to have someone to talk to, and as a would-be writer I found their ideas interesting. After a time, in spite of their horrible cigar smoke, I became quite attached to the tribe, particularly after the night I came down from Little Long Lac on a CNR spur line to the Lakehead.

I was the only passenger in the lone sleeping car attached to a mail and baggage train. After supper I took out my typewriter and began to write a letter to Graham Spry, thanking him for the books about Canada he had lent me to read: *In Search of America* by Philip Frederick Grove, which had made a profound, if depressing, impression on me, and *The Year Book of the Arts* by Bertram Brooker, which I had found inspiring. When I glanced up from my letter, I realized that the Pullman porter was sitting right across from me and staring at me intently. He was an odd-looking, pockmarked man with a huge tumour on his neck. Maybe he was just lonely, or perhaps not well, but in any case he began to talk about God rather incoherently. After he had talked and talked I began to feel nervous, and went back to the men's smoking room. As the night wore on I wanted to go to bed but was afraid to undress. It was not until two in the morning, when a couple of travellers climbed on board at some lonely little station, that I felt safe enough to turn in.

Among all the people we met on that tour, the person who stands out most clearly in memory is Edgar Tarr of Winnipeg. He was a quiet, wise, thoughtful man, a Canadian nationalist but also an internationalist, one of the founders of the Canadian Institute of International Affairs. He was a member of what was known as the Winnipeg Sanhedrin, a group of men dedicated to Canada, who were led by John W. Dafoe of the *Winnipeg Free Press*.

After talking with all and sundry, from East to West, about the depression and the sort of society we both wanted, J.B. and I became aware that it was quite impossible for people in our generation to communicate with anyone over forty. We thought that the old men had made a mess of things, and we were determined to do a better job. We were utterly committed to doing something about poverty and injustice, and it never crossed our minds to opt out. At that time I swore a mighty oath that I would always remember what it was like to be young. I have never forgotten.

Crossing Canada, most of the time alone, was an overpowering experience. The size of the country was awesome. There was so much of everything. There seemed to be days and days of bush and muskeg in Ontario, days and days of flat, brown or snow-covered prairies, and great rows of dog-toothed rocks barring the way to the West Coast.

On the 12th of October I learned about winter in Canada when the train was snowed in for two days just outside of Saskatoon. J.B. was lecturing at Manyberries, and when it became obvious that I wasn't going to reach him, I decided to send a telegram from the railway station.

I had to walk about half a mile through the train yard in the driving snow. The station was warm and steaming with the breath of men. It smelled of sweat, unwashed clothes and bodies, and despair—what J.B. and I called the "unemployed smell" after we met it later in Montreal. Many of the men wore khaki greatcoats from World War I. Others were dressed in shabby, cast-off garments. They were the unemployed who had ridden the rails or climbed on top of open cars to cross the country in their search for jobs that were not there. We had seen them daily on trains as they sat huddled against the icy wind and, as time went on, with a cold feeling of dread inside us, we felt a kinship with them.

When he was in a city, or any town where there was a newspaper, J.B. always went to call on editors to ask for a job. Everywhere it was the same story. Editors were impressed by J.B.'s qualifications and said they would like to hire him but it was out of the question. They had reduced their staffs because there was practically no advertising and people weren't paying up on their subscriptions.

J.B. and I were both horribly worried, but tried to hide our anxiety and cheer each other up. When a cheque for $100 for an article he had written for *The Bookman* caught up with us in Calgary, he kept saying that his pen could always keep us from starving. We spent $75 of that $100 on a mouton coat for me because I had only a tweed coat which felt like paper when I went out into the cold.

We had decided to use some of our savings to buy me a CPR ticket from Calgary to Vancouver by way of the Okanagan. J.B. was speaking at Banff, Kelowna, Penticton and Vernon, and we wanted to see the Rockies together and enjoy the roller-coaster ride through magnificent scenery on the Kettle Valley line.

At a Canadian Club dinner meeting in Penticton I sat beside Grote Sterling, Minister of Defence in R.B. Bennett's cabinet. When I said I had been born in Philadelphia, he asked if I had ever heard of a family called Willing. I said my great-great-grandmother was a Willing. It turned out that he was a descendant of her sister who had eloped with a young British army captain by the name of Sterling. My new-found cousin invited us to his home for lunch the next day. It gave me a strange feeling to see there a Georgian silver gravy boat that had belonged to the Willing family. The twin of it had sat for years on the sideboard in the dining room of 1732 Pine Street.

The day after that, when the Kettle Valley train stopped to take on water at Summerside, a man called Cooper climbed aboard the balcony at the rear of the passenger car. He had heard, from a member of the Vernon Canadian Club, that J.B. would be riding on the train, and was curious to find out if he was, by any chance, a relation. It turned out that they were related through J.B.'s mother's people, the Armstrongs. Meeting kinsmen in a country where we thought we had no family connections cheered us at a time when we were feeling pretty low. It seemed to me that the two coincidences had been arranged by Fate to give us a sense of belonging in Canada. We never saw or heard from either of our distant relatives again, but at the time they did us a lot of good.

After J.B. spoke in Vancouver and Victoria we took the boat to Prince Rupert. On the way J.B. came down with a terrible cold and stayed in bed over the weekend. I was taken to see the sights, notably the ten miles of road, the first lap of a hoped-for highway to Vancouver. Judging by the traffic, the jaunt was the big Sunday thrill for everyone in the town who owned a car.

That day the president of the Canadian Club asked me if J.B. still had a beard. I replied that he had never had one. After a few minutes of double talk, I understood, to my dismay, that the club thought they were going to hear Admiral Byrd of the Antarctic the following evening, probably because J.B. had been billed to lecture on the naval conference of 1927. When I got back to the hotel J.B. was feverish and miserable, and I didn't dare to tell him about the beard business for fear of upsetting him. His rather academic speech on the problems involved in international disarmament must have come as a surprise to the men in the audience. However they applauded loudly and kept asking J.B. about world affairs until after midnight.

Later, on the train to Edmonton, I fainted a couple of times, so when we arrived I went to see a doctor. After a series of unpleasant tests I was diagnosed as having severe anemia. The doctor told me to stay in bed for several days and then curtail the trip. I was disconsolate at not being able to go to the Peace River with J.B., and heartbroken about having to leave him and go back to stay with Mother while he finished the remaining three weeks of the tour and kept on trying to find a job.

I stayed three days alone in the Macdonald Hotel in Edmonton while J.B. went to Peace River Landing, and during that time I decided I would have to write a novel in order to help earn some money. I wrote an outline on a pad and when J.B. came back for the weekend we worked together all day and half the night discussing what should go into it. It was to be a satire about Philadelphia society.

Going back to Philadelphia alone, I sat for hours listening to the clanking of train wheels, the hissing of steam and the lonely cry of the engine whistle echoing over the prairies. I could see form and beauty in the long flat reaches of land covered with snow shaped into patterns by the driving winds. But I found infinitely sad the farm houses, unpainted and isolated in the midst of desolation. And the sight of clusters of desperate men on the top of the trains that passed depressed me greatly. I felt young, lonely, ill and vulnerable.

The following weeks in Philadelphia were a horror. It was bad enough to be sick with worry about J.B. and his struggle against his fear of the future without finding Mother lacking in understanding and sympathy at a time when I needed her support. She kept saying, "J.B. should be ashamed of himself for allowing you to travel all by yourself like that. He ought to be ashamed of himself to have made my healthy, laughing sunshine child so pale and sad."

I kept replying that J.B. didn't order me around, that he treated me like an adult, that we had decided together about my travelling the way I did, and that it had been what I wanted to do. I tried to explain that it had been a wonderful experience to be able to see all the magnificent country and to meet so many different kinds of people. I became furiously angry when she said she wondered if J.B. was really trying to find a job. I shouted at her and told her she was disgusting when she said, "He needn't expect me to give him any money. I've hardly enough myself to keep my head above water. You don't seem to understand that all of my dividends have been cut or just haven't paid anything." I found it intolerable when she kept probing and probing to find out if something was wrong with our marriage.

Having always had a warm and loving relationship with Mother, it was devastating to find myself fighting her viciously, the way she and her sisters fought—just what I had promised myself I would never do. I could feel myself turning into the sort of person I didn't want to be. I kept thinking of Father saying *"empire sur vous-même"* and being crushed by the knowledge that my self-control was diminishing after every argument with Mother. Since my marriage I had begun to think and act like an adult, and had been treated like one by my husband, and now I began to feel and behave like an adolescent.

I understand now that Mother was sick with worry about me and my marriage and, above all, by the strange, social upheaval taking place all around her. It was a frightening, unhappy time for her—as it was for J.B. and me. It must have been desperate for her to find me turning to her for comfort and security when she was herself so insecure and in need of consolation. I understand that now but then I believed she had failed me, and told her so.

A week or so after the New Year I received a telegram that did me more good than all the liver shots the doctor had been sticking into my rump. It was a typical Bird message. *"Courage, Madame, j'entends le papier."*

This was of course a *double entendre*. We had both been brought up on the story about the American lady on a train in France who was desperately impatient to get into the lavatory which had been occupied for some time. A Frenchman, waiting in line, attempted to encourage her by leaning close to the toilet door and then saying happily, *"courage, Madame, j'entends le papier."*

J.B. obviously meant that there was real hope of getting a job on a newspaper.

A couple of days later a letter arrived saying he had gone to see the editor of the *Montreal Star*. "Can you use an editorial writer or a reporter?" he had asked.

The editor had replied, "Maybe. Sit down over there and write a couple of editorials about anything you want." So J.B. had sat down at a typewriter, written two editorials, and had got the job. The pay was about half of what he had been getting either in Washington or New York but it was in Canada and the sort of work he wanted above all else to do.

In his letter he said to come home at once. I took the train the next day and at Rouses' Point became officially a landed immigrant.

Montreal

We started life as new Canadians at Povey's Lodge, a rooming house on Peel Street near Sherbrooke Street, a site now occupied by a tall glassy building. There was a variety of restaurants, notably a Honey Dew and a Murray's on St. Catherine Street, where we usually ate breakfast and lunch. For dinner we wandered far afield looking for inexpensive meals that were fit to eat.

We went often to Jules Stien's then on Berri Street, east of St. Lawrence Main, where the young French Canadian intellectuals gathered because the four courses and glass of wine were cheap and had a genuine *français de France* accent. We went frequently to Chez Ernest, then on Dorchester Street, where Ernest gave me a recipe for a depression Bolognese sauce which contained celery and carrots to stretch the amount of meat that went into it. We also went to The Samovar on Peel Street, where we enjoyed pink borscht and balalaika music, and to a Romanian restaurant way north on the Main, where we ate sizzling steaks steeped in garlic.

Soon after I arrived in Montreal, J.B. was given an assignment by the *Montreal Star*. He was to live among the unemployed and write a series of articles about what was happening to single men. At that time there was no unemployment insurance, no family allowances, no universal old-age security, no medicare, and no public assistance. Welfare—what little there was of it—was supplied by religious organizations, which meant that you were out of luck if you were an atheist or a person who had no religious affiliation.

J.B. plunged into the job with vigour because unemployment was something he knew about. In order to look the part he shaved his moustache and let his beard grow to the dirty-looking stage. He bought a dilapidated overcoat from a second-hand store and a new pair of dungarees which he shabbied up by rolling them around the furnace room floor. Mr. Povey, a cheerful cockney, thought J.B. was a detective and gave us respectful assistance.

In those days homeless, penniless men, many of whom had left their families and come to the city in search of work, were fed by the Grey Nuns on Dorchester Street and were housed in the Dufferin School and in the Meurling Refuge where they could spend the night free of charge. They usually lined up for a meal, such as baked beans, before going into the dormitories at around five in the afternoon. The food was better at the Dufferin but the sleeping was better at the Meurling because clothes and bedding were fumigated daily, so there were fewer bedbugs, lice or fleas.

The men were let out of the refuges early in the mornings after being given a cup of coffee and bread. There was no place for them to go during the day so they walked the streets, stood in line at unemployment offices, or rang doorbells in the hope of handouts. Later, when we found an apartment, we gave sandwiches to men almost every day, and at night, after the refuges were full, we would give a few cents so that a man could find a bed at the Salvation Army hostel. The "Army" did a fine job in Montreal during the dirty thirties.

While getting material for his articles, J.B. conscientiously lived the desperate life of the unemployed. It was a cold February that year in Montreal, with much wind and snow, and walking the streets all day on a practically empty stomach was an exhausting, spirit-destroying ordeal. When the snow on the streets thawed on a sunny day feet became wet, and then freezing cold, as the thermometer dropped toward zero after dark.

From time to time J.B. dropped in to see how I was getting on and to take a long hot bath. He brought the "unemployed smell" with him, so we hung his clothes out the window to air and to keep them from smelling up the room.

During that period the wives of friends such as Brooke Claxton, Raleigh Parkin and Frank Scott often asked me to their houses for meals, realizing that Povey's Lodge was a confining, depressing place. But Hilary Belloc was the person who helped me most at that time. Hilary, the son of Hilaire Belloc the English author, had been at Oxford with J.B. before being "sent down" for keeping a rope ladder in his room and climbing in and out of his window after the college halls were closed at midnight. For years after that he "sailed the seven seas" and led an adventurous, Bohemian life. Suddenly, in his late twenties, he decided to settle down and study mining engineering. Since he had fought with his father and refused to accept any financial help from him, he had to rely on his own small savings. He planned to go through the course on $300 a year and naturally had made himself familiar with all the cheapest "greasy spoons" in Montreal.

He was a short, muscular man with blue eyes and blond hair which made him look young and rather naive although he was, in fact, experienced and sophisticated. He had a brittle, Irish sense of humour, and a loud, high-pitched, explosive laugh, which would burst out when he told about his adventures in Tahiti and New Caledonia. In spite of his pose as a hard-boiled guy, he was essentially kind and warm-hearted, and realizing that I was lonely and disoriented, often took me out for dinner. We went "Dutch," of course, since he had so little money. Most of the restaurants we went to were on the second floors of old houses. They looked awful, but the food was plentiful, if badly cooked. We could get a three course meal of soup, lamb chops or a couple of hamburgers with potatoes and canned peas, stewed fruit and pale coffee for about thirty-five cents.

One bitterly cold night I invited Hilary back to Povey's Lodge for a glass of beer after dinner. We were sitting propped up on each end of the bed when the door flew open and a disreputable-looking man wearing a khaki knitted cap, and with a huge scarf over his mouth, burst into the room. He towered over Hilary who had sprung to his feet, fists up, shouting, "You can't come in here. Get the hell out."

"Really, Hilary," said a quiet English voice, "if I can't come into my wife's room, I don't know who can."

J.B. had been in a fight in a waterfront pub where he had been learning the art of panhandling from a pal picked up in the bread line. We gave him a glass of beer and he told us his story with gusto.

The series of articles, entitled "Down and Out in Montreal," pulled no punches. They shocked many people, but they were read. Although the advertisers didn't like them because they were "bad for business," they created so much interest that J.B. wrote another series showing what was happening to white-collar unemployed. Actually a great many of the men in the bread lines were technically white-collar and in the flop houses J.B. met English public school boys and university graduates.

The new series presented certain problems. White-collar workers were

screened before they were given food coupons and the right to a bed in
one of the rooming houses. A man had to state his religion and give the
name of a priest or parson who would, presumably, be asked for a
recommendation, before any relief could be provided. (J.B. gave the
name of a clergyman he had met in Banff, and the name of one who
lived in London, Ontario, hoping that since they were so far away, the
authorities would be too busy to check.) The risk of being recognized
was another problem. J.B. wore his own clothes for this part of the
operation since they were shabby enough to convince anyone of his
authenticity. On one occasion he had to do a quick turn to avoid
Raleigh Parkin who was walking across Dominion Square on his way
to the Sun Life Building. At the time J.B. was carrying a large package
of Bath buns which he had been asked to deliver to one of the relief
agencies. He was touched when he delivered them and the girl in the
office gave him one as a reward.

The series drew attention to the incredible hardship that the unemployed were suffering because there was no place for them to go
during the cruel winter weather. This aroused public opinion and a day
shelter at Vitre Street was provided. Later J.B. made speeches about
the ghastly effect of intellectual stagnation on intelligent men who just
sat all day long in a dreary hall doing nothing and with nothing to look
forward to. After a while a series of lectures were provided for them by
a friend of ours, Colonel Wilfred Bovey, the director of extramural
relations at McGill University. There were lectures on literature, art,
history and current events. But economics and politics were taboo
subjects because the authorities were afraid the men might get "ideas."
They were afraid of communism and even of socialism. Participatory
democracy as we know it today had not yet been invented. There had
been disturbances in Montreal; some people talked darkly about the
danger of revolution; and there was a rumour that Sir Herbert Holt,
the financier, had said, "Why don't they call out the militia?"

During the first few months in Montreal I did what I could to help
unemployed people in a practical way. A couple of times a week I
worked as a volunteer in the basement of an Anglican church where a
kind old dowager called Mother Molson, a member of the beer family,
had organized a food depot for indigent families. Only Anglicans were
given baskets. This led to sudden conversions. We found ourselves
feeding families with ten, eleven and twelve children who had formerly
gone to a Catholic Church but who had now become Anglicans.

Parents and children lined up in front of the half dozen workers who stood behind a long table laden with supplies. We asked them how many there were in the family and then filled baskets with canned goods and winter vegetables according to a chart which told us how much was allowed for a family of a designated size. It did not indicate how much food to give if there were more than eight children so we would sneak in an extra cabbage or can of tomatoes for the big ("blueberry") families. One day a mother told me there were no baby clothes in her house and showed me how she had to use newspapers as diapers for her new baby. So I took up a collection for a layette among the workers.

What upset us all was that every day we ran out of supplies before all the waiting families could get their share. We would cut rations for the early arrivals in order to try to let everyone have a little, but that didn't work because always more and more people kept on coming and we had to turn many of them away empty-handed. It was a dreary business and it gave me nervous headaches. I felt absolutely beaten when I got home.

By this time J.B. and I had found an apartment on Milton Street near McGill University and were living comfortably, which made me feel guilty, although I realized that even if I starved myself it would not make any difference.

Once, John Farthing, the son of the Bishop of Montreal, who later wrote *Freedom Wears a Crown,* came to lunch to talk about ways of getting a different kind of welfare for people. He couldn't eat what I had cooked for him because he was so upset by the long line of hungry men in front of the Anglican cathedral. He said he knew this emotional reaction wasn't helping anyone, including himself. It must have been a passing misery, since he did a great deal to help by working efficiently with organizations trying to find food and lodging for unemployed people.

As time went on I decided that there was something horribly wrong with the system, and studied economics and political science seriously. I borrowed books from the public library and from our friends, and seemed always to be going places with books under my arm. When I got onto a bus or a streetcar, the conductors, thinking I was a student, would give me children's tickets, which I thought was a great way to save money until J.B. pointed out that I was cheating.

After living on Milton Street for two years we moved to a delightful six-room apartment nearby on Lorne Crescent. (The rent had been reduced from $85 to $55 a month. Those were the days of deflation.)

It had a wood-burning fireplace in the living room and window seats under six windows through which poured the afternoon sun.

Our apartment was always full of people. At one period I seemed to spend my time pouring afternoon tea for economists. That was when the Kredit Anstalt Bank in Austria went broke and Britain went off the gold standard. T.E. Gregory, the English economist, later adviser to the Government of India, came for tea and told us the best investment at that time was to buy wedding rings and put them into a safety deposit box. We did not follow his advice.

Hilary Belloc and I walked a lot that winter, exploring Montreal from the waterfront to the top of the mountain, talking, talking as we strode along in the cold. We founded a Society for the Suppression of the Discussion of the Gold Standard. The rules were simple: nobody in my house was allowed to talk about the gold standard until after the second cup of tea. A great many people joined, because though everybody talked a lot about the gold standard, few understood it.

The seven years we spent in Montreal, from 1931 through 1937, were exciting in spite of the depression, or maybe because of it, since it acted as a spur. We were greatly concerned about conditions and were anxious to help to change a society which had so obviously failed.

I must have had incredible energy when I was in my twenties because during that period I wrote four full-length novels. All of them were rejected; they came back to me with kind letters from a succession of publishers. I looked at them recently and I'm glad they were not published. I am not a novelist. My plots are hackneyed and my characters are not people but ideas. The books read like treatises and the characters sound like college professors lecturing. I find it interesting, however, that even so long ago I was writing about the need to scrap the B.N.A. Act and write a new constitution in order to give the province of Quebec a better deal. I also wrote about the necessity for English-speaking Canadians to learn to speak French so that they and people in Quebec could communicate with one another.

I was always terribly disappointed when a novel bounced back but not for long because I had usually started on another and forgotten the one that was finished. I was helped by having the satisfaction of seeing some of my writing in print. *The Saturday Review of Literature* was still sending me books to review and *The Canadian Forum* published some of my short stories. Recently a short story, *Beauty Parlor,* written under the by-line Florence Rhein, was included in a retrospective volume of selected material published by *The Canadian Forum*. I had forgotten all about it and read it with interest in the light of my subsequent career since it was about three women and what happened to them during the depression.

During those years in Montreal when I was not studying economics or political science I read a great deal, usually in bed late into the night. There was a D.H. Lawrence cult going on at that time, so I read Lawrence and discussed his attitude toward sex with my friends. Frank Scott lent us a copy of *Lady Chatterley's Lover* that had been smuggled into the country because it was then banned in Canada. Since I had never heard of the famous four-letter word before and I did not think there was anything wicked about sex, I was not shocked and couldn't understand why it was considered indecent. However I thought the chapter in which the gamekeeper and the lady ran around naked in the rain was funny, even silly.

(Many years later Frank Scott argued and won the case of *Lady Chatterley* before the Supreme Court of Canada so that today she is quite respectable. By an odd coincidence he spent the evening before the Supreme Court hearing in our house in Ottawa where he recited a satirical poem about "Lady Chat" which he had written to commemorate the occasion.)

In the 1930's it was also fashionable to have read or to have said one had read *Ulysses*. People were always smuggling in copies from France. We thought James Joyce was wonderful and quoted him a great deal.

During this period all of us were afraid of another war. A number of my young women friends formed the Peace Study Group in order to explore the causes and cures of war. At our fortnightly meetings one of us would deliver a paper and there would be discussion afterwards. Our views covered the political spectrum from centre to extreme left.

It was about that time that the LSR, the League for Social Reconstruction, was founded in Montreal. It was modelled after the British Fabian Society and became the intellectual spearhead for socialism in Canada, bringing about the Regina Manifesto and the birth of the Co-operative Commonwealth Federation, the mother of the present New Democratic Party. Several members of the group belonged to the LSR, so that their papers usually blamed war on the iniquities of capitalism. One member was an avowed communist who tended to break up the meetings by doing all the talking and laying down the law. I discovered that it was quite impossible to talk rationally to communists because they had all the answers down pat and would not deviate from the party line. I could not convince them of my point of view any more than they could convince me of theirs.

I had read Karl Marx with interest and thought that his description of England during the industrial revolution should be required reading for everyone because it is such a brilliant, poignant description of the life of the worker, but I could not believe that violent revolution is the way to improve a society. I certainly didn't accept the idea of a dictatorship of the proletariat, because I didn't like dictatorship then any more than I do today. I never joined the LSR because I was not committed to Fabian socialism. I have, as a matter of fact, never joined any political party, because when I began writing and lecturing about public affairs I wanted to be as objective as possible, and to feel free to praise or criticize governments and policies, something which would have been difficult for me if I had had a party affiliation.

Back in the thirties I was, of course, only slowly working my way toward what became a most interesting and rewarding career. Although I was quite unaware of it, I took the first step when I prepared several talks on different political systems for the Peace Study Group. Evidently some of the members thought well of them, because I was invited to give four lectures on current events by the Montreal Junior League. I worked hard preparing those lectures. I was excruciatingly nervous beforehand and was seized with violent diarrhoea before each one.

I was surprised and terribly pleased when the lectures were well received and I was asked to give a series to the board members of the YWCA and to the McGill Graduates Association. I charged $25 a lecture, which enabled me to lecture for free to groups of working girls.

I spent the first $250 I earned by lecturing on a dining room table and six chairs. They were designed by myself and executed by a French-Canadian craftsman called Crevier. We have used them ever since.

For three or four winters after that I lectured on current events to Women's groups. I enjoyed the research involved in preparing the talks and was exhilarated by audience feed-back and especially by the question period, but I went on having butterflies in my stomach. I have never wholly outgrown nervousness before a speech or a broadcast though I feel fine once I start to talk.

During that bitter decade we were able to see at first hand what was happening to thousands of women. We paid our cleaning woman, an English girl in her twenties, Chrissy Wyatt, a dollar and a half a day, the going wage. She was pregnant and in poor health. Pale, thin as a bone is thin, she seemed always to be in pain because her teeth had to be extracted one or two at a time as they crumbled in her mouth. Since she couldn't afford false teeth, she looked more and more like an old hag every day. I forced milk and eggs on her when she came to me once a week, but the rest of the time she seemed to live on tea, bread and jam. Her husband was unemployed so she was the sole support of the family. I was sure that her baby would die from malnutrition before it was born and was astonished when I went to see it after Chrissy came home from hospital. He was a beautiful, healthy little boy.

That visit upset me, though, because the Wyatts lived in one room furnished with a bed, a crib made out of a box, a large radio, and a two-ring electric cooking unit. Their chesterfield and other furniture had been taken away because they had not been able to keep up the instalments. When I told one of my affluent friends about this she said furiously that people as poor as that ought not to be allowed to have a radio and should use the monthly payments on it for food. She said I was talking nonsense when I explained that the radio supplied the only entertainment the Wyatts had. She said that poor people didn't need "luxuries" of that kind. We had quite a fight about the difference between luxuries and necessities: I kept saying, rather sententiously I fear, that man cannot live by bread alone.

After the baby was born the Wyatts went back to Liverpool. I can't remember how they managed the fare; perhaps they were deported because they were indigent. It made us sad because we knew they had come to Canada with high hopes—as we had—of making a good life for themselves.

Our next cleaning woman, Maude Whiteley, was also the sole support of her family of four children; her husband, Walter, a ship construction worker, had been let out of his job. She was a tough, brave, big-hearted cockney brought up in Bethnal Green, a slum area of London.

Mrs. Whiteley's children were handsome and intelligent; their clothes, washed by hand, were clean and well pressed. Although she was always exhausted and suffering from all sorts of minor complaints, she kept going by sheer guts, attacking the dirt in our apartment at top speed, talking all the time. And always she made me a steak-and-kidney pie before she went home at five o'clock. She told me her husband just sat around all day smoking and looking off into space; he had given up trying to find work because it was all so hopeless.

I first became aware, in a personal way, of the iniquity of Quebec law in regard to women when Mrs. Whiteley's oldest boy, Ronnie, was knocked down by a car. Mrs. Whiteley telephoned us about it and we rushed down to the hospital. The boy's head had been injured and he needed brain surgery immediately. Every minute of delay lessened his chances of recovery. He was in the operating room and the surgeon was dressed and standing by but he was unable to operate because the law required the permission of the father. The mother had no legal right to authorize an operation. Walter Whiteley had gone out and no one knew where to find him, so we stood around praying he would be found in time.

The Montreal police did well that day; because they looked into every bar and moving picture theatre in the vicinity. They finally found him at a movie and raced him to the hospital to sign the permission. The boy made a good recovery but we felt the law was iniquitous.

In Quebec, up until the sixties, a married woman was forbidden by law to give permission for her children to undergo surgery; nor could she authorize an operation on herself without her husband's permission. In those days the Civil Code of the province also decreed that minors, people in prison, idiots and married women could not enter into a contract.

Remembering Kate Cox, my New York cleaning woman, I decided that laws as well as the attitude of society needed to be changed. I found it revolting that people took it for granted that "working class" women were exhausted by child-bearing and hard work. I had a strong feeling of empathy with Chrissy and Maud Whiteley, as I had had with Kate Cox. We talked together as friends. I felt with increasing conviction that I had a responsibility toward them and other women like them because through an accident of birth I was lucky enough to have more money and a better education than they.

Not long after Ronnie's accident, Walter Whiteley inherited a few hundred dollars from his father. He invested it in a cigarette and candy store, and Mrs. Whiteley gave up cleaning in order to help him. After that Vera brought comfort to our apartment. She was a Barbadian, a quiet, slow-moving woman, and a fine cook. She worked half a day every day except Thursday and every other Sunday, for $5 a week, considered a good wage at that time. Because she enabled me to have more time for my writing, I could earn more than before and was able to pay her out of my earnings.

I am more productive and useful, and certainly a much happier and more interesting wife, if I can study and write rather than do housework. Obviously good food and a clean, well-run house contribute greatly to

the enjoyment of living, and there is nothing demeaning about housework, but I find it frustrating and tiring, and prefer, whenever possible,
to pay someone to do it so that I can be free to do the things that give
me greater satisfaction and permit me to use my education and experience.

After Vera had been with us for about a year she began to be sick in
her stomach, and admitted tearfully that she was pregnant. When I
asked her if she thought the father of the child might marry her, she
said indignantly, "Marry him? Why, I ain't even speakin' to him." That
seemed to me to be a thoroughly reasonable point of view.

Vera worked right up to the last day before going to hospital. The
baby was stillborn and after she was able to come back to work we
never mentioned the matter again.

Although J.B. was earning much less than he had when we were
married we were living very comfortably compared with many of our
friends. After all we had a large apartment, drove a car and had someone to cook dinner for us. At that time Blair Fraser, a brilliant newspaper man, was earning $25 a week by hosing coal, and he had a wife
and baby to support. My brother, John, also with the responsibility of
a wife and baby, was earning 35¢ an hour and working a ten-hour day
six days a week.

J.B. was not only writing editorials but was being used as a "trouble
shooter," which meant he was assigned to cover any unexpected news
break which took place in Canada or the United States. His copy was
always published, so it came as a shock when Lord Atholstan, the
owner of the *Montreal Star,* who had at first held out against wage cuts,
eventually cut the wages of all his employees. We had always resented
the way J.B. received his salary in a small brown envelope instead of
being paid by cheque, so we were not only depressed by the cut but
also humiliated because now the envelope clanked with silver as well as
bills; his pay had gone down from $65 to 59.80 a week.

The depression years were a traumatic experience for many young
people because of the feeling of insecurity and helplessness they brought.
For me, personally, the Italian invasion of Abyssinia and the Spanish
Civil War were equally traumatic. Both wars deprived me of a sort of
emotional and intellectual virginity. In recent years the American role in
the war in Vietnam has shocked me deeply; I consider it stupid, unnecessary, cruel and degrading. But it has not torn me apart emotionally
the way the Abyssinian War and the Spanish Civil War did. With age,

emotions grow less intense, dulled by exposure to horrors like the cruelties perpetrated on the inmates of Belsen and Buchenwald, and on the Jews in Warsaw. In order to avoid going mad one has to learn to accept the things one cannot change, while plugging away patiently at the things one hopes to do something about. Many young people have, of recent years, felt about Vietnam the way I felt about Ethiopia and Spain and I have understood and sympathized when they demonstrated. I would have joined them if I had thought it would do any good.

In the 1930's, like so many of my generation, I was a devout believer in the idea of collective security, and thought, idealistically and naively, that the League of Nations, even without the United States, could bring about lasting peace. Woodrow Wilson was one of my heroes. I believed in self-determination for nations and felt that nineteenth-century colonialism had no place in the twentieth century.

I was therefore all the more deeply depressed by the failure of oil sanctions, the abdication by France and Britain when Mussolini went into Ethiopia, and the long-drawn-out death throes of the League. To this day I have the sick feeling of remembered disillusionment when I think of a news photograph of Haile Selassie, a tiny figure in white, begging the assembly of the League for help which was refused. My stomach still turns over with nausea when I remember the newspaper stories about the bombing of barefooted Ethiopian natives and their straw huts, and the way Mussolini's son, a bomber pilot, boasted about his prowess, describing the beauty of bursting bombs and flying shrapnel, and laughing about the way the blacks ran like ants when he dived down and peppered them with machine-gun fire.

I was also emotionally involved in the cause of Republican Spain. As far as I was concerned, the nationalist regime had been elected by the people and was the legitimate government of Spain, while Franco was a fascist and a dictator determined to destroy democratic government. I found it utterly disillusioning when Britain, France and the United States embraced a policy of non-intervention and then stood quietly by while the Soviet Union sent troops and war machines to support the government, while Hitler and Mussolini supported Franco in order to train their troops and pilots and try out their armaments. I was horrified and incredulous when refugees were dive-bombed on the road to Guernica.

In Montreal, as everywhere else, people were in sharp conflict about the war because the elected government of Spain was communistic and anti-clerical. There were frequent fights over the issue between McGill students and students at the University of Montreal. When La Palencia, a Spanish woman on a lecture tour to raise money for the nationalist government, was scheduled to speak to the McGill undergraduates one afternoon, the University of Montreal students threatened to break up the meeting. Only McGill students were allowed to attend, and the city riot squads were milling around.

I wanted to hear La Palencia, so I stuck a few textbooks under my arm and walked into the hall. I was deeply moved by the sincerity and passionate pleas of the thin, intense Spanish woman dressed in sombre black, and by her thin, ravaged face. As she talked about what was happening to her fellow countrymen, I kept thinking of Goya's paintings of the horrors of war.

That evening, after speaking, La Palencia was almost mobbed by French-speaking Catholic students. A couple of McGill professors smuggled her out of the lecture hall by a side door and rushed her on foot to her hotel. One of them was kicked in the stomach while trying to prevent her from being struck by a member of the mob.

Most of my friends felt as I did about the Civil War in Spain. We thought Norman Bethune was a hero when he organized, for the Spanish government, a mobile blood transfusion unit which he commanded in the field himself. Beth was a communist, and although, like J.B., I was not a communist or even a socialist, I admired him because his political convictions were based on the strongest humanitarian motives. He was not an armchair communist but a courageous man of action dedicated to saving, not destroying life.

Beth was a complex and fascinating character, as the books and films about him have shown. He came often to our apartment because he was trying to persuade J.B. to go around the world with him in a sailboat. (It was a sort of escape fantasy; both of them knew it would never take place.) Inevitably, as the evening wore on, the conversation would turn to the misery so many people were enduring as the result of poverty and ignorance. Beth was a person who seemed to have been born three drinks below par. Between the third and the eighth drink his conversation was forceful, convincing, and often brilliant. After the eighth drink his character deteriorated, as it does with most people when so much alcohol enters their blood, and he became unpleasant. One evening he polished off a bottle of brandy he had brought as a present, and being aware he was too drunk to drive safely, accepted our invitation to spend the night with us. He evidently did not suffer from hangovers, because he was up at six the next morning, took a walk on nearby Mount Royal and was cooking breakfast by the time our alarm clock rang at seven. He looked like a healthy, pink-cheeked baby, relaxed and cheerful, as he took off for the hospital in his Model A Ford roadster to perform a number of difficult operations.

It was the tragedy of his patients that had made Beth hate capitalism and all its works. He used to tell us about his frustrations as a physician, explaining that although he knew how to cure many people of tuberculosis he often could not bring his patients to lasting health because they returned from hospital to the unhealthy conditions which had caused them to contract T.B. He used to expatiate on the effects of malnutrition on mind and body if a person's parents and grandparents as well as he himself had not had enough of the right kind of food. He once turned on me and said, "Anybody can have your kind of beauty. Your straight bones, strong teeth, shiny hair and clear skin are only a matter of a few generations of having enough to eat. Any woman could look like you if she was given orange juice and milk and cod-liver oil when she was a baby."

Norman Bethune was, I think, a man in search of truth as well as one who loved his fellow men. There were many facets to his character, and some of them I did not like. I used to get angry at him because he enjoyed the conquest of women. He had great vitality, being a passionate man with the ability to make women feel valued, and so was attractive to them. Inevitably, I think, he hurt several of the ones with whom he had affairs. I suppose he suffered from some sort of insecurity about his own virility, having once been ill with tuberculosis, and so had a Don Juan complex.

When he resigned from the Roman Catholic hospital where he operated in order to go to Spain, the Sisters gave him a cigarette case as a farewell gift. We wondered if they were so innocent that they didn't know he was a communist or whether they knew and didn't care because they were so conscious of what his skill as a surgeon and his dedication as a physician had done to relieve suffering.

It was characteristic of Beth to go on to China, where he met his death.

In those days, Beth was regarded by many people, and certainly by the powers that be, as a reprehensible, seditious character because of his political beliefs. I think he would have laughed if he had known that, in 1972, three decades after his death, the memory of his martyrdom in China was honoured by a capitalist Canadian government. I have a hunch he would have said, with a cynical laugh, that the recognition was based on the hope of better trade relations with China and of selling wheat, rather than on any real appreciation of what he had done since, after all, everyone had known for years about the way he had practised the art of healing in China under ghastly circumstances.

Those years in Montreal were a time of great intellectual ferment. They were exciting years because we were young and confident that we would be able to help clean up the mess made by an earlier generation. We really believed that.

Although Canada continued to sink into the black bog of depression, there were encouraging vibrations from south of the border after Franklin Roosevelt was elected in 1932. The low points for all of us were reached during the Hoover administration when the President called out troops against the hunger marchers who had camped on Anacostia Flats on the outskirts of Washington, and when banks in the United States shut their doors.

During the thirties the mystique of the New Deal acted as a tonic for Canadians and even made R.B. Bennett take heed, although too late to save his party from defeat. Most Canadians listened to Roosevelt's Fireside Chats and became ardent Democrats.

At that time I thought, as I do now, that Franklin Roosevelt was a great man and that Eleanor Roosevelt was a great woman.

When Mrs. Roosevelt embarked on her career as the eyes, legs and conscience of her husband, she was greatly criticized and made fun of, not only by the political opponents of the President but also by a great many conventionally-minded people who were upset because she didn't adhere to the accepted role of a wife and mother.

At that time, as I began to find myself as an adult, she was a bright star to steer by. (I find it interesting that some of my woman friends who used to sneer at "Eleanor" now have changed their minds about her after having read the two-volume biography by Joseph Lash. Of course we live in a very different climate as far as women are concerned than we did in the 1930's, and people are beginning to realize that women need not and should not accept a passive role, that they should use their skills, talents and minds the way Eleanor Roosevelt did.)

During the time J.B. and I lived in Montreal, we worked hard, but we also had a great deal of fun. We took up skiing and skied in the evenings on Montreal Mountain, a stone's throw away. Often on weekends we went north to St. Sauveur where we usually stayed at a boarding house kept by Madame David. The Banque Canadienne Nationale took up half the ground floor, and I was once startled to find a revolver, kept handy to protect the bank, in the bathroom where Madame had absent-mindedly left it. Sometimes we stayed with George and Mary McDonald, ardent skiers until well on in their sixties, even though George had been so badly wounded in the First World War that one arm was practically useless. And sometimes we stayed with Jacques Bieler and his brother André, the painter, in their chalet which André had decorated on the outside with a huge fresco of St. Christophe, the patron saint of skiers.

Soon after I arrived in Montreal Marian Scott, the painter, took me shopping for ski equipment. We bought a pair of wide, rather worn skis at a second-hand store, a pair of dark blue, woolly slacks that collected snow when I fell, which was often, and then became soaking wet when I went indoors, a dark blue melton cloth jacket, and the cheapest harness and boots we could find. The whole outfit amounted to about the cost of a good parka today but I was quite happy with it.

I didn't think I could afford to take lessons as most sensible people did, but with coaching from friends, I learned to do a snowplow and to turn on the trails. There were no ski tows in those days, so we went across country and climbed the hills. I used to get terribly tired because I fell so much that I could never keep up with other people. J.B. and my friends would wait impatiently until I came plodding along, panting and exhausted after having extricated myself from a snowdrift, and then they would start off again without ever giving me a chance to rest. In spite of weariness and aches I loved those ski weekends. The country was beautiful on a sunny day and the companionship was wonderful. In the evening, we would drink hot rum punch and talk our heads off or go to the St. Sauveur pub to drink beer and sing.

When we didn't take the train north to ski we usually danced on weekends. We went to inexpensive night clubs in the East End or to dances put on by the Claxtons, Parkins or Scotts. We danced to the radio or to records played on the kind of phonograph that has to be wound up by hand. We drank a punch made with red wine, rye and rum. It generated considerable power, with the result that the dances went on until the morning hours.

For several winters, while he was still studying mining engineering, Hilary Belloc and I continued to take our long walks through the city. When the snow came we went skiing on Montreal Mountain in the afternoons. On summer week-ends J.B. and I went with him on canoeing picnics on the St. Lawrence. We took bathing suits, bottles of beer and sandwiches, and made a day of it. We missed him sorely when he graduated from McGill and went to Norwalk, Connecticut, to stay with a friend, Harrison Smith, the publisher.

After he had been in Norwalk for a time Hilary wrote asking me if I would send his mongrel dog, Trotsky, to him as he planned to drive to California to marry his cousin Hope Bartinet.

(To break him into domesticity, Hope had given Hilary the dog when it was an engaging little puppy and to everyone's astonishment, it had grown prodigiously until, as J.B. said, it was the size of a Connemara donkey. When Hilary would come to see us in our second story walk-up apartment, we used to tie Trotsky to a bannister and give him bones to chew on the landing. The people who lived above us were jolted when they came up the stairs.)

When I received Hilary's letter I went around to the nearby boarding-house where he used to live and where he had left Trotsky in the care of his landlady. I walked the huge beast down to the CPR to arrange for passage and was told that, since the week before a valuable dog had escaped from a baggage car, the authorities now insisted that all animals be confined in a crate for shipment. I had quite a time finding a packing case large enough to hold the dog, then transporting it and Trotsky, plus water pan and dog biscuits, back to the station in a taxi. I was worried when I found that the only through train to Norwalk arrived there early in the morning, and I sent a wire to Hilary: "Be sure and meet train arriving Norwalk 4 a.m. as Trotsky is in packing case."

An hour or so later the telephone rang and a man's voice said, "In re your telegram to Norwalk, who is this Trotsky?"

I explained that he was a dog. A little while later J.B. telephoned to say, "What on earth have you been up to? The Mounted Police have called to enquire about a telegram you sent saying Trotsky is in a packing case."

It happened that this was just the time that Leon Trotsky had dis-appeared from Norway on his way to Mexico and the police in many countries were trying to find out where he had gone. We were amused by the episode although we didn't think the authorities were very bright to imagine we would have broadcast it on the wires if Leon Trotsky, dead or alive, really had been stuffed into a box.

In 1935, J.B. and I had a deluxe holiday in New York thanks to the federal election. We had saved two hundred dollars for a trip to New

York which we planned to take when the election was over. One morning J.B. telephoned and said, "Are you in a gambling mood? Do you want to take the chance of having one whale of a theatre bat or no holiday at all?"

I said I wanted one whale of a theatre bat. He explained that "some dumb bloke" on the Montreal Stock Exchange was willing to bet $200 even money that R.B. Bennett would get more than 60 seats. The Conservatives had won 137 seats in 1930 but J.B. was sure that Bennett was going to go down in spectacular defeat in spite of his last-ditch attempt to adopt some of F.D.R.'s New Deal measures. After all, the unemployed and the farmers and their wives could vote even if they couldn't eat.

After J.B. accepted the bet I began to have misgivings about being rash. We were both edgy on election night when a big Tory vote in the Maritimes began to be announced on the radio. We had an early supper so that J.B. could go down to the newspaper to work, and as he went out the door he said, "Do you mind terribly if we don't get that holiday after all?"

I replied nastily, "Oh no. Of course not. It should be worth two hundred dollars to you to find out that you don't know your job as a newspaper man."

Afterwards I wandered around town with friends visiting the headquarters of some of the candidates and late in the night stood outside the *Montreal Star* building on St. James Street where the election results were being displayed. I suspect that my loud cheers when Bennett got only 39 seats were due not so much to any abiding faith in Mackenzie King as to delight in knowing our deluxe holiday was safe.

A dollar certainly went far in those days. We stayed in luxury at New York's Chatham Hotel for four nights. A masseuse came to the hotel to give me a treatment for a neck stiff from skiing. We went to the theatre three times, and dined in expensive restaurants on rich dishes like roast duckling with wild rice, accompanied by a good Burgundy. We went dancing at the Roosevelt Hotel where we had danced when J.B. was carrying on his whirlwind courtship. I bought a beautiful pair of gold slippers. In spite of these excesses we did not spend all of the $400.

The dollars left over from the trip led to a funny coincidence when the maid of honour at our wedding, Eleanor Lewis, a former classmate at Bryn Mawr, came up from Philadelphia for the weekend. We invited Francis Cundle, a nice young stockbroker, to come for dinner and go with us to see a new musical, *Life Begins at Eight Forty,* and then to a six-day bicycle race. Feeling flush, we had bought a magnum of Mumm's for dinner.

When the cork popped, Eleanor said, "Do the Birds usually have such a high standard of living?"

"No, it's not our style," said J.B., "it's just that some poop on the stock exchange offered two hundred dollars on Bennett's nose and I put it on Bennett's bum."

"Good God," said Francis Cundle, "I was the poop on the other end of the bet."

With the exception of that champagne dinner we entertained in a simple way, though often. A great many people of different kinds came to our apartment for tea or to drink beer after dinner in the evenings. The local branch of the Canadian Institute of International Affairs used to meet in a room in one of the McGill University buildings just across the way, so that frequently the visiting speaker and a select group of members would come back to the apartment for beer and sandwiches after the meeting was over.

Our best friends were usually there: Frank Scott, long-legged, thin, intense, striding up and down like a panther, talking brilliantly with flashes of wicked wit; Brooke Claxton, already with his eye on a political career, solemn, full of anecdotes about Canada in the past; Raleigh Parkin, egging everybody on with "(A), (B), (C)," arguments set forth in a careful, orderly way; Terry McDermott, a teacher of history at McGill, asking Socratic questions that infuriated everyone but occasionally led to the clarification of thoughts, which is what he wanted; Eugene Forsey, a young professor of economics at McGill, advocating socialism as a cure to all ills in a high-pitched insistent voice; Carl Goldenberg, bland and bright-eyed behind huge glasses, a coming lawyer who brought his gifts as a moderator to calm an over-emphatic argument; King Gordon (later to have a career in international relations), a young professor of theology always ready with a practical argument; Monteath Douglas, thoughtful, a man of few but wise words, a banking and business economist and always a humanist.

Those men all cared deeply about Canada and have since given much of their minds and energy to improve life in this country. Most of them have lived to see the acceptance of social measures that then were the stuff of dreams.

When we had been in Montreal for three or four years we wanted to own a part of our country. After scouting around we bought a lot a hundred feet wide and a hundred and fifty feet deep beside the road on the outskirts of St. Sauveur in the mountains north of Montreal. It cost $100. There was for us something symbolic about owning even so small a parcel of Canada; it was a sign that we had put down roots, that we were committed to a lasting attachment.

One day in early spring when I drove through St. Sauveur on my way to Ste Agathe I saw that a small deer had jumped the fence surrounding our property and was cropping the long grass. After that, with mock gravity we alluded to our "estate" as The Deer Park. We planned to build a small shack on it but during the 1930's we never had enough money for the project. A couple of years after we moved to Winnipeg we decided to sell The Deer Park, and since Brooke Claxton wanted it for his son John, we let him have it for the price we had paid for it plus the cost of the tiny taxes we had paid over the years. We were aware that the value of the land at St. Sauveur had greatly increased as the place had become a popular ski resort, but we had an almost mystical feeling that it would not be right to make money out of a bit of Canadian earth bought for such personal reasons.

During the Montreal years we managed to travel a little because the dollar stretched so much further than it does today. I had my first introduction to the Caribbean when I was convalescing from a bout of influenza. J.B. presented me with a ticket for a month's cruise on the *Lady Rodney,* one of the CNR Lady boats that carried freight and a few passengers on a round trip from Montreal and Halifax to British Guiana.

The beauty of the islands and the warm sea water hooked me on the West Indies; I'm an addict.

I have been to the Caribbean seven times since 1934 and have watched with mixed feelings what has happened there. On that first trip I was shocked by the terrible poverty and obvious poor health of the islanders. On every island I saw people with elephantiasis, blind people and spindly-legged, pot-bellied children, many of them with running sores on their bodies. I was disgusted by the way the tourists and white-skinned residents treated the blacks, clapping their hands to summon a waiter and speaking to them rudely or patronizingly. When I got home I wrote a story about those rum-drinking, indolent, arrogant whites, and it was published in *The Canadian Forum.*

In the summer of 1936 J.B. and I went to Europe again for the first time since our honeymoon eight years before. We sailed for England on one of the Cunard Line's Cabin Class A boats, the *Ascania*. We were very hearty: played deck tennis, danced, walked miles on the deck and provided a skit for the ship's concert. At meals we sat at a small table with Tommy Mathews, the registrar of McGill University, and Leonard Murray (years later the admiral unfairly held responsible for the rioting in Halifax on V.E. Day). All four of us loved the sea and ships, good food and drink, and good talk—we all talked a lot.

We were three days late in arriving at Southampton, as we were held up by fog on the Grand Banks. In the 1930's, even on a cabin class boat, everyone dressed for dinner, and since there was no laundry on board, the three men at our table pretended to be worried about the state of their boiled shirts when it became apparent that the ship was going to be delayed. In the true British racing tradition, they became fiercely competitive in what we called the Dirty Shirt Derby, the winner to be the man with the shirt that was the most presentable by the end of the voyage. J.B.'s shirt won, thanks to his steward, Porter, who used stale bread every morning, accompanied by a flood of comment, to clean the visible parts of the starched front of his entry. The three backers of their shirts kept urging one another to order spaghetti or beef stew with lots of gravy in the hope that a heave of the ship would splatter a rival's entry with indelible stains.

Porter was one of the old-time Cunard stewards, a First World War navy type, efficient and outspoken, with a dry, cockney sense of humour. I had a very low rating with him at the beginning of the voyage because of what I had done to J.B.'s large travelling flask: Just before sailing I had used a funnel to decant some Chanel No. 5 from a large to a small bottle. J.B. had later used the same funnel to fill his flask with cognac, and on the first night out he found out what I had done when he had a drink before dinner while I was down the corridor having a bath. He poured out his troubles on Porter's shoulder and the contents of the flask down the wash-basin, and when I came back to the cabin I was met by Porter holding the flask at arm's length. Figuratively holding his nose he said, "You ought to be ashamed of yourself, ruining Mr. Bird's good brandy like that."

When the Dirty Shirt Derby took place Porter was in the position of a jockey, carrying our colours as it were, and looked forward to his share of the purse. My enthusiasm for the sporting event made him loyal to me and the shocking affair of the Chanel No. 5 was not mentioned again.

We had a happy time in London on that trip, going to the ballet at Covent Garden, to art galleries, to the theatre and to visit friends in the country. After a couple of weeks we went to Antwerp to stay with one of J.B.'s sisters. There was a powerful radio in the living room so we spent a great deal of our time listening to programs broadcast from the capitals of Europe. It turned out be dreary listening since we kept hearing "ancestral voices prophesying war." From Italy it was Virginio Gayda; from Germany it was Goebbels. We became convinced that war was inevitable. We felt sure that the great art galleries would soon be destroyed and the stained glass of the great cathedrals shattered by bombs. So we decided to go to the Netherlands to say farewell to the Vermeers (at that time Vermeer was J.B.'s favourite painter) and then to France to take a last look at Chartres.

In Paris we went again and again to the Louvre. We followed an almost daily routine. First we looked at the paintings of the Italian Quatrocento that meant so much to me because of G.G. King's course in Renaissance painting at Bryn Mawr. Next we looked at the great Dutch masters to keep J.B. happy. Then we went up to the top floor to look at the Post-Impressionists we both enjoyed so much, and it was there we spent the longest time.

On the plane from London to Brussels, J.B. had sat beside a man who coughed in his face and sneezed all over him, and by the time we got to Paris, he was suffering from a running cold. He didn't want to pass on his germs to me so when we arrived at the L'Aiglon, a small, very cheap hotel in the Latin Quarter, he asked for a room with twin beds. That was impossible, the desk clerk said, because there were only double beds in the hotel. But, he added, shaking his head and looking at me sympathetically, if Monsieur insisted, it could be arranged to have a cot put in our room.

Monsieur did insist. While we were unpacking, the chambermaid and the *valet de chambre* appeared carrying a huge armchair. With much head shaking and sympathetic glances at me, they installed it in a corner and then did something mysterious to it which caused a narrow cot to shoot out from its entrails.

The cot was so narrow that J.B. had to lie on his side crunched between the arms of the chair. All night long he coughed and groaned. In the morning he woke me by saying in a stricken voice, "I think one of my lungs has collapsed. I'm sure I have pneumonia."

"I guess we ought to go to the American Hospital at St. Cloud or some place. I don't know where," I said, desperately.

"I'm a very ill man," said J.B.

He felt better after he had had coffee and a brioche, and decided that he did not have pneumonia after all but had merely been nearly suffocated by the narrowness of the cot. That night he coughed less but still groaned a great deal because he could not turn over or lie on his back. As the day wore on, however, his health began to return and we went out for a cheerful dinner in an inexpensive bistro on the Left Bank. Afterwards we wandered through the streets arm in arm until we came upon one of the little carnivals which appear suddenly for two or three days in empty squares in French towns. This one had a carousel and a number of little booths of the kind where people shoot at targets or throw balls at ninepins in order to win prizes. One booth had a hoop-la game: the idea was to throw a ring over the neck of a bottle of champagne which you then won as a prize. J.B. turned out to have a hitherto hidden talent for ring throwing and, egged on by an admiring crowd, won six bottles of dubious champagne.

We strolled back to the hotel, swinging a bottle or two in each hand. When the concierge at the L'Aiglon unlocked the door for us, J.B. said, "I've won all this sweet champagne and we can't possibly drink such muck."

"I can sell it to American tourists," said the concierge, "I'll give you a large bottle of good champagne in exchange."

A little while later he arrived in our room with an ice bucket and a bottle of the best dry Mumm's. After we had polished off the contents, J.B.'s cold was so much better that we decided I wouldn't catch his germs if he did not sleep in the cot.

The next morning when the maid arrived with our coffee she took one look at the empty cot and then turned to us beaming congratulations. When we were dressed and went out into the corridor on our way to the Louvre, the man who was cleaning the halls put down his broom and stepped up to congratulate us. Downstairs the desk clerk came around the corner of the counter to wring our hands. The concierge, obviously taking credit for the *rapprochement,* added his felicitations. It was like a René Clair movie; all we needed was some sprightly incidental music.

Except for that summer trip abroad and a trout fishing holiday in the Laurentide Park, J.B. and I spent our vacations in Rhode Island with my mother. She was lonely and wanted us very much and I felt I should spend as much time with her as possible. I also adored Saunderstown where there were so many people like the Lockwoods, the Copes, the La Farges and the Wisters, for whom I had great affection.

For three years the visits south were not wholly happy, however. I was miserable because Mother and J.B. kept up an unrelenting warfare. She blamed him for my having left the United States. She accused him of neglecting me because he had so often left me alone when he went out of town to cover stories for the *Montreal Star*. She was fiercely protective of me and possessive, saying J.B. should not "allow" me to live such an independent life. J.B. kept trying to explain to her that he was not neglecting me when he went away on assignments because that was the way he earned his living. He said he wanted me to stand on my feet and be a mature person, to have a life of my own as well as the one he shared with me, that he didn't want a child-wife. After a while he would lose his temper and become overemphatic and then withdraw into himself and not talk any more, while Mother would burst into tears.

I used to get angry at Mother when she was critical of J.B. because he was not earning as much money as Father had at his age. I always blew up and was rude when she said we needn't ask her for money, something we had never done or ever would have done. She had kept on giving me the same allowance I had had when I was at college but often threatened to cut it off as her dividends were progressively cut.

I also used to get angry at J.B. because he couldn't understand that Mother was critical of him for my sake; she wanted me to have the sort of life she had had.

It was, of course, a classic mother-in-law situation, but for me it seemed like a unique personal misery to have the two people closest to me making themselves unhappy over me.

It is remarkable, I think, and a credit to both of them, that they fought it out until each reached an understanding of the other's point of view and then called it quits. They began to respect each other, and in time, a lasting affection developed between them. They worked out their own relationship independent of me. The other day, when rearranging a bookshelf, I came across a copy of *The Rise of American Civilization,* by Charles and Mary Beard. On the fly-leaf is written in Mother's handwriting: "For J.B. Forgive her. She loves him. Bessy."

We never dared tell Mother that five years after we went to Montreal J.B. turned down a job with a salary somewhat larger than the one Father had earned at the same age. A rich organization was looking for a public relations officer, had been impressed by J.B.'s column in the financial pages, and offered him a huge salary for those days—$12,000 a year, plus paid-up membership in one of the big Montreal clubs and in the Dixie Golf Club, plus all the usual expense account perquisities.

It was very tempting for us both. I said J.B. should take it because after five years we would have saved so much money that we wouldn't have to worry about bread and butter any more and he could then return to newspaper work and do his own thing. J.B. persuaded me that he did not have the P.R. mentality and could not spend his time deodorizing a big corporate body. He insisted that if he took the job he would change, become a different kind of person and be caught forever in a sort of life which would not give him the kind of satisfaction he had as a newspaperman reporting accurately or writing editorials he believed in. I saw his point of view and agreed with it. Looking back on it I am quite sure we made the right judgement when we decided against his accepting the offer.

It was a different matter when in 1937 "Biff" MacTavish, the editor of *The Winnipeg Tribune,* came to see J.B. "Biff" was looking for an associate editor who would be qualified to take over from him when he moved to another Southam paper. He offered J.B. the job and, after long discussions with me, J.B. decided to take it. He had happy memories of Kansas and the American Middle West, and felt that this job, with its promise of a better future for him, was a great opportunity to increase his knowledge of Canada.

I did not want him to leave *The Star.* I loved Montreal; I had made many friends there, was happily settled in the apartment on Lorne Crescent, and was enjoying a mild success with the lectures on national and international affairs. I found Montreal a cosmopolitan, sophisticated city, and enjoyed the French flavour. Winnipeg seemed very far away from my family and from the world I had always known. I liked the people I had met there on the Canadian Club tour, but I had found the Prairies depressing; there was so little variety in the landscape and the wide open spaces gave me agrophobia.

On the other hand I agreed with J.B. that he would find it hard to work for the future publisher of *The Star,* J.W. McConnell, a tycoon who stood for many of the things we thought wrong with Canada. We both felt that J.B.'s integrity would undergo a destructive attrition if he were required to write editorials he didn't believe in. We talked about it calmly, weighing the pros and cons, as we had done when we faced a decision about immigrating to Canada. The pros obviously outweighed the cons, but I still didn't want to leave Montreal, even though I always welcomed a new experience. I finally gave in, however, when J.B. promised that we would not stay in Winnipeg for longer than five years.

When he told Albert Carman, the elderly editor of *The Montreal Star,* that he had decided to go to Winnipeg, Carman urged him to stay and offered him a raise. "I expect you to fill this very comfortable chair some day," he said.

It was a tempting future, except that J.B. was convinced that Lord Atholstan, the owner of the paper and a very old man, would soon die. J.W. McConnell, who had already bought the paper, would then take over. J.B. was sure it was better to resign with a job ahead rather than be forced to leave after disagreement with McConnell and have to look for a job in a buyers' market.

Once the decision to go to Winnipeg had been made, we had high hopes for the future, as well as considerable apprehension about cutting loose from our familiar moorings after seven years. But we laughed our heads off when J.B. opened his last little brown pay envelope. Inside was a slip of paper with the message: "Remember the banana. The one that leaves the bunch gets skinned."

This was a typical Atholstan touch; he delighted in such little ploys.

Winnipeg

We decided to go to Winnipeg from Montreal by ship through the Panama Canal. On the way we spent a few days in New York and were wined and dined by our friends. One night at dinner I sat beside a plump, middle-aged man called Buckminster Fuller. He told me he was an inventor and had sunk every penny into a new kind of car, his brainchild, by which he set great store.

"For the last two weeks I've been sleeping in subway trains," he said. "I go round and round and round. It's very exhausting but I'm broke."

I wondered if he was being a trifle dramatic because his dinner-jacket was well pressed and his stiff shirt unrumpled and clean.

After dinner he took us for a ride in his "dymaxion" car, which had the engine in the rear. He drove down Third Avenue and then suddenly made a hairpin U-turn around one of the pillars of the el. It was a startling experience for us and evidently not just for us, because a cop on the street corner shouted, "Jesus Christ. Did you see that?"

I've been told, though I don't know if it is true or not, that Buck Fuller sold the patent for his car to a big automobile company that wanted to prevent any rival firm from getting hold of it. However, it was never manufactured because the cost of re-tooling and converting factories would have been astronomical.

Buckminster Fuller has, of recent years, become a sort of guru, along with Marshal McLuhan, and that night he already showed a tendency to pontificate. He kept insisting that I put eggplant-coloured paint on the floors of the old house we hoped to buy in Winnipeg, but he could not tell me how to mix the paint to achieve that rich purple-black shade.

We sailed from New York on an American ship scheduled to stop at Cuba, Panama, Acapulco, Los Angeles and San Francisco. Going through the Panama Canal was an interesting experience, but Acapulco was the high spot of the trip for J.B. and me. The ship anchored in the beautiful harbour and we went ashore to wander through the market and have lunch in the single small hotel on top of a cliff looking down on the Pacific. On the harbour side the big curved stretch of beach was deserted, so we put on our bathing-suits behind a sand dune and went swimming in the soft, blue water. It was lovely to swim there, just the two of us alone, and then to lie on the sand and let our bodies be dried by the glistening sun. Pictures of Acapulco as it is now have made us feel we never want to go back again to see what "progress" has done to such natural beauty.

When we docked at San Francisco, Hilary Belloc met us with a beat-up old touring car, a Stutz, which Harrison Smith, the publisher, had given him. We stayed a couple of nights with him and his wife, Hope, and drove far and wide in the Stutz, a thirsty car which drank an inordinate amount of gasoline. We were entranced by the wild flowers and picked a dozen varieties in five minutes when we stopped for a picnic lunch.

From San Francisco we went by train to Portland and Seattle, by night boat to Vancouver and then by train eastward to Calgary and Winnipeg. It took a great deal longer than it would take to fly from Montreal to Winnipeg today but it gave us the feel of the continent, which air travel never seems to do.

On our arrival, we stayed in a rooming house while George Ferguson, the managing editor of the *Winnipeg Free Press,* the rival of the *Winnipeg Tribune,* drove us around and helped us to find a house.

During the first few weeks I was grateful for western hospitality. In the east, people we met at parties in New York, Washington and Montreal would say cordially, "We must have lunch together some time. I'll give you a call." And that was that and you never heard from them again. In Winnipeg people said, "Come for supper on Sunday night at 6:30," or "Come for Sunday lunch," or "Come for a drink tomorrow afternoon." It helped to be asked to people's houses like that, but even so it took a long time for me to become adjusted to the new environment although superficially I settled in very quickly.

Within six weeks we were installed in a rented house in River Heights, close to Haskins Avenue, in those days the dividing line between the built-up area of the suburbs and the open prairie. It was a square, two-story little rabbit-hutch. There were three bedrooms upstairs and a maid's room and lavatory in the basement which was dry and clean. Remembering the dreary "maids' rooms" in the attic of "1732" Pine Street in Philadelphia, I put bright yellow, painted furniture and gay chintz curtains in the downstairs room.

We bought an Irish-terrier puppy with a high-falutin' pedigree name and rechristened him Apeneck Sweeney, after the character in T.S. Eliot's poem. And J.B. gave me a huge Oldsmobile, heavy, shiny, with all sorts of gadgets that went wrong, very unlike our faithful Albie which we had sold for $25 to Davidson Dunton, J.B.'s successor as associate editor of the *Montreal Star*.

It did not take me long to find a young Ukrainian housekeeper, Anne Herby, who had been taught to cook and do housework in a school for domestics the city was running in an effort to reduce unemployment among young women. She was kind and competent, and I had plenty of free time to walk on the prairie with Sweeney, play tennis with J.B., write, or anything else I wanted to do. The trouble was that there was nothing I wanted to do except go back to live in Montreal. J.B. was happy, engrossed in his new job, learning to know the town and the province, meeting new people every day, feeling useful and fulfilled, stretching and filling his good mind with new ideas and impacts. But I made his home life miserable by complaining about everything. I hated the poky little house and said so, day-in and day-out. I groaned constantly about the dreariness of the "great open spaces" and the dullness of the social life.

I could see beauty in the wide sweep of the prairie and wholeheartedly added my voice to the nightly paean of praise for the spectacular western sunsets. But the flatness and the stunted trees depressed me; I found the landscape alien and forbidding. I liked the people I met and responded to their warmth, but I missed my friends in Montreal and their conversations about art, poetry, music, ballet, travel and politics.

Winnipegers seemed to me to be divided into two groups. One consisted of people who had either been strikers or had sympathized with them during the Winnipeg strike in 1919. They were serious and solemn, and talked about wheat, grasshoppers, rust, hail, rain or the lack of it, the Crowsnest Pass and railway rates, and the price of wheat at the lakehead.

The other group consisted of people who had been strike breakers in 1919. They were richer and more amusing than the others. While consuming large quantities of whiskey, they talked about wheat, grasshoppers, rust, hail, rain or the lack of it, the Crowsnest Pass—and rail-way rates, and the price of wheat. It seemed to me that everywhere I went there were only two topics of conversation: "the crop" and the price of wheat at the lakehead.

After living in Montreal for seven years, where the problems of French Canada seemed of vital significance to all of Canada, I found it upsetting that most Winnipegers were not interested in Quebec or sympathetic towards the people who lived there; they were culturally, though not politically much closer to the wheat farmers of the Dakotas and Minnesota just across the back-fence, whose economic problems they shared, than they were to their fellow-countrymen a thousand miles away, whose language they did not speak and whose aspirations they rejected.

During those early months in Winnipeg I felt isolated in a cultural desert. Later I found that my first evaluation of the place was subjective and false. Wheat was certainly the main preoccupation of a great many people, since the economy of the area was almost totally dependent on it, but many of them were also interested in the same things as I was. The men in the Sanhedrin, such as J.W. Dafoe, Edgar Tarr and George V. Ferguson, were internationally-minded—partly, of course, because Manitoba was dependent on world markets in order to sell her wheat surplus. There was good music in the city; the Ukrainians, Poles and Germans in the north end had brought the musical traditions of the old world with them, and the annual Music Festival was always a moving experience because of the beauty of the children's voices. There was an amateur drama group whose members, for years, were the backbone of CBC radio drama when it was at its height. There was a little theatre group, the Cercle Molière of St. Boniface, which put on excellent plays. There was also a budding ballet, which a few years later began to blossom under the tutelage of Gweneth Lloyd. During my early days we went to the ballet out of a sense of duty and were embarrassed by the wobbling efforts of spindly-legged little girls to dance on their points, though we were delighted by the new choreography that had freshness and charm. These days, whenever I go to a performance of the Winnipeg Ballet I marvel at Gweneth Lloyd's courage, faith and good sense in deciding to build a ballet in Winnipeg where there was so much latent talent among the children of European immigrants.

As time went on I came to appreciate the dynamism of Winnipeg people, but during the first few months there I felt alienated because I was not yet part of a group of like-minded people the way I had been in

Montreal. I had no writing assignments, no lectures to prepare, no ideas for short stories or novels. I felt dull and useless, convinced that I would never write again. This sort of psychological block is common among writers and I have had it often, but now I do not panic unduly about it since I know it will pass. But that summer after we went to Winnipeg I blamed geography for the failure that was in myself.

I kept saying to J.B. that we were too far away from everywhere. I used to drive at high speed across the prairie in the big, powerful car in the hope that it would help me to be less discontented and disoriented; but all that speed didn't help me to escape from myself or take me anywhere. No matter how fast or how far I drove, I was always the same person, and the country didn't change as I covered mile after mile of flat roads past identical fields of wheat, identical houses and barns protected by windbreaks, and identical vertical grain elevators beside the same railway tracks stretching away to infinity.

After two months, in July, I took the train east to stay with Mother in Rhode Island. I had a glorious time swimming in Narragansett Bay, sailing in the thirty-five foot Herreshoff sloop belonging to my brother Shan, playing tennis, going out for dinner. I reverted to my girlhood and lived in a comfortable, silken cocoon with all my creature comforts looked after by Ben Bush and an excellent cook. The weeks slipped by. I worried about J.B. alone in the heat of a Manitoba summer but I couldn't bear to think about going back to Winnipeg. I knew I was living a parasitical sort of existence and was not putting up a fight to make a significant life for myself in a new environment, but I kept postponing my return to responsibility even though I knew I couldn't go on living in Saunderstown forever.

One day at breakfast Mother said, "Florence, I want to ask you a question. Do you love your husband?"

"Yes," I said. "Yes, I do. I love him very much."

"Well then, don't you think you had better take the next train back to Winnipeg?"

I looked at her and she held me with her steely, dark blue eyes.

"Yes," I said, "that's what I'm going to do."

It took me three nights and two days to get to Winnipeg by train and during that time alone I did a lot of thinking about the kind of person I wanted to be. I have always needed a few days alone, from time to time, in order to take a long, deep look at myself, and that journey was providential at that particular phase of my life.

For a long time after I went back to Winnipeg it was tough going for me, and consequently for J.B. I was restless, underemployed intellectually, frustrated by not using my potential, and therefore complaining and unreasonable.

I began to feel happier when, in September, J.B. and I drove all over Manitoba in order to get to know something about the people who read *The Winnipeg Tribune*. I was stimulated by the trip, as I had been by the Canadian Club tour eight years before, and I wanted to write about the wide beauty of the prairies in autumn and the warmth and courage of the people who live there. When we got home I wrote four articles that J.B. used on the editorial page of the paper. He did not pay me for them, nor did he ever pay me for anything else I wrote for the *Tribune*, either then or after he became editor-in-chief. He does not believe in patronage or in nepotism.

In order to protect him from being held responsible for my ideas, I decided to adopt a pen-name. Before that time, I had written under my maiden name, Florence Rhein. Obviously, if I used Florence it would help to identify me. In any case, I disliked it because it sounded pretentious and reminded me of Florence, the stupid, snobbish, society woman who married the musician in *The Constant Nymph*, a book I had just read. Rhein I did not consider a good pen-name because few people know how to pronounce it at first try and usually forget how to spell it. After much thought, I decided not to use any of the four names my parents had given me but instead to call myself Anne Francis after both my great-grandmother, and my mother's sister, who had written short stories for magazines under the name of John Francis. She took a man's name as a *nom de plume* because, at the turn of the century, publishers had a preference for male writers and society frowned on an unmarried woman who wrote fiction instead of marrying and fulfilling the traditional woman's role of wife, housekeeper and mother. I liked the idea of bringing to life the name of Anne Francis as a writer, which my aunt had suppressed in deference to sex prejudice.

My first winter in Winnipeg was a shock. I had thought Montreal was abominably cold in January and February, and had not been aware that Winnipeg has much longer, colder winters. It was a disagreeable surprise to find that the mercury could drop to forty below zero and that there were whole weeks in which it never went up as far as zero during the day. The natives all went around saying, "It's dry cold, so you don't feel it." But we felt it all right, although it didn't keep us from leading an outdoor life. We found there was a cheap winter rate at the

Cambridge Riding Academy on the prairie, half a mile away from our house, which enabled us to ride as often and as long as we wished. J.B. and I rode together practically every weekend and I usually went out a couple of times during the week. We often rode when it was twenty below zero and regarded zero as balmy if there was no wind. We wore RCMP felt-lined boots, woollen underwear over a cotton undershirt, a balaclava helmet, a windbreaker, and huge eye-goggles rimmed with padding. Wooden stirrups replaced the metal ones that would have caused frostbite.

The Lord Strathcona Horse, stationed in the barracks at Tuxedo, was not yet motorized and its horses kept open the trails through the bush, enabling us to ride even when there was a lot of snow. Apeneck Sweeney, our Irish terrier, used to go with us. In winter he had a great deal of trouble with ice forming between his toes, and from time to time he would sit down on the trail to try to chew out the ice pellets. Once he sat down suddenly and my cow pony, Daisy, trotting briskly behind him, stepped on his tail. Sweeney, the horse and I all went through a rapid form of levitation but fortunately I came down with the right part of me in the saddle. Sweeney's tail was never the same again; it had a permanent kink in it that added to the rakish look he had already because one of his ears never remembered to stay properly pricked up.

Sweeney was a disreputable character, very intelligent, very Irish. He had a large vocabulary, and had learned to jump hurdles and do all the usual tricks. He was polite to people and dreadfully rude to other dogs, picking fights with animals far larger than himself. He was seldom without a torn ear or a bloody wound and when we clipped him in summer we could see that his body was covered with scars. He was death on cats until he met up with a hellion of a tom cat who lacerated his nose. After that he pretended not to see a cat, even when it was only a few feet away. If he didn't see it he was under no obligation to give chase.

Sweeney was a womanizer and wandered far and wide where his nose told him to go. "He can smell a bitch eight miles away, down wind," the veterinarian told me when I complained that he kept running away and either ended up in the dog pound or was taken in by kind people. We were always getting calls from Sweeney's benefactors who had found our name on his collar and telephoned us to say he was eating well and had made himself at home but they would be glad if we would come and get him. Once he visited the Convent of the Sacred

Heart on Armstrong's Point—an odd coincidence, since there is a reference to the Convent of the Sacred Heart in T.S. Eliot's poem about Apeneck Sweeney.

Another time he fell in love with a Kerry Blue belonging to a friend, Mrs. Frank Ryan, and sat so long in front of the house that his private parts froze to the door mat. Mrs. Ryan had to thaw him out with kettles of warm water. After that he always sat down very carefully, sideways, with his tail and one leg tucked under him to make sure that an awful thing like that would never happen again.

On one occasion, when we went on a trip, we left Sweeney at a kennel from which he escaped. He found his way first into the vault of the Royal Bank where J.B. had an account and then into a beverage room, obviously looking for his master. Another time, soon after J.B. became editor of the newspaper, we took him with us when we went to have a Christmas Eve drink with Wesley McCurdy, the publisher of the *Winnipeg Tribune*. I was, of course, self-conscious and eager to make a good impression on my husband's boss. When Sweeney saw the Christmas tree in all its glistening glory with the elegant gift-wrapped presents under it he did what every red blooded dog does to a convenient tree.

One winter's day he disappeared. An hour or two later the phone rang. "This is Mordue of Mordue Brothers, the funeral directors," said a lugubrious voice. "The boys were coming home with the hearse this morning when they saw my Irish terrier on Broadway Avenue. They picked him up and brought him home but he isn't my Irish terrier, he's yours as I can tell by the name on his collar."

I promised to pick Sweeney up later in the afternoon when I went into town. When I arrived at the funeral parlour, a harried-looking man in striped trousers and a cutaway coat answered the door.

"Thank God you've come," he said. "Your dog is in the basement. We had nine funerals today and each time the organ began to play that damned dog began to howl."

One evening when we were giving a cocktail party someone telephoned to say Sweeney was at a house on the other side of town. We couldn't leave our guests, so I phoned for a taxi to go and get him. It was an office party in honour of visiting Southam brass and many of the great and the good of Winnipeg were invited. When a taxi drew up at the door late in the evening, Wes McCurdy peeked around the edge of the Venetian blind to see who was arriving. He was taken aback when the driver opened the back door of the cab and Sweeney stepped out, walked with dignity up the front steps and waited quietly until the driver rang the doorbell and the maid opened the door.

When we gave dinner parties Sweeney used to sit down in front of each guest and yawn loudly as the hour came around when we began to hope our friends would decide to go home. Konrad Lorenz, the Austrian ethologist, believes that dogs can sense the feelings of their masters. He cites, as an example, his Alsatian who used to nip visitors without apparent provocation when Lorenz began to be bored by their company. At the time, we thought Sweeney was probably bothered by cigarette smoke as the evening wore on and was yawning from lack of oxygen, but later, after reading Lorenz, we decided he was probably reflecting our mood. After all, he always seemed full of fun when we were in good spirits and moped when we felt glum.

During that first winter in Winnipeg I began to make friends and to feel I had a place in the community. I was invited to join the Social Science Study Club, a highbrow version of the Peace Study Group in Montreal. Alderman Margaret McWilliams, a formidable, strong-minded woman, was one of its founders. Later, while her husband was Lieutenant-Governor of Manitoba, the Social Science Study Club broadened out into the Winnipeg Women's Branch of the Canadian Institute of International Affairs and she was elected its first president. I was vice-president.

I wrote a little that year, mostly editorial-page essays and art criticism for *The Winnipeg Tribune,* but I felt I was only using a fraction of my ability, and it irked me.

In September 1938, during the month of the Munich crisis, I came up against hard reality. J.B., at thirty-six, had just been made the youngest newspaper editor in Canada and was carrying heavy new responsibilities. The week of Chamberlain's visit to Hitler he was looking so tired and nervy from lack of sleep and exercise that I persuaded him to go riding with me after work. It was glorious autumn weather and I thought nothing would be more relaxing than a ride on the prairie.

That afternoon, Josie Welsh, the groom at the riding stables, mounted J.B. on Champ, a reliable old rodeo pick-up horse, a huge animal, and put me on Greylegs, a big strong jumper J.B. had ridden occasionally. J.B. had warned me against Greylegs because the horse had such a big barrel and a hard mouth, but I liked him because he was fast and powerful, so that riding him was exciting, like going down a steep hill on skis. After I had mounted I mentioned to Josie that I had no curb rein and he said that a snaffle was all I needed.

We started out, happily heading for the open prairie instead of the bush trails in order to have a good canter and work off some of our worries about what was happening in Europe. Sweeney was with us and kept making side excursions or rushing ahead looking for jack rabbits and gophers. We let the horses have their head and it was glorious fun for a while until I realized that Greylegs was racing ahead, galloping faster and faster in spite of my efforts to rein him in. He was, in fact, out of control. J.B. behind me called out, "You're riding too hard. Slow down." And just then, Sweeney, away ahead, flushed a rabbit and came tearing out from behind a bush. Greylegs, like Buck Fuller's "dymaxion" car, made a hairpin turn. I went off, and as I went, I swung my foot clear of the stirrup to avoid being dragged, landing hard on my back. I lost consciousness and when I came to, J.B. was leaning over me. I felt sure my pelvis had been broken because my back hurt and I wasn't able to move my legs.

J.B. spoke to me very quietly. "I'm going to get help," he said. "Don't be afraid. I'll be back soon."

It was strange to lie there alone, listening to the click of Greylegs' bridle as he grazed nearby. His feet made loud, thumping noises, the ground acting like a sounding-board, and I was terrified that he would step on me although I knew that a horse does not step on a person if it can possibly avoid it. After a while J.B. came back with an old man who lived in a shack beside the railroad tracks across the prairie. They brought a shutter with them and shoved it under me very gently and wrapped a blanket around me. It had been a hot day while the sun was up but now it was getting low in the heavens and the air was cooling rapidly. I was shivering, and my teeth chattered—from shock, no doubt, as well as from the cold earth under me.

"Listen," J.B. said, in the same quiet, steady voice as before. "I'll have to ride to the nearest telephone. I'll have to leave you again. Do you understand?"

"Yes," I said, "I understand."

I heard him talking to Champ as he mounted and then the sound of hoofbeats fading away into the distance. The old man stayed with me and entertained me with gruesome stories about people thrown by horses on the prairie who had died or been crippled for life. He said several times, "I don't hold with horseback riding myself."

After a while I heard the sound of hooves vibrating through the earth, a voice saying "Whoah, boy, Whoah," and then a girl was kneeling beside me.

"Want a cigarette?" she said.

I said "Yes," and she put a lighted cigarette between my lips.

"Can you handle it yourself?"

"Yes. My arms are all right. It's my back."

"I had a bad fall last year," she said. "I broke all sorts of bones, but I'm fine now and riding again. I'm going to take your horse back to the stable now."

I never saw the girl again but she helped me over a bad place that evening.

Some time later I heard the sound of an automobile engine, the slam of a car door, and then J.B. and a policeman were looking down at me.

"We'll put her onto the back seat," the policeman said.

"If you so much as lay a finger on her I'll knock you down," J.B. replied moving so that he was straddling my body. "She is going to stay right where she is until the ambulance comes. She's hurt her back and can't be moved without a stretcher."

His voice was hard and queer and he was almost shouting. I thought he must have gone out of his mind. I had never before heard him sound like that.

"Have it your own way," said the policeman.

It seemed to take a long while for the ambulance to bump out across the prairie. When it arrived, skilled hands eased me onto a stretcher. It was a police ambulance, and Mr. Speed, the River Heights cop who patrolled the area on a bicycle in summer, sat beside me and J.B. sat next to him. It was rough, slow, painful going on the prairie, but fast going when we reached city streets.

"I hear a lion roaring," I said, as the machine picked up speed.

Mr. Speed leaned over and held my hand, saying gently, "It does sound like a lion, doesn't it? But it's only the siren to clear the streets so we can get you to a doctor as quickly as we possibly can."

When I was finally stretched out on a bed in the Winnipeg General Hospital, I looked up to see John McEachern, our family doctor, and Dr. McCharles, a surgeon, looking down at me with worried faces. I was annoyed by what I considered an irrelevant impertinence when one of them leaned over, pulled up the bedclothes and tickled the soles of my feet. When I wiggled my feet in protest, McCharles said, "Thank God."

He told me afterwards that they had been afraid my spinal cord had been injured and that I was paralyzed.

The next morning, George Stephens, the director of the hospital, a friend of ours, came into my room.

"You're a lucky young woman," he said. "If John Bird hadn't stopped them from jack-knifing you onto the back seat of the police car, you would probably have been paralyzed from the waist down and in a wheelchair for the rest of your life."

After many X-rays, the doctors found that I had not, as feared, smashed any vertebrae although I had cracked the fifth spinal process. They decided, after consultation with an orthopaedist, that I ought to wear a steel brace for six months and stay in bed, with a board under the mattress, for most of the day, only getting up for two or three hours.

My back hurt for several months and the brace was uncomfortable and tiring, though good for posture. I had never faced a long period of being kept in bed before, and it required a bit of figuring out before I was able to adjust my sights to a new way of life.

I had just been invited to join the Winnipeg Junior League and had accepted because I was impressed by the good job it was doing in the community and also because many of my new friends were members. When I lived in Philadelphia and in Montreal I had tended to look down my nose at Junior Leagues, regarding them, though I didn't know much about them, as snobbish clubs of fat-cat women who amused themselves by playing the role of Lady Bountiful. Certainly the members of the Winnipeg Junior League belonged to an economically privileged group, as I did, but many of them were intelligent and hard-working. They took a professional attitude towards social welfare and community planning due to the training course they had to pass before being accepted, and because for several months during the year every member was required to put in several hours a week of serious work as a volunteer in a community project. The entire training and work program was designed to get away from the old-fashioned Lady Bountiful idea. Some of the outstanding graduates of the Winnipeg Junior League were: the late Margaret Konantz, elected to the House of Commons in 1963; Agnes Bendickson, in 1973 president of the Canadian Council on Social Development; Jean Plaxton, in the Department of the Secretary of State; and Mary Ferguson, the only Canadian to be president of the Association of Junior Leagues of America, who has all her life been a valuable member of a legion of boards concerned with social development.

At the time of my riding accident, membership in the Winnipeg

Junior League was a godsend because it gave me a lasting interest in community problems and, most important at that juncture, the opportunity to be one of a group of people doing something I believed in. Fortunately for me, the course in Community Needs, which had to be taken by provisional members, only required my attendance for half a day at a time, so I was able to go to all the lectures and field trips. When the half day was over I went home exhausted and crawled into bed until the next day. I learned a great deal from the lectures given by social workers sent from the secretariat of the Association of Junior Leagues in New York, and began to understand some of the inner workings of the Winnipeg community after visiting the Juvenile Court, the Family Bureau, the Children's Aid Society, the YWCA, and other community-oriented organizations. (The winter after, when my back was strong and I was riding again, I became the education chairman of the League and learned a great deal more about Winnipeg by planning and organizing the course for provisional members.)

While I was still partially laid up after the accident, I wrote another novel. It was about Canada. At the end of it the hero and heroine, Montreal intellectuals both, did not walk into the sunset as they so often did in the romantic, silent movies of the period, but took the train north to start a new life close to the strength-giving earth, away from the hurry and fret of city life. (I didn't go into the matter of how they were to earn a living.) It was a romantic, impractical resolution of a plot based on a sort of Rousseau-like concept of the healing qualities and the worth of primitive life.

I thought it was a good ending then. I do not think so now. For a long time, the frontier was an escape hatch to imagined freedom. It represented the fresh start that was supposed to change people into finer, happier, more liberated human beings. I believed that too for a long time, but now I think there is no escape from ourselves and no "geography cure."

I'm glad now that my last novel was not published because it reflected my own immaturity, but at the time I was sad when it was rejected. On the other hand, writing that book was a valuable exercise because it forced me to discipline myself and made me use my mind at a time when it would have been easy to let it go slack. I'm convinced the brain is like a muscle and in order for it to function well you have to keep it toned up by regular exercise.

In the spring of 1939 King George VI and Queen Elizabeth came to Winnipeg on the Royal Tour. They arrived on the 24th of May. For weeks before, everyone was in a highly nervous state over the lilacs. They seemed to be the only topic of conversation. Would they or would they not be out when royalty came to call? In Winnipeg, the lilacs are expected to be in bloom to celebrate Queen Victoria's birthday, and usually show loyalty to the Crown by turning the city briefly into a sweet-smelling garden of purple and white. Winnipeg is then *en beauté* like Kew in lilac time. That year they held back because of cold weather. The King and Queen arrived in a practically flowerless city with rain pouring down on them as they drove in an open car from the railroad station to the official receptions.

There were two receptions that day. The first was given by the Mayor, John Queen, and the second by the Premier, John Bracken. We were invited to attend the Premier's party and were required to sit on funeral-parlour chairs in front of the Legislative Buildings for two hours until the King and Queen arrived and went into the rotunda. We had been instructed to get all dolled up for the occasion, the men in striped trousers, cutaway coats and top hats, the women in short cocktail dresses. It was raining so hard that I wore a raincoat over my best dress and held an umbrella over my best hat. J.B. refused to share the umbrella because he didn't think it wide enough for two people. He maintained an unflinching calm while the rain pelted down on the silk hat he had not worn since our wedding—and has never worn again. After we had sat there for half an hour I could see the topper was slowly warping and crinkling and looked as if it might melt away. When I cried out at the spectacle, J.B. said with solemnity, "A plugged hat is the least I can sacrifice for king and country."

While all of us, at least a couple of hundred people, waited for our sovereign to appear, we listened to a play-by-play description of the Mayor's reception being broadcast on a loudspeaker. Everyone laughed when the commentator said the King was wearing a naval uniform as it was obviously appropriate garb for a day when there was so much water around.

Prime Minister Mackenzie King accompanied the King and Queen on the trip and followed them around wherever they went like a faithful terrier. His presence at Mayor Queen's party was too much for the commentator who began bravely by saying, "The King, the Queen and Mr. King have now arrived at the city hall and Mr. Queen is on the steps to meet them. The King is now shaking hands with Mr. Queen, and now the Queen is shaking hands with Mr. Queen, and now Mr. King is shaking hands with Mr. Queen. And now the King and Mr.

Queen and the Queen and Mr. King are moving into the reception hall. Now the King and Mr. Quing, I mean Mr. Keen and the Quing . . . I'm sorry I mean. . . ." He floundered on becoming more and more confused and desperate while Their Majesties' loyal subjects in front of the Legislative Buildings rocked with laughter.

Premier Bracken's reception was marked by a crass official bungle. Mayor Queen had made a special trip to Minnesota to invite Governor Stassen and his wife to come to Winnipeg to meet the King and Queen, and to attend the reception given by the Premier of the province. Mr. and Mrs. Stassen were in the reception line when Eustace Brock, the naval aide-de-camp, came up to them and told them they had to get out of line because it had just been ascertained that, according to protocol (presumably laid down by Mackenzie King and the White House), no American official was to be introduced to the King and Queen until President Roosevelt met them at Ogdensburg on their way to Hyde Park and Washington.

Mr. and Mrs. Stassen left the line and went home embarrassed and furious at what they must have considered an incomprehensible insult rather than the act of petty officiousness which it was. I went to a luncheon that day given by one of the Minnesota grain people for a number of Americans who had come up from St. Paul and Minneapolis with the Governor. They were angry, and when the martinis began to flow they became very outspoken in their indignation. Governor Stassen's embarrassment must have been considerably increased that evening when he saw on the front page of a Minneapolis paper a large photograph of himself shaking hands with King George. An overzealous news editor, anticipating the event, had faked the photograph from two separate photos in the newspaper morgue.

War Again

By the summer of 1939 it was apparent that "peace in our time" was a fantasy, and that the carving up of Czechoslovakia to appease Hitler in the hope of avoiding another world war was a gambit played from a position of weakness, indecision and despair. Remembering the voices we had heard on the radio in Antwerp in 1936, we felt certain that the next territorial demand would come when the crops had been harvested in Europe. All summer long we were depressed by forebodings that it was the last period of happiness we would have for a decade.

On September 1st, Hitler's Panzer divisions moved into Poland. On the 3rd, Britain declared war on Germany.

September that year was a golden month in Manitoba. On the Sunday Britain declared war on Germany, we were working in the garden, preparing the ground for spring seeding and clipping the shrubbery. We kept the radio turned on all day. From time to time neighbours crossed lawns to talk in low voices, and then hurried indoors or stood by an open window, listening, when the sound of a voice reading the news came over the air.

J.B. and I found ourselves savouring, with extraordinary intensity, the warmth of the sun, the smell of the freshly turned earth, the flowers, the sight of young children playing in the street. We became newly aware of our paintings on the walls and the books on the shelves in the living room and they assumed new significance. We felt a great emotional outpouring between us, a feeling of shared grief and love as if we were about to be parted from each other and everything we valued.

After lunch Leonard Brockington telephoned and asked if he could drop in. Brock, a lawyer, had been first chairman of the Broadcasting

153

Commission (later to become the Canadian Broadcasting Corporation), and was at that time the counsel for the Winnipeg Grain Exchange. He had been a tall man until arthritis bent him nearly double. He walked with a cane and had difficulty in standing for any length of time but he did not allow his affliction, by that time arrested, to prevent him from doing anything he wanted to do.

Brock had been born in Wales, and until his death he kept the rich, musical tongue of his people. There was magic in his voice. What's more, he had a verbatim memory and loved the sound of words. That afternoon he was tense, choked with grief and foreboding for the years ahead. All three of us were in a deeply emotional, sentimental mood, and after we had talked for a while, Brock and J.B., who also has a fabulous memory, began reciting poetry. J.B.'s taste and mine ran to T.S. Eliot and the modern American and Canadian poets, but on that day, when England was now at war and Canada soon would be, the two men quoted, from Browning, Matthew Arnold, Shakespeare and Housman, the much-quoted, hackneyed passages about England and war which at that time had new power to stir our hearts. Later Brock read four verses from Masefield's "August 1914," his beautiful, resonant voice giving the lines a moving impact.

Just as he finished reading the telephone rang. It was the managing editor of the *Tribune* for J.B. He took the call upstairs. A few minutes later he came down again, having changed his clothes.

"The *Athenia's* been torpedoed. We're getting out an extra," he said in that tense, quiet voice he uses when he is suppressing his feelings. "Joan and Frank Aykroyd are on board."

He picked up the car keys off the hall table and said, "So long, Brock. Sorry to walk out on you," and was gone. Joan and Frank Aykroyd were old friends of the Montreal days and the news about them brought war home to me in an immediate, personal way. I was aware that all our premonitions of what lay ahead were beginning to materialize. When Brock had gone home I sat down on the bottom steps of the stairway, put my head in my hands and cried.

The Aykroyds survived. They were put in separate lifeboats and were taken to different ports when they were picked up by rescue ships, so that neither knew the other was safe for some time.

The next week we bought a sketch of the Rocky Mountains by Lawren Harris from the Picture Loan Society in Toronto. We paid a hundred dollars for it in instalments of five dollars a month. We also bought a recording of Beethoven's *Fifth Symphony,* unaware that its four opening notes—the V-for-Victory Code—would become the theme of the BBC broadcasts to occupied Europe. We felt those two purchases were symbolic; we hoped to preserve a little sanity and a few lasting values during the madness that we knew lay ahead.

After Canada declared war on Germany on September 10th, Winnipeg men began to enlist in droves. One afternoon we went to see the recruits for Canada's First Division march down Portage Avenue on their way to a training depot. They were the children of the depression. Most of them were the young, the unwanted, who had graduated from school only to stand around idly, hopelessly, on the corners of Main Street because there were no jobs for them. They looked unhealthy, undernourished and pigeon-chested, wearing badly fitting uniforms or parts of uniforms—a Falstaff's army. Row after row of them shuffled past without a band to keep them in step. (For a time after Canada went to war regimental bands were taboo—too emotional.) I found myself weeping as the volunteers went past because I knew that in a few months they would be stronger and healthier, fattened for the slaughter. I thought it dreadful that they had never been given a chance to have a reasonable life in their youth and were now only wanted and given paid employment, proper nutrition, and medical care because they were needed to fight for their country. It was a tragic irony that the youngsters rejected in peacetime were the first to be recruited to defend Canada in time of war.

Not long after the war started, Margaret Hyndman, a Toronto lawyer, had the excellent idea that women should register for voluntary service. She prepared a long questionnaire which would provide the federal government with a record of the skills, training and experience of women who were prepared to give voluntary service to the war effort. When she came to Winnipeg to explain the project, she said all the registrations were to be sent to Ottawa to be put on file. Margaret McWilliams, Mary Ferguson and Margaret Konantz were determined that the registrations be kept in Winnipeg where a Central Volunteer Bureau would be set up to make use of women volunteers as soon as they were needed. They were convinced that the best use of woman power would not be made unless each community was organized on a local basis. Like most Winnipegers, they were suspicious and resentful of dictation from Ottawa or Toronto, and were determined to handle their own affairs.

At a meeting of representatives of local organizations it was decided to use Miss Hyndman's questionnaires, keep them on file in Winnipeg and set up a Central Volunteer Bureau to serve as a placement service, a clearing house of information, and a central agency to co-ordinate war and community work in Winnipeg. A committee was appointed to carry out the registration and set up the Central Volunteer Bureau. Margaret Konantz was the chairman, an admirable choice; she was as strong as a bulldozer, with unlimited energy and imagination and a genius for organizing. Monica McQueen, a social worker, and Sally Heppner, a valiant volunteer were on the executive. I also served as publicity chairman. Mary Ferguson was pregnant and did not take public part in the operation although she acted as an invaluable brain trust.

Within a week or two we had found office space and had borrowed tables, chairs and office equipment. I wrote press releases, advertisements, newspaper articles, and speeches which I and members of my committee made at eighty-five different public gatherings, urging women to register for voluntary service. Day after day women poured into the office to fill in the questionnaires. Within a few weeks we had a personnel pool of 7,000 volunteers.

It took time to organize the Central Volunteer Bureau. Money to finance the project was obtained from volunteer organizations, business concerns and, later, the federal government.

Monica McQueen became the first executive secretary, with a small salary, and she gave the Bureau a good start. But after her husband, the economist, Professor Pete McQueen, was killed in the plane crash at Armstrong, she needed a better-paid job to help her educate her children, and became director of the Winnipeg Council of Social Agencies. Gertrude Laing (who many years later was a member of the Royal Commission on Bilingualism and Biculturalism) succeeded Monica as executive secretary. She has written a booklet about the remarkable work of the Winnipeg Central Volunteer Bureau, which became the model for the Women's Voluntary Service Centres Eleanor Roosevelt helped to organize after the United States entered the war.

At first some of the Winnipeg organizations that had traditionally used volunteers were jealous of the C.V.B. and did not want to co-operate with it. It took considerable persuading to make them understand that volunteers would be employed more efficiently and there would be less overlapping of services if a central agency were responsible for co-ordinating all the volunteer community and war work in the city. They held out for a time, being convinced that women would be more loyal to their own organizations. That sort of argument ceased in 1940 when the "phoney" war ended and the Winnipeg Grenadiers were taken prisoners in the fall of Hong Kong.

The First World War had been a knitting war for a vast army of women. This time, remembering the uneven sizes and strangely constructed feet of many socks and the large number of sweaters suitable only for either giants or pygmies, the government wisely decided to supply the Armed Forces with factory-made issued garments. At first this decision led to considerable frustration for women who had a great personal need to do something about the war effort and were determined to knit. A perceptive physician explained to me that it was important to find war jobs for women for the sake of their mental health and morale and that knitting was valuable therapy. He pointed out that during the First World War there had been a much higher incidence of stomach ulcers among the people living in neutral countries than there had been in countries where people could work out their anxieties in action.

In the first months after the Second World War started, there were few jobs available for volunteers, so that the work of the CVB was not demanding. It was, in fact, an anticlimax for the CVB executive as well as for the 7,000 volunteers who were waiting impatiently to be called into service: having beaten the drum to stimulate women to register, we had few jobs to offer them. We tried to look ahead, however, and prepare for the future by writing and lecturing about the importance of community service so that women would understand that "holding the home front" was essential to the war effort and was indeed the "war work" they wanted to do. Courses in motor mechanics, elementary plumbing and household maintenance were organized for women. The Red Cross gave courses in home nursing, and the St. John's Ambulance Corps gave courses in first aid. The Family Bureau gave courses in the techniques of "visiting" to members of the women's auxiliaries to the Armed Services. The visitors were told where to refer the wives and common-law wives who had not received their separation allowances, who had financial or health problems, or were having difficulty in bringing up children in a fatherless household. They were also told what to say and what not to say to grief-stricken wives when the expected casualties occurred.

As the war went on, the workload of social agencies increased because of the many unhappy family situations which developed.

Courses in social work and on-the-job training were given to many volunteers who co-operated closely with the professionals and became, in time, remarkably professional themselves.

After the fall of France, when Britain became the target of nightly air raids, there were plenty of jobs for women volunteers, and the CVB was able to fill them quickly and efficiently because of its files and its care in trying to place the right person in a job.

All through the war I wrote, as an unpaid volunteer, a weekly column for the *Winnipeg Tribune* about women's war effort. It was called "Holding the Home Front" and the Tribune's cartoonist, Mozel, illustrated it. A volunteer wrote a similar column for the *Winnipeg Free Press*. Gathering material was an inspiring, moving operation. Women worked themselves to the point of exhaustion at a legion of jobs, without hope of glory or desire for recompense, providing necessary community services as well as war service. They worked for the Red Cross, making bandages, knitting or helping the doctors and nurses in the blood bank. They packed Bundles for Britain, Survivors' Kits of clothes and toilet articles for the seamen hauled out of the ocean or from lifeboats after they had been torpedoed, and food parcels for Canadians in the Armed Forces who had been taken prisoner in Europe. As Japan had not signed the International Red Cross Convention, food parcels could not be sent to the Winnipeg Grenadiers and the Royal Rifles from Montreal, taken prisoner after the fall of Hong Kong.

There was a good deal of absenteeism among volunteers during the last months of the war when everyone was exhausted and there was a let-up in tension as we became more confident of victory. I therefore wrote a scathing column, pointing out that community and war services were still badly needed and there could be no rest for the weary. There was a warm response from laggard volunteers when I mentioned that there was practically no absenteeism in the ranks of the women's auxiliary to the Grenadiers. For five and a half years those women, whose men were starving in Japan, went right on packing food parcels for prisoners of war in Europe.

The Central Volunteer Bureau had on file a list of women who had indicated on the questionnaires that they would receive servicemen on leave as guests. After the Commonwealth Air Training Plan got underway, Winnipeg was flooded by young British, Australian and New Zealand airmen on forty-eight hours' leave from Rivers, Paulson, Carberry and Brandon. People opened their doors to them. As a rule the men would return to the same house every time they had a "forty-eight."

Many of the hostesses were the wives or mothers of men who had enlisted and gone overseas; for them the young guests in air force blue were a comfort. I wrote many happy and many sad stories about them. Happy, because the boys were so glad to find themselves in a family atmosphere. Sad because after they went into combat in Britain, they usually wrote to their Canadian "families" and then, very often, the letters stopped coming and we knew what had happened, or letters came from their parents to say they had been killed in action or taken prisoner.

Again and again, during those years, I would write about the need for some job to be done, and immediately women would respond and fill the need. Once they rather overdid it: in my column I said there was a shortage of bottles, and asked women to bring any clean, old bottles they could find to the CVB. In two days' time it was impossible to get into the office because of the thousands of bottles delivered by women from every corner of the city. Evidently many women hoarded old medicine bottles, feeling that it was sinful and wasteful to throw them out, and they were delighted when they could get rid of them not only with a free conscience but with a sense of virtue. I felt like the sorcerer's apprentice as I tried to stop the flow of bottles because they kept right on coming even when I cried, "Hold! Enough, enough!"

Marg Konantz finally had to find a depot for them, and hired a truck to take them there. That gave her the idea of the Patriotic Salvage Corps. It didn't take her long to organize the Salvage Corps which turned waste into cash to support the voluntary services in the city. From this idea came her idea of organizing the city under block captains responsible for seeing that women put their salvageable materials out in front of their houses the day the trucks, driven by girls in white uniforms, came down their street. As far as I'm concerned, modern efforts to salvage and recycle materials are old hat after Winnipeg. For years, like every other housewife, I saved fats in covered tins, washed old bottles and tied newspapers in packages. Between collection days our basement looked like a junk shop.

The first radio broadcast I ever did was a fifteen-minute effort to explain the workings of the Patriotic Salvage Corps. A sympathetic, patient young CBC producer, Andrew Cowan (much later head of the Northern Network system of the CBC), put it on the air after many rehearsals. I was so nervous that my stomach turned to water, my tongue stuck to the roof of my mouth and my hand shook so badly that the script rattled and sounded like a windstorm over the air.

As German submarine warfare and the bombing of Britain accelerated, the number of volunteer jobs for women increased. A big canteen was opened in the annex of Eaton's store where older women served home-made cakes and sandwiches and younger women danced their feet sore with boys from Shilo and the air training centres. The Winnipeg Branch of the Canadian Federation of Artists, of which I was vice-president, painted their volunteer contribution; a huge, satirical mural on the walls of the canteen. In some quarters it was regarded as risqué and very avant-garde. It shocked some people, but the soldiers liked it.

As more and more men went into uniform, women were needed not only to do jobs as unpaid volunteers, but also to do the work of the men who had gone overseas. The papers were full of stories about "Rosie the Riveter," and pictures of women working in factories. The federal government found money to provide a network of day nurseries for the preschool children of mothers working in war industries and the industries gave women flexible hours and part-time work. It was considered the patriotic and laudable duty for a married woman with children to take on a man's job in order to free him for active service. However, there was considerable worry about the "latchkey" school children who came home to an empty house, and had to let themselves in to wait alone until the mother or father came home. It was felt that some provision should be made for after-school supervision of the children.

After a time women were recruited for the service auxiliaries to the Army and Navy and the womens division of the Air Force. A number of my friends joined the CWAC, the WCRNS, or the Women's Division (RCAF), took the officer's training course and were sent on active duty as noncombatants. A good friend, Alice Sorby, became a Lieutenant-Colonel of the CWAC and led a contingent overseas. A small, wiry woman, smart in the uniform designed by Creed, Alice was quietly efficient. It was a shock to the old guard when she strolled in the officers' mess the first time, but after a while the men got used to having women invade the sacred precincts.

The CWACs who were cooks and dietitians greatly improved the meals served to the Armed Forces stationed in Winnipeg, and the other service women also did an excellent job. Nevertheless, there were constant undercurrents of disapproval and murmuring about the immorality of the women who were privates or non-commissioned officers. They were often accused of only having joined up in order "to get a man." On one occasion the newspapers carried a front-page story about a couple of CWACs who had been picked up by the Military Police and charged with being drunk and disorderly on a streetcar. After a number of indignant people wrote to the newspapers about the awful women in uniform, I telephoned the captain commanding the CWAC in Winnipeg to get her side of the story. She said bitterly that her young women were certainly no worse and probably better than the young male soldiers.

"It's just the old prejudice against women," she said. "If one of my women gets tight and cuts up rough in public, everyone accuses all of them of being immoral hussies and the dregs of humanity. If half a dozen soldiers get drunk on a Saturday night, as they always do, nobody says anything and the papers don't bother to print anything about it. People just shrug their shoulders and say, 'Boys will be boys'."

Women in the army were discriminated against in another serious way. Up until 1969 it was against the law to give birth-control information or contraceptives to anyone. In Winnipeg old Mrs. Speechley was the local Marie Stopes who, along with about a hundred helpers, successfully evaded the law and much public criticism for many years. A thin, intense woman, with grey, windblown hair caught in a loose bun at the nape of her neck, invariably wearing a high-necked shirt and a shapeless skirt, she must have looked like an angel in shining raiment to the poor women, worn out by childbearing, to whose homes she brought contraceptive devices. Although her work was illegal and frowned upon, it was taken for granted for the army in Winnipeg to issue contraceptives to the male soldiers, and to require them to attend lectures about the dangers of contracting venereal disease. But the women in the army were denied this information. It was, of course, an example of the practically universal acceptance of the double standard. Some of the young CWACs I interviewed about this discrimination were very angry, saying they needed contraceptive information even more than the men, since they would have to leave the army if they became pregnant, and they were just as susceptible to VD as the men were.

As far as I was concerned, during the first two years of the war, my work for the CVB and writing the column added up to a full-time unpaid job. I thought I had as much on my platter as I could possibly do, but I found I was wrong about that when, in the summer of 1940, my life was complicated by the war in a rather unexpected way.

Early in 1940 we had written to J.B.'s sister Noel, who was living in

France, asking her to send her ten-year-old daughter to us for the duration of the war. We had a spare room which I used as a study and we felt it wrong to have an unoccupied bed at such a time. We were incredulous when Noel wrote back saying she thought it best to keep the child in France where she was doing well in school. She wrote, "We are not worried. There is no great danger. After all, we have the Maginot Line."

We had heard about the Maginot mind but had hardly expected to encounter it in J.B.'s family.

We felt frustrated and deeply concerned for Noel and her family when Hitler's Panzer divisions by-passed the northern part of the Maginot Line in June and occupied Belgium, the Netherlands, and half of France. However, they escaped, after many adventures, and went to the Belgian Congo where Noel ran an inter-allied hostel for seamen at Matadi until the war was over.

Another sister, Dolly, who lived in Antwerp, took refuge with her husband, Cam Petersen, in a small summer cottage they owned at Kapellenbosch. They lived there like peasants while Cam worked secretly with the Belgian Underground. The South Saskatchewan Regiment liberated them in 1945.

After the fall of France and the Low Countries, we wrote to Charles Croft, J.B.'s best friend at Oxford, inviting him to send us his two oldest boys, then aged nine and seven. Although our study was small, we figured we could put two beds in it and set up the typewriting desk in my room.

The Crofts were good friends of us both. Charles had called on me when I was in London before I was married and I had liked him immensely. When we were on our honeymoon in 1928 we had arrived in England just in time to go to his and Phyllis' wedding. In fact we had driven to the church with the groom and the best man.

On our trip to England, four years before, we had stayed with Charles and Phyllis in Plymouth where they lived in a big, rambling house with a large garden stretching the length of a long city block.

Charles, like J.B., was tall and lean, with an Irish sense of humour. Phyllis was a short, roly-poly young woman, very cheerful and full of fun. She wore orange dresses to match her hair or green and orange prints to bring out the colour of green-amber, wideset eyes and a Devonshire cream complexion. She had a slight nutmeg powdering of freckles across her nose.

Life had been comfortable and relaxed for the English professional class before the Second World War. Phyllis then had a general house-work girl and a nurse for the children. The night we arrived there was a black-cock with bread-sauce and a Nuits-Saint-Georges for dinner for the four of us, which was accompanied by much hilarious toasting of absent Oxford friends and formal, rather bibulous speeches by the two men.

There had been only two little boys at that time: Desmond, a solemn, round-faced five-year-old, and Jonny, an active three-year-old with big, sad eyes. Benny, the third boy, was born soon after. Desmond and Jonny were the boys we had urged Charles Croft to send to us.

In July, when we had a letter from Charles Croft saying he was going to send his two sons as soon as possible, I thought I had better go to Rhode Island to see Mother while the going was good, and invited a friend, Sally Coyne, to come with me. We travelled east by CPR and, as the train was winding its way around the edge of Lake Superior, a telegram was handed to me that had been picked up at a small station where we stopped to water the engine. It was from J.B., and read, "Stay me with flagons. Comfort me with apples. Cable from Charles Croft asking us sponsor whole family, wife, three boys and grandmother. What shall I answer?"

I looked at that telegram and wondered how we could fit all those people into our small, three-bedroom house. I knew that a refugee was only allowed to bring fifteen dollars out of Britain and I didn't see how we could possibly feed and clothe five more people on J.B.'s quite modest salary. After talking to Sally about it for an hour or so I went into the lavatory and was sick.

"It's those damn curves around the lake," I said. "They make me trainsick."

I tried to think of all the reasons why we should refuse to sponsor the Croft family but none of them gave the slightest tip to the scale com-pared with the single argument that if your best friend asks you to shelter his family when there's a war on, you say, "Yes, of course."

The clincher was that the Crofts' home town, Plymouth, a vital target, was already being flattened by bombs.

With the gravest misgivings I wired J.B. saying I thought we ought to cable Charles to send the family. He was of the same mind as I and sent the cable as soon as he heard from me.

I spent ten days with Mother in Rhode Island and then went back to

Winnipeg to make arrangements to receive our war guests. (War guest was a euphemism for refugee that everyone used at that time in the vain hope of taking the sting out of reality.) I beavered around borrowing a couple of beds and a crib for the four-year-old and clearing out bureau drawers and already overcrowded cupboards.

After the sleeping plan had been rearranged, the bedrooms looked even smaller than before. It required skill to navigate around the beds through the narrow channels where one could walk. There was enough sleeping space for Phyllis and the three boys but obviously no place for Granny Lee, Phyllis' mother. However, the Central Volunteer Bureau came to the rescue and found an elderly widow, living alone in a large house, who was willing to open her doors to a stranger.

In the midst of an August heat wave, we received a message from Halifax that the Croft family had landed and was on its way west by train. When the thermometer hits the high nineties Fahrenheit, the natives of Winnipeg always tell you that it is dry heat so you don't feel it. This is a local myth, a twin of the one about not feeling the dry cold when it is forty below. During the first day or two of a heat wave it was possible to keep our house reasonably comfortable by shutting all the windows and drawing the shades until it began to get cooler outside, usually around 9:30 or ten when it began to grow dark. Even the frequent, violent thunderstorms failed to cool the air for more than a few hours.

On the blazing hot morning when the Crofts arrived, Sally Coyne brought her car to the station to help us transport them and their luggage. Our car was inadequate for such a sudden increase in the size of our family. In order to economize on gas, then rationed, we had sold the Oldsmobile and had bought a small Studebaker roadster. Fortunately it had a couple of folding seats for children at the sides of a small space behind the front seat.

The station platform was a bedlam of wild-looking, unkempt women and washed-out children who seemed to be in a state of shock after a nerve-racking crossing and three nights on the train. Some of them were milling around a huge pile of suitcases, dufflebags and paper parcels. Others were standing forlornly, looking dazed. We soon spotted Phyllis because she was wearing a favourite orange linen maternity dress she had worn when we had seen her four years before. She and a thin dark woman were standing close together, obviously searching the crowd for us while three small boys eddied around them.

It was a shock to us both when we realized Phyllis was large with child and evidently ready to give birth very soon. She was obviously worn out after having made an enormous effort, requiring great physical and moral courage. Granny Lee, aged fifty-nine, looked as if she hadn't had a good night's sleep in her life. Both women were in such a state of nervous exhaustion that they couldn't stop talking and went on talking steadily for days.

Desmond, aged nine, was still as tow-headed, cherubic and round-faced as we remembered him. Jonny, aged seven, was thin, big-eyed, worried-looking, one of those little boys who make even the toughest-hearted woman feel protective and maternal. Benny, aged four, was a blue-eyed, wistful character, with a will of iron, as we discovered later. All three boys were pasty-faced with purple circles under their eyes, and were suffering greatly from the heat in their English-weight grey flannel suits and woollen knee socks. They were quiet and subdued at first, eyeing J.B. and me warily, although they soon came to life and became active and full of questions.

We drove them to our little house which shrank visibly as we all poured through the door. There was no place to put all the trunks and suitcases and everyone kept falling over them and apologizing nervously. Our house and small garden must have been a dreadful comedown for Phyllis after her spacious house in Plymouth, not at all what she must have expected. When I showed her to her room, the first thing she did was to pull up the shades and open the window. I explained that she was making the house hotter by letting in the sun and sweltering noon heat, but she replied that she would suffocate in such a horribly small room without air.

During the next few hours Phyllis talked and talked. She told us the voyage over had been a nightmare. She said most of the English mothers on board had always employed nannies, as she had, to look after their children. As a result the children were upset by being deprived of the experienced authority of their nurses and the mothers were upset because they couldn't handle their children who refused to obey them and ran wild all over the ship. The mothers yelled at them and spanked them and the children screamed and kept on disobeying. The women were afraid of submarines, afraid their children would fall overboard, afraid of the unknown future ahead. They were distraught and heartsick at leaving their homes and their husbands. In addition, Phyllis was afraid her baby would be born at sea without a doctor in attendance. She showed me a bottle of chloroform her family doctor had given her, with instructions to inhale the anaesthetic if her labour pains became unbearable. "He said my hand holding the bottle would drop down when I became unconscious so I wouldn't breathe in so much that it would kill me," she said.

"The whole voyage was awful," she went on. "All the food was the usual shipboard food, very fancy. The children wouldn't eat it. The last four days were the worst. They ran out of milk and oranges. The children kept crying and the mothers kept slapping them and yelling at them. And the boat was zigzagging around in the most awful way because of submarines. Oh, it was awful."

"It was such a relief when we landed in Halifax," she said, "and the black porters on the train were so kind. I could get the right kind of food for the children, and it was wonderful coming through all that wild country. The children kept saying, 'This is the new world!' And they were thrilled, as we all were, by the sunrise this morning, it was so beautiful. And it was strange; there were no trees after we came out of the forest."

She told us proudly that she had had to make all the arrangements to cross the Atlantic by herself because Charles Croft had left Plymouth at very short notice in order to go overseas with the Eighth Army.

It was then we heard what had happened. In July, shortly after receiving our letter asking him to send us the two eldest boys, Charles had been given his marching orders. When he left he had told Phyllis to send the boys to Canada right away. But after he had gone Phyllis decided that she must keep her family together at all costs. She was determined to go to Canada, since her husband had left England, and Plymouth was being so badly bombed that frequently she had to huddle with the children in an air raid shelter in the garden or go down into the cellar. Her mother, Granny Lee, had planned to go to stay with her son, a farmer in Kenya, but agreed to go first to Canada in order to help Phyllis with the children and the expected baby.

At that time we were blessed with a cook-housekeeper, Louise Bricknell, who had come to us when Anne Herby had married. Louise was a métis, with Indian, French and Scottish blood. She also was a sort of saint, gentle, cheerful, yet firm with the boys, answering the newcomers' questions patiently, and encouraging me when I was depressed and worried by unforeseen problems—and for a long time there were new unforeseen problems almost every day. She also cooked wonderful meals, great morale builders for all.

On the first morning after Phyllis arrived, she came down to breakfast and asked, "What was the noise in the night that sounded like an air raid siren?"

Just then the eerie shriek of a train whistle echoed across the prairie.

"That's it," Phyllis said.

"It's probably a freight train on the CNR tracks," replied J.B.

Benny looked up from his porridge and asked, "Can we go down into the cellar when the war comes?"

"The war won't come here," J.B. said.

Benny began to cry. "But can we go down into the cellar if it does come?" he asked.

"You can go into the basement any time you want," J.B. said.

Later Louise told me that after breakfast Benny had gone down the basement stairs by himself and had come up happy.

"It's all neat and clean," he said, "because this is the new world."

Once they got over their fatigue from the journey, Desmond and Jonny seemed to adjust to life in Winnipeg very quickly and were soon playing with other children on the street. But Benny, who had been told that his mother would be going to hospital to get a new baby, was upset and afraid that his mother would desert him. He would not let her out of his sight, and followed her around all day. When she put him to bed at night he cried until she went upstairs to him, or he came downstairs and looked around the edge of the bannister to make sure she was still there. When he did finally go to sleep after his mother went to bed beside his crib, he had nightmares and cried out in a strange, thin voice. He was a pathetic example of what war can do to a small child.

For an entire fortnight after the Crofts arrived it was so hot that when we went to bed we left all our doors and windows open, in the hope of catching a cross-draught if a breeze sprang up. J.B. always fell asleep the minute he put his head down on the pillow, but I usually lay awake for a long time and woke up frequently. Often I could hear Phyllis sobbing quietly and was reminded of my childhood when I used to lie awake and listen to Kaekey crying in the night during the First World War.

One night, just before dawn, Benny had a nightmare and fell out of his crib which had one side left open at his request. I jumped out of bed when I heard his body fall on the floor and rushed across the hall to find that Phyllis was ahead of me and was crouched on the floor holding him in her arms. In the half light of the room it was like a Flemish painting: the exhausted, sweating woman with her distended belly, wearing a white cotton nightgown, rocking a child back and forth, her head bent over it as she murmured comforting words.

There were many arrangements to be made during the weeks Phyllis was waiting for her baby. Anna Wilson, our family doctor, agreed to take the case. She examined Phyllis the day after the Crofts arrived and found her in excellent health. However, Phyllis was upset when she found that she would have to go to hospital. She had always had her babies at home because, she said, her doctor husband thought there was more danger of infection in a hospital and also because he regarded childbirth as a natural, normal function that should, as much as possible, be separated from the concept of illness. Understandably she was terrified of going to a Canadian hospital and was sure the baby would die or she would contract puerperal fever.

This was a difficult period for all of us, a time of great worry. We were all under pressure and it made us edgy and irritable. From time to time it had its funny side, as when Phyllis turned on me indignantly and told me I was the most extravagant housekeeper she had ever met. I, in turn, became indignant at such an unjust accusation, as I had been watching the pennies carefully and was pleased with myself for being able to supply good, nutritional meals very cheaply.

"You've had salmon, chicken and peaches all in the same week," Phyllis said when I demanded examples of my extravagance.

I tried to explain that there was a glut of peaches and I had bought a huge basketful for canning and had served the leftovers for dessert. I said British Columbia salmon was in good supply and chicken was cheaper than meat. I didn't think she believed me and I only understood her scepticism when J.B. told me that in England you had to pay as much as a shilling for a single peach while Scottish salmon was a traditional luxury item and chicken was regarded as party fare.

As time went on tensions began to build up and I realized it would be almost impossible for two such strong-minded women as Phyllis and myself to share the same inadequate accommodation without conflict.

One afternoon I picked up J.B. with the car after work, but instead of playing tennis, as we usually did, we drove along the Assiniboine River until we found a tree to shade the car. There we parked and talked. It was clear to both of us that we couldn't keep Phyllis *and* four children with us indefinitely. There simply wasn't room. We realized more tensions would grow as time went on. We knew that it was essential for J.B. to have a modicum of rest in his own home when he was carrying such a heavy load. As well as running a newspaper in wartime he was giving a weekly fifteen-minute radio commentary sponsored by *The Winnipeg Tribune.* He went on at 11:15 p.m. On the other four week nights, members of the *Tribune's* editorial staff broadcast and J.B. had to stay up to hear what they said in order to encourage or criticize them. He usually telephoned them at the studio immediately after the broadcast, and then needed to have a snack and a drink, and unwind by playing recordings of Mozart concertos and Beethoven symphonies. It was usually long after midnight before we were in bed.

That afternoon when we sat in the car by the river, we talked our way through to the decision that we would have to find the money to rent a house or apartment where Phyllis could look after her children.

When we broached the idea to Phyllis that evening, she burst into tears, saying she was at the end of her tether, that she was usually unwell for a long time after one of her children was born, had never cooked or done her own housework, and had always had a nurse for her babies. She pointed out that Louise was a wonderful "nanny" who could help her with the baby, so the only thing for her to do was to stay on with us.

I explained that we would be even more crowded when there were four children. I realized, feeling like a heel, that she had a terrible feeling of rejection and was frightened, clinging to any straw of security. I wondered if we should not try to find a big house where all of us could live together and then turned down the thought because I knew it wouldn't work.

I was torn with sympathy for Phyllis. I felt intensely, seeing how disturbed she was, what it must be like for her to say farewell to husband, home, cherished possessions, to come to a place so different from what she had expected, to friends preoccupied with their own lives and with needs so different from her own.

Objectively, I was impressed by the way her whole body and mind were utterly concentrated on the preservation of the child inside her and keeping around her the children already born. She was an earth mother, fiercely protective, fiercely possessive.

I realized, as I listened to her, that she was indeed not well enough to run a household of small children and look after an infant, even if her mother, an artistic, temperamental woman, helped her. I understood her dismay, remembering my own inexperience when I first married and went to live in New York. After talking over the matter with J.B. again and asking the advice of some of my Winnipeg friends, I suggested to her that we might be able to find a boardinghouse where she would not have to cook meals and do the housekeeping. She jumped at the idea. For me the next question was where to find a suitable boardinghouse as well as money to pay for board and lodging. Granny Lee wanted to be with Phyllis to help with the baby, which made sense but also raised added accommodation difficulties.

For days I followed up ads in the newspapers and scoured the town, only to find that boardinghouses were either full or that landladies refused to take any children, let alone a baby. Then, providentially, two large rooms became vacant in a boardinghouse kept by Mrs. Rutherford, a warmhearted Englishwoman who felt it was her patriotic duty to help a fellow countrywoman in dire need. After endless discussion, Phyllis decided to take one room for Benny, herself and the baby, while Desmond and Jonny stayed with us. Granny Lee would take the second room.

J.B. and I began to feel more relaxed as we saw our way clear for at least a short time ahead. There were fewer tensions between Phyllis and me, and the house was quieter thanks to the generosity of a Winnipeg friend, Ruth Riley, who had sent Desmond and Jonny to stay on a farm for a fortnight.

It was a help to all of us when the heat wave broke and we were able to get some sleep and have a little privacy by closing our bedroom doors at night. We all knew that Phyllis' time was near so I was prepared on the night she crept into our room, leaned over my bed and said in a low voice, so as not to wake J.B. "The water has broken in my womb. I think you ought to phone Dr. Wilson."

When I told Anna Wilson what had happened, she said, "Get her to the hospital as quickly as you can."

We dressed and took Phyllis' little suitcase, which had been packed for a fortnight, and went out into the silent street where the car was parked in front of the house. I drove fast to the Winnipeg General Hospital on the other side of town. It was still dark night, just before the greying of dawn, and the streets were deserted. Phyllis was very quiet, very self-controlled, very brave. I felt as if my heart had sunk into my stomach. Inside the hospital an old man took the suitcase, gestured Phyllis to a wheel-chair and pushed her into an elevator. Before the door shut between us, I kissed her, said, "Good luck," and went back to the car. Driving home, I thought about the loneliness of a woman in labour in a bare room in a strange country, with only strangers around her and her husband far away under fire in a place unknown to her. Her daughter, Phyllis Bird Croft, was born many hours later.

During this period my friends in Winnipeg and the United States rallied to help us in the most remarkable way. I learned a great deal about human generosity and kindness during the war as well as about the strength of women.

A young registered nurse offered to take care of the baby for a fort-night free of charge after Phyllis left hospital and went to Mrs. Ruther-ford's boardinghouse. Some friends brought presents of baby clothes. Others arrived with good warm clothes for the boys. The wife of one of the editors on *The Winnipeg Tribune,* who had a small boy of her own, took Benny into her house while Phyllis was in hospital so he would have companionship at the sand pile.

When Desmond and Jonny came back from the farm they fitted into our household very easily. I entered them in Queenston Public School, a few blocks away, where they were with the friends they had already made on our street. At that time Sweeney was of the greatest help with them. We had been afraid that, being such a one-man dog, utterly devoted to J.B., he might be jealous and become disagreeable or even dangerous. But he accepted the Croft children as members of his own family.

Desmond and Jonny made a fuss over Sweeney in a way that made us realize he was important to them. One day, when they thought I was reading, I overheard a conversation which made me understand why. The boys had been throwing a ball around the combination living-dining-room for the dog to retrieve, and had dropped to the floor to rest when Jonny said dreamily as if a long-suppressed memory was forcing its way back into his consciousness, "We used to have a dog called Bottle when we lived in Plymouth."

He was silent for a minute and then said, "Desmond, what happened to Bottle?"

I looked up from my book to see that Desmond's face had turned red as he said in a furious, choked-up voice, "You know perfectly well what happened. We couldn't bring him with us so we had to have him put away."

It occurred to me that Jonny had not understood what was meant by the term "put away."

It turned out that the two Croft boys enjoyed walking on the prairie as much as we did, so that autumn the four of us and Sweeney went out most afternoons after J.B. got home from work. We were usually joined by half a dozen children who lived on the street. J.B. told them about the birds and flowers we saw on our way. He is a walking story-book of fascinating information about natural history and always talks to children as if they were adults. The members of the walk-club were interested in what he had to say and treated him as an equal, talking to him the way they did to one another.

Later they became members of the Elm Street Bird Club, founded by J.B. after so many children kept coming to him with questions about birds. The club members not only went on bird walks with us but took part in an annual competition by writing an essay about birds or bird behaviour they had observed on their own. Prizes, Taverner's *Birds of Canada* and a bird chart, were presented to the authors of the two best essays at either a wiener roast on the prairie or an ice-cream bust in our house, depending on the weather or the voracity of the latest hatch of mosquitoes.

On many weekend evenings we played games with Desmond and Jonny—word games and other mind-stretchers of the kind my brother John and I used to play with Aunt Folly when we were children. We enjoyed those evenings as much as the boys did. On week nights, after their school homework was done, we often read aloud to them before they went to bed or told them stories.

We rode horseback in the winters throughout the war, often with Desmond and Jonny Croft and always with Sweeney. We went riding on the Christmas Day of 1940 after we had heard on the radio that Hong Kong had fallen and the Winnipeg Grenadiers and the Royal Rifles had been taken prisoner by the Japanese. Many of our friends were with the Grenadiers and we were depressed and unhappy that morning but we did not think it right to disappoint the little boys, so we rode as we had promised them we would.

It was a very cold, clear day, after a light snowfall the night before. The trees were covered with a soft, white powder that glistened in the sunlight under the blue sky and turned the prairie into a fairyland of beauty. That beauty was almost unbearable because of what the men across the Pacific were enduring and what their wives were suffering behind the closed doors of little houses in different parts of Winnipeg. There was something terribly poignant about the clear English voices, brittle as the icing on the trees, of the children, refugees from war, who laughed and talked as they rode beside us.

"Merry Christmas! Merry Christmas!" they had said that morning but there was no merriness in our hearts.

Eleven months later, on December 7, 1941, J.B. and I had just come in from riding when we heard that the Japanese had bombed Pearl Harbor. We were feeling relaxed and yet exhilarated by the cold air and exercise and were hungrily eating beef sandwiches and drinking beer when the incredible news came to us over the radio. J.B. tore upstairs to take off his riding boots and dress to go down to the office to help get out an extra. I drove to Ruth Riley's house and the two of us sat all afternoon listening to the radio and talking about the wey we felt. Ruth and I are both American-born Canadians. At that time, General Harold Riley was the Commandant of the military district and Ruth had been up to her neck in war work as I had been. As Canadians we both felt utterly committed to the winning of the war. Yet that afternoon we both found in ourselves, to our astonishment, a whole range of emotions that had not yet been touched. Knowing my younger brother, Shan, I was sure that he would not stay out of the fight, and the sharp pain of that knowledge made me have a fresh understanding of the way J.B. had been feeling for two years. Up until then, I had thought I did understand, as I certainly did intellectually, but it was not until my own blood was threatened that I understood emotionally.

During the five years that Phyllis Croft and her four children were in Canada, we were always aware that if Charles Croft were killed—and there was every likelihood that he might not survive the desert campaign—J.B. would be responsible for his family for a long time. We knew it might be a very long time if Britain were defeated, as seemed possible then as we began to hear leaks about the devastating effects of the submarine campaign and the bombing of the West Coast ports. In order to prepare the boys for an uncertain future where an elitist education such as we had might be a disadvantage, we felt they should go to a Winnipeg public school along with the children of most of our friends. We felt that learning to understand and get along with different kinds of people is as important as book learning. We had come to the conclusion that Canadian public schools prepare children much better for life in this century than the class-conscious, socially segregated private schools. Phyllis agreed to this wholeheartedly. Many Canadian private schools were providing free tuition for English war guests, so it was not a matter of money, as far as we were concerned, but of what sort of education would be most useful in an unpredictable future.

Not knowing what sort of world Desmond and Jonny might inherit, we did our best to make them as self-sufficient as possible. On Sundays, when Louise was off duty, I gave Desmond a primary course in cooking and assigned both boys a share of the household chores to make them feel part of the home team. I felt then, as I do now, that it is just as important for a man to be able to cook and run a house as it is for a woman, since so often the traditional roles are, and should be, inter-changeable.

J.B. and I were quite aware that we were faced with a delicate psychological situation for ourselves as well as for the children. We wanted to give the boys a feeling of security and that required making them aware of our affection. At the same time we understood, being childless, that we must not allow ourselves to become so deeply involved with them that we began to regard them as our own children and become possessive. We considered it essential to prepare them not only to stay in Canada if necessary, but also to go back to England, and above all never to allow them to feel that we were more important to them than their parents. That was easier for me than for J.B. because Phyllis was nearby and saw them constantly. On the other hand, their father was far away and his image was bound to fade as time went on so that J.B. would become the essential father figure children need so much.

J.B. was sensitive to this problem and talked a great deal about Charles Croft, telling the boys slightly embroidered tales about the prowess and exploits of their father when he was at university. In these graphic accounts of college rags and student pranks Charles somehow appeared up front every time. J.B.'s affection and admiration for Charles made this easy for him. Both of us would have felt a devastating sense of failure if the two older boys had not been able to adjust them-selves to life with both their parents in England when the war was over.

J.B. and I had done our best to have children of our own. We enjoyed a splendid, uninhibited sex life—we had that "fullness of life" my mother used to talk about—but we missed out on children. Giving birth to a child is for a woman one of the great human experiences, and since I have always wanted to embrace experience, to feel, to know and to understand all that there is for a human being to know, for a time I regretted never having given birth to a child. I wanted J.B.'s child but was not interested in adopting children in order to have children in the home or to satisfy some sort of maternal urge or to conform to social pressure. As it is, my life has been so full that the initial, brief regret at not having had children of our own passed very quickly. I think now that my life would have been less useful, less interesting and certainly more restricted if we had had children.

As it is, we have been fortunate in having a few close friends among the younger generation. Desmond and Jonny gave us great pleasure during the war because they were so intelligent, sensitive and receptive. The bond between us and the young Crofts has widened our horizons and has been one of the greatest continuing joys of our later life. Desmond became a distinguished physician and his research has given him an international reputation. He has visited us in Canada a couple of times, and we have often stayed with him and his wife in London. Benny is also a brilliant research physician. We lost touch with Jonny for a while when as a young man he settled in Kenya but have seen him occasionally since he became a probation officer in London.

We also have a long-lasting, warm and loving relationship with J.B.'s niece and nephew who stayed with us in Ottawa for many months. We are both devoted to my niece, Rita, the daughter of my brother John, who in many ways is like a younger edition of myself. And we have great affection for Shan's son, Peter, and his youngest daughter, Jane.

Phyllis Croft was not well for a long time after her daughter was born. After a year or so, however, she regained her strength and energy and carried on with her plan to keep the family together. Jonny went to stay with her in the boarding house when, to our amazement, Granny Lee, full of spirit, went to Kenya as planned, seemingly quite unperturbed by the prospect of such a long and difficult journey on seas teeming with German U-boats.

One day in the summer of 1941 Phyllis asked us to come and see her. When we arrived, she announced that Charles had somehow managed to send her a little money from Africa. She told us she had decided to live in a small place where life was simpler and less expensive than in Winnipeg, and had rented a small house at Stonewall. She had decided to keep the two younger children and the baby with her and to send Desmond to stay with friends on a nearby farm so that she could see him more often than if he stayed with us in Winnipeg. She thought that at first three children was all she could manage but planned to have him with her later if all went well.

The house at Stonewall turned out to be a tiny workman's cottage, with running water in the kitchen but without an indoor toilet or bathroom. J.B. and I were impressed by Phyllis' courage in deliberately taking on so much privation in the rugged Manitoba climate, but had grave doubts about her ability to make a go of it. Certainly at first she had a terribly tough, lonely and worrying time which left her often on the edge of physical and nervous exhaustion. But somehow her extraordinary will to survive, her sheer gut courage, carried her through.

She grew amazingly. Phyllis was, in fact, one of the great success stories of the war. She learned to cook and to feed her children adequately in spite of ration books and an infinitesimal budget. In the summer she cultivated a large vegetable garden and did a lot of canning. After two years, she had at last all her children around her again; Desmond left the farm and went to live with her. He was by then a strong boy of twelve and his help was needed not only with chores but as an intelligent companion.

As time went on, Phyllis also made a place for herself in the community. She took up curling and played an active part in amateur theatricals. She was an inspiring example of the way a woman, who for years uses only a small portion of her ability, can realize her hitherto undeveloped potential under the pressure of harsh necessity.

During the late summer and autumn of 1940 and the winter of 1941 I was on the run all day and every day making arrangements for the Croft family, handling the publicity for the Central Volunteer Bureau, writing my weekly column about the volunteer work of women and attending interminable, incessant committees dealing with the placement of volunteers, the care of English "war guests" and the expansion of services for men in the Armed Forces.

During this period something occurred which increased my understanding of what can happen to a woman who is poor and ignorant, and who is by law denied the help she needs. Our dear housekeeper, Louise Bricknell, had to undergo surgery, and while she was in hospital I hired a young woman, Emma, to take her place until she was well enough to work again. Emma was a cheerful, obliging person, but rather stupid and forgetful. However, I thought I was lucky to have found her; housekeepers were scarce because so many women were working in factories, driving taxis and trucks, and quite generally taking over the jobs left by the men who had enlisted.

When we first arrived in Winnipeg, the going wage for a maid was fifteen to twenty dollars a month and sometimes as low as twelve for a girl fresh in from the country. At that time, when I said I thought that no young woman could stay respectable on that sort of pay, I had been ticked off severely by the wife of the publisher of *The Winnipeg Tribune* who told me that by raising the going wage I was making it hard for other people to employ household help. During the dirty thirties, when deflation made the price of wheat and everything else dirt cheap, many housewives exploited servants as they have always done when they could get away with it. After the Second World War created labour shortages, the same housewives were astonished and loud with complaints when they found that women preferred almost any other kind of paid employment to working long, unspecified hours for a pittance, under the constant, often nagging supervision of another woman.

I realized when I hired Emma that she was not very bright, but she was a pair of hands that freed me from household chores and gave me the time I needed to carry out other obligations which seemed to me to be more important and certainly more satisfying. She was a scrawny country girl, but she put on weight after she came to us, probably, I thought, because I was making good use of our ration books to enable us to have plenty of nourishing food.

One night, just before dawn, I was awakened by Emma's voice saying over and over again, "Mrs. Bird! Mrs. Bird!"

She had crawled half-way up the stairs and was holding onto the banister, unable to go further. When I put on my dressing-gown and went to her she kept saying, "Oh Mrs. Bird, help me. Oh God, please help me."

She was obviously in agony. I helped her back to her room and told her to lie down. She threw herself on the bed and her body began to arch in spasms of pain. She made little gasping sounds like an animal. Her face was flushed, and when I touched her she felt burning hot, I realized that she was running a high temperature. Tears ran down her cheeks and sweat stood in beads on her forehead. There was blood on the bed and her nightgown was soaked with it.

I went upstairs and telephoned a doctor who came quickly. He did not stay with Emma for very long. When he left her, he telephoned for an ambulance.

"What's wrong with her?" I asked.

"She's having a miscarriage," he said, "probably self-induced."

I was horrified. "You mean she has committed an abortion on herself?" I asked, wondering if I could have misunderstood him.

"It often happens," he said. "Sometimes they do it with a knitting needle, sometimes with a coat-hanger. It's against the law, of course. She could be put in prison for it. But I'm just saying it's a miscarriage. I don't know what started it and neither do you. My only interest is to keep her from dying."

As he put on his coat, he said, "You're going to have a bit of cleaning up to do down there. It would be kind not to discuss it with anyone, not unless you want to get the poor woman into more trouble than she is in already."

I stayed with Emma until the ambulance men put her on a stretcher and carried her away. She was quiet now and her face was no longer flushed, but white and strangely sunken.

When I went downstairs to clean up her room, I found that the bed was soaked with blood. There were buckets of bloodstained towels in her room and more of them in the bathroom. I wondered how it was possible for one small body to lose so much blood and yet retain life. I wept with pity as I sponged the mattress and washed the sheets and blankets.

Emma did live. I went to see her while she was in hospital, but after she was discharged she went back to her people who lived on a farm.

In March, 1941, J.B. went to England to report the spring blitz on London. I tasted then a little of what so many other women had been going through for two years and were to endure for another four. I knew from his dispatches that he was roof-watching on the nights he wasn't finding out what went on in the deep shelters of the London Underground railway or among the demolished buildings after the "all-clear" sounded. Every morning I would read, with a feeling of dull terror, the huge headlines about the rain of death over London, the fires and the people being dug out from under the rubble. Later, in the evening papers, with a flood of relief, I would read what J.B. had written and be comforted by the thought that he had come through another night and was still alive. Yet I was lucky compared with Phyllis who went for months without a word from Charles. I had thought I understood her suffering and that of my other friends whose husbands were on active duty, but it was only when my own man was in palpable danger that I understood emotionally as well as intellectually what it is like to walk with fear day in and day out and to sleep with it during the night.

Being busy was a help because it kept me from thinking too much. Like my friends, I did all the things that needed to be done and didn't complain: there were so many other women who were having a much worse time. For hours on end I would forget that J.B. was in London and then, all at once, I would remember with a feeling of utter misery and depression.

When J.B. came home in June we took a week off to fish at the Lake of the Woods. There both of us felt as if our senses had been reborn so that we were newly aware of the spruce trees, the contours of the rugged shore line, the shimmer of the water, the physical delight of being young, with lungs full of clean air, muscles relaxed from much exercise, stomach content with much eating and drinking. It was wonderful to be together again.

The war taught many Canadian women, including me, that up until then we had only used a small amount of our potential ability and energy. We found we were able to do things that we had never done before or considered doing. And we knew that as women we had made a great contribution to the war effort. This knowledge had a lasting effect, not only on women but on our whole society. When the war was over it was taken for granted by governments and industry that all the married, gainfully employed women, who had successfully filled men's shoes in factories and at other jobs hitherto not open to women, would consider their place to be in the home and stop working as soon as the men in the Armed Services returned from overseas. That did not happen. A few married women did return to full-time work in the kitchen, the laundry and the nursery, but not nearly as many as had been expected and not to anything like the same extent that American women did. Many Canadian women had found they could run their homes, bring up their children and work for pay, often without the help of a husband, and they saw no reason why they should not go on doing what they were able to do.

After the First World War there was a song about soldiers: "How are you going to keep them down on the farm now that they've seen Paree?" For Canadian women after the Second World War the song should have been: "How are you going to keep them shut in the home now that they have had money of their own, the feeling of independence, new interests and the satisfaction of working for a goal as part of a team?"

The answer was that by 1957 the participation rate of women in the labour force was as high as it had been in 1947. And every year since then an increasing number of married women have gone to work.

It is a sad comment on our society that it required the tragedy of the First World War to give women their political rights and the disaster of the Second World War to force governments and women themselves to begin to recognize women's economic rights as individuals and their potential contribution to the economy of the nation.

During the First World War so many women replaced so many men so well that no government would have had the gall to insist that the "ladies" were either too delicate or too dumb to vote and hold public office. Consequently Parliament gave women those federal rights in 1920. It was not until 1928, however, that the Judicial Committee of the Privy Council in Britain overruled a decision of the Supreme Court of Canada and declared that women are "persons" and so have a right to sit in the Senate of Canada. It was not until 1940 that women in Quebec were given the franchise. Regrettably in the years since then women have not fully exercised their political rights, and only a few of them are found in the power structure of political organizations and government.

Since the end of World War II, women have made an enormous contribution to the economy, but in spite of equal pay laws and the noble sentiments expressed in the Canadian Bill of Rights and the United Nations Universal Declaration of Human Rights, they still do not have their economic rights. For example, they are frequently paid less than men when they do work of equal value and responsibility and are often not given the promotions they would have received if they had been men with similar qualifications.

The truth is that women are still in a transitional stage between the not-so-distant past when they were second-class citizens and the still distant future when they will participate fully, without discrimination in every aspect of our society.

Broadcasting

When Desmond and Jonny Croft were staying with us they used to ask us about Greece, Crete and Africa, where their father had been with General Montgomery's Eighth Army during the long campaign. They wanted to know why there was a war which had changed their lives so much and, worried and perplexed, kept asking us about the news they heard over the radio which they didn't understand. We found that when we explained as best we could what was happening and why and told them about the history of the places where the Allies were fighting in Europe and Africa, they seemed objectively interested and less nervous and apprehensive.

Those were tense days for intelligent children because of the anxiety of adults, communicated to them by a sort of emotional osmosis, and the prevailing atmosphere of worry due to the news, which was nearly always bad. Fear was all around us in the air. For me, Lorne Greene is not a father figure, the just and wise man of Bonanza, but is instead the voice of doom reading the CBC ten o'clock news at night, bringing the shock of the fall of Hong Kong, the Dieppe raid, the destruction of convoys by wolf-packs of submarines, the burning of London, the bombing of Coventry, the attack on Pearl Harbor. The news of death, destruction and defeat went on and on. As I listened night after night I kept thinking that background newscasts, written in simple language and delivered in a calm, assured voice, might help children to understand what was happening and so allay their fears.

One day, in the summer of 1941, I read about a survey of newspaper readers and radio listeners made in rural Manitoba. It showed that only five per cent of the families in the country took newspapers regularly,

181

while about 90 per cent had radios. Many of those people were New Canadians whose mother tongue was either German, Ukrainian or Polish. I thought those people, many of whom still had a limited command of English, might listen to the sort of newscast I had in mind for students in junior high and high schools. I developed a Messianic fervour about the idea. After churning it over for many days, I remembered that audiences in Montreal had liked my lectures on international affairs, and with that memory came the conviction that I ought to write and deliver the background newscasts myself. It never occurred to me to doubt my ability to do it.

I had only made one broadcast in my life, the amateur one about the Patriotic Salvage Corps, and knew nothing about the process involved except that we listened to the radio constantly and had strong theories about what was good and what was bad. I knew the CBC wouldn't consider putting me on the air so I decided to persuade a local station to hire me. The Government of Manitoba owned CKY, a station covering most of rural Manitoba as well as the Winnipeg area; so, acting on the sound principle that if you want to get things done you go to the man at the top, I went to see Premier Bracken. He was enthusiastic about my idea and told me the provincial government had for some time been concerned about the way many people on the prairies were listening to German propaganda beamed by short wave from Europe. He gave me every encouragement and made an appointment for me to see Ivan Schultz, the Minister of Education, since I had said that the broadcasts ostensibly should be aimed at school children. Mr. Schultz liked the idea and said he thought such a program could, if properly done, help morale as well as have considerable educational value as a supplement to history and current events classes in the schools. He said he would speak to Mr. Backhouse, the manager of CKY, and arranged an appointment for me at the studio.

Mr. Backhouse obviously regarded me as a nuisance. He listened to me in silence, with a bored expression on his tired face, as I explained in detail the sort of thing I wanted to do. I could feel his antagonism, and became more and more hesitant, repetitive and disjointed in my exposition. After I had come to a halting stop, he said, not unkindly but certainly devastatingly as far as I was concerned, "Mrs. Bird, you're just a society woman with a bright idea. You haven't the slightest idea of how much discipline and hard work goes into writing and delivering a series of broadcasts day after day, week after week. You couldn't possibly stand it. You wouldn't be able to last a month."

I wanted to cry. I wanted to knock him down. I thought that some-how he must have found out about my having left Bryn Mawr to "come out" in society, and wondered despairingly if I would ever be able to live down that year when I had been so young, so troubled, so selfish and so unhappy after Father died. I realized I could never make Mr. Backhouse understand that for the last twelve years I had disciplined myself to write and to study, and had learned a great deal about history and public affairs. I was aware I didn't look like the prototype of a serious professional woman and realized that I still had a Philadelphia drawl with the precise diction of Bryn Mawr College superimposed on top of it, which made me sound affected to some people. I thought of my five novels and all those rejection slips and wondered if I were going to be rejected again. I was like the proverbial drowning man whose life is supposed to pass before him in the few seconds before he becomes unconscious.

Fortunately my adrenal gland always gives me the fighting juice I need when I'm on a spot, so that afternoon I did not cry and I did not give Backhouse a clip on the jaw as I wanted to do. And I didn't resort to feminine wiles or turn on charm, because I thought that would be disgusting; that was not the way I wanted to get the job. I only said, very quietly, "I know I can do it. I'm sure it's worth doing. Please, just give me a try."

I guess Ivan Schultz had asked Backhouse to put me on the air as an experiment because when I refused to be daunted and kept saying, "I know I can do it," he didn't argue, but said I could start after Labour Day in September. I said it had to be a professional, not a volunteer arrangement, so he offered to pay me $20 a week for a five-minute broadcast every Monday, Wednesday and Friday at 5:15 in the after-noon. After taxation, he said, my take-home pay would be $18 a week. I was entirely satisfied with the offer, being aware that getting the pro-gram on the air was the important thing, although it was of course essential to be paid even so small a sum in order to establish the agree-ment on a professional basis. Right then I was also motivated by an intense fury, by a fierce passion to show Mr. Backhouse what I could do. Unwittingly, he had used the one argument guaranteed to make me dig in my heels.

It never occurred to me that at the age of thirty-three I had found myself a career.

I wrote my first broadcast very quickly and easily on a Monday morning and was pleased with myself. But when I timed it on the electric clock which hung over the refrigerator in the kitchen, I was stunned to find that it took me ten minutes to read it. I went upstairs and cut ruthlessly, retyped it, and timed it again. It was two-and-a-half minutes too long. I stood, looking at the teapot-shaped clock, with its relentless second hand. I was sure something was wrong with it and compared it with my wrist-watch. There was nothing wrong with it.

By three o'clock in the afternoon, after working since nine in the morning, I had managed to cut the script down to five minutes. But I had tried to stuff too many ideas into it, and it was disjointed after the cutting—in no way what I wanted it to be. I felt perhaps Backhouse had been right. In fact I might not last a week, let alone a month.

When I arrived at the studio at half past four, nobody seemed to know that I was expected. The receptionist told me to wait on a bench in the outer office. There I sat for half an hour looking at the clock and wondering if anybody was going to tell me what to do. When Andrew Cowan had produced my Salvage Corps broadcast for the CBC he had carefully gone over the script with me, helped me cut it, suggested changes in the text, and had in fact edited it professionally. He had timed it twice to make sure I would not feel hurried and had corrected my pronunciation of a couple of words. He had brought me a glass of water when I went into the studio, and had quite generally held my hand when he saw how nervous I was. I didn't know that CKY didn't have producers, and became even more unnerved than I was already when a young announcer came down the corridor and told me to follow him.

"You're in there," he said, pointing to a door. "You'll have to get off the air in four minutes and forty seconds, so keep your eye on the clock."

"I thought it was a five-minute broadcast," I said, feeling my throat beginning to shut with nervousness.

"I have to have twenty seconds to sign you off and make the station identification," he said.

"What on earth shall I do?"

"Cut it. You're not on for another ten minutes."

He disappeared into a door beside the one he had shown me. I was trembling so badly I could hardly hold a pencil, but I cut out what I thought was twenty seconds' worth and timed it on the clock in the hall. It only took ten seconds. "I'll have to talk fast, that's all," I thought, as the second hand on the clock seemed to tear forward and I realized I had only thirty seconds before air time.

I went through the designated door into a tiny studio. There was a lectern, and I stood there, looking at a window opening into the control room where the engineer was sitting. I could see the announcer out of the tail of my eye in another studio at the side. The second hand on the clock made another unbelievable jump ahead and I heard the announcer say, "We now bring you *Behind the Headlines* with Winnipeg commentator Anne Francis."

The red light on top of the lectern turned green and a horrible croaking sound came out of my mouth. I read too fast, stumbling often, in my attempt to make up those ten seconds. I went on and on forever, so it seemed. At last I said, "This is Anne Francis speaking from Winnipeg," and the show was over.

During the last thirty seconds, when I had been racing that relentless second hand, I had been aware that the door behind me had opened stealthily and that someone was standing behind me breathing down my neck. As I picked up my script and went out I could see two figures filling the small space in the studio.

The announcer had neglected to tell me that Mercer McLeod and his wife collaborated on a slightly dramatized form of short-story reading which went on the air right after me. They had to get to the lectern and be all set to go while I was getting out of the studio. Later I found out that on some days they used to bring props with them, bells and things, which they occasionally dropped by accident.

Behind the Headlines was scheduled to come on right after a five-minute spot in which Gordon Sinclair, then a roving reporter for *The Toronto Star,* gave a short, snappy talk about his adventures shooting lions in Africa, charming snakes in India, or climbing the Himalayas. It was a good spot because both Gordon and the McLeods had a strong following, but that day I felt it was too much to have unexpected company behind me as I wound up my broadcast. However, I was determined not to let anybody know how nervous I was—unaware that my trembling hand and shaky voice advertised my "butterflies."

Fortunately, that first day J.B. had come down to the studio, and was waiting outside the door making V-for-Victory signs. He gave me many encouraging words as we drove home, and was full of suggestions about the script which helped me a great deal.

It took many weeks before I was able to get on to the knack of writing a four-minute-and-forty-second broadcast in less than four hours, after I had done the necessary research and checking. It took even longer to learn to put myself on and off the air, since there was no producer, without having my insides turn to water with nervousness. At the studio my comings and goings three times a week were treated with indifference.

Nobody told me whether I was good or bad or had any suggestions to offer.

Several things that happened during that time taught me a lot about the broadcasting game. Once when I was describing the work of the St. John's Ambulance Corps, I wanted to say "the halt, the lame and the blind," but instead said "the halt, the lime and the blamed," and then laughed loudly, almost breaking the microphone. That taught me not to write clichés because your mind goes to sleep on them and your tongue can make a mistake. It also taught me not to hesitate or stop talking, and certainly not to laugh after making a fluff.

Another time I forgot to check the sequence of the pages of my script and when I turned a page found that the next one was upside down. In my effort to get it right side up, ad-libbing all the time to avoid dead air, I hit the microphone with my engagement ring, making what sounded rather like a bomb explosion to the listeners. Afterwards J.B., who listened loyally on the radio in his office whenever he could, said that my ad-libbing had been fine, except that I had reversed the British and the Germans and had the wrong side advancing across the desert. That taught me to make sure the pages of a script were in the right succession and right side up before I started to broadcast.

Once a handsome young announcer named Tommy Benson, later to become CBC brass, went to sleep in the adjoining studio. I kept looking at him in consternation, slurring my words and stumbling as I kept wondering what would happen when it was time for him to sign me off the air. I needn't have worried because he woke up with a jerk when I finished, gave me a mocking gamin glance, leaned toward the mike and said in a mellifluous voice, "Listen to Anne Francis again on Friday at the same time." That taught me to concentrate on getting my words off the paper and not to worry about what other people were supposed to do.

When I took on the broadcasts, I resigned from the executive of the Central Volunteer Bureau and all the committees concerned with community welfare and war work but kept on writing my Saturday column about women on the home front. After a month or two I was able to write a five-minute script in a couple of hours, which gave me more time to read and study and get on top of the subjects that flashed into the news. I used to look at the teletype in the radio station a few minutes before air-time and learned how to rewrite a paragraph quickly if there was a new development in the news, using my stop-watch to time what I had cut out or put in. I had invested in a stop-watch after I began to get a trickle of favourable fan letters and found it was a relief not to have to stand in front of the refrigerator looking at the clock when I timed the script.

I wrote and delivered the scripts on Mondays, Wednesdays and Fridays and wrote my column on Thursdays for the Saturday paper. That made Tuesday my day off. When someone asked me what I did on my day off, I said I went shopping for the week's supply of food, did the mending and darning, answered letters, paid the bills, had my hair washed, and went riding or took a walk on the prairie.

"I have a lovely relaxed day on Tuesdays," I said.

As the winter of 1942 wore on I began to receive letters about *Behind the Headlines* from all sorts of adults as well as children. School teachers urged their pupils to listen and then to write compositions about what they thought of the program. Their remarks, sent along to me by their teachers, were encouraging. The one I liked best came from a girl in junior high school who wrote, "I like you because you don't talk to us as if we was two years old." I liked that because it indicated that even though I used simple language I was not talking down.

Desmond and Jonny Croft were helpful critics, listening faithfully and never hesitating to say what they thought if they found me obscure or dull.

After eight months, although I was learning a lot by a hit-and-miss, trial-and-error method, I realized that I needed a producer to help me edit my copy and improve my delivery. I thought that, since the reaction to the series had been so good, I might have a chance to get a contract with the CBC for the following winter season. Accordingly I went to see Bud Walker, then head of the Western Network. He said he had been listening to me, liked the broadcasts, and was prepared to give me a fifteen-minute spot every Monday, Wednesday and Friday for thirteen weeks, beginning the following September. (It was May by then and winter programs were going off the air.)

After my last broadcast on CKY, I went to see Backhouse to tell him the CBC was putting me on in the autumn. That was one of my finest hours. He shook me by the hand and said, "Mrs. Bird, I owe you an apology. I never thought you could do it. The broadcasts have been a remarkable success."

That time I was even nearer to crying than when he had said I was just a society woman with a bright idea.

In the summer I went to New York for a few days and worked on my voice with Gloria Chandler, the radio consultant for the Association of

Junior Leagues. She believed in my broadcasts and did everything she could to make my voice sound as if I weren't sucking peppermints or trying to swallow gumdrops when I talked. She was a tough coach and helped me a lot. My ambition was to speak international English without any strong regional accent.

In the autumn of 1942, a few days before my new program *Headline History* was scheduled to go on the Western Network of the CBC, I had a telephone call from Bud Walker's secretary saying that the program might be cancelled, and was, in any case, not going to go on as planned. I was desolate and desperate; I couldn't imagine what had happened and didn't know what to do about it. Four days later I had a call saying all was well and the program would start the next week. I found out later that the head of the department of public affairs in Toronto—or perhaps it was the head of the news department—had reached the conclusion that a woman could not handle news in wartime and had decided to scratch the program. When the word came to Winnipeg, Bud Walker took the next plane to Toronto and gave his personal guarantee that I could do it. The following week, *Headline History* went on the air. It stayed on for twenty-six weeks that year and for twenty-six weeks each of the following three years.

I soon found that a fifteen-minute broadcast, even when I broke it up in the middle with a couple of minutes of music, required much more solid information than a five-minute talk. In order to find the material I needed I spent a great deal of time in the Winnipeg Public Library where the reference librarian was a whizz at finding me all sorts of interesting, colourful books and magazine articles about the places in Europe and Africa and Asia that came into the news spotlight. I used to telephone her early in the mornings, and by the time I reached the library, an hour or so later, my work table would be piled high with books, the relevant passages marked by strips of paper. She also dug up biographical material if I decided to talk about a personality. The Sunday edition of *The New York Times* and the magazines and books in our own library usually supplied me with the political background of the events. I had a great deal to learn, and as a rule studied on the nights I didn't go out or have friends in for a drink or a meal.

Headline History was produced by Dan Cameron, the brother of the CBC's perennial reader of the news, Earl Cameron. He was an extraordinarily handsome man, dark-haired, dark-eyed, whose naturally saturnine features were softened by his kindness, gentleness, and irrepressible sense of humour. Like Bud Walker, he believed a woman *could* analyze the war news from an historical perspective and was determined I could prove it.

Dan turned out to be a tough, demanding perfectionist—just what I needed. He put in a lot of effort on my scripts, working through them with me patiently and relentlessly. I often swore at him when he tore my paragraphs to pieces or tossed out the purple passages I had slaved over for hours, but I knew I was learning what I needed to learn and struggled on under his insistent demands that I do better. When I went on the air he would give me the confidence I needed by either smiling at me through the glass or looking deeply interested. I was always nervous but I began to suffer less when the light in the studio turned green. In those days all broadcasts were live—not put on tape before air time as so many are today.

After I had been doing *Headline History* for a year, I re-angled the scripts for American audiences and sold them to three American radio stations in parts of the country far removed from one another. The extra pay enabled me to engage a secretary, Margaret Brend, who saved me a great deal of time and increased my productivity considerably.

One autumn, J.B. and I took a ten-day fishing holiday at Kenora. We felt we had to get away from the unremitting pressure of the dreary news, and we didn't read a newspaper or listen to the radio once during all that time. When I came back one of my first broadcasts was about General MacArthur in the Philippines. I said that when he returned to the islands, MacArthur would not set himself up as a Gauleiter but instead would make sure that Manuel Quezon, the elected president, would return to office. After I got home the telephone rang. It was George Ferguson, of *The Winnipeg Free Press*. He said that he and Bruce Hutchison had been listening to my broadcast, which was excellent, but still they thought I ought to know, because I was sending scripts to the States, that Quezon had died of T.B. at Saranac a couple of weeks before. I thanked him, wired the American stations to kill the unfortunate sentence in my script, and telephoned Dan Cameron to say I was prepared to resign at once. He assured me that would not be necessary because, he said, everybody made mistakes and he himself was equally guilty for not having known that Quezon was dead.

In 1945, when Franklin Roosevelt died, Dan asked me, on very short notice, to give a tribute to the American President on behalf of the women of Canada. Roosevelt was one of my heroes, so I was emotionally involved as well as upset by having to dress, write a five-minute talk in an hour, and drive to the studio. When I read the script through in rehearsal, my glasses kept misting up so I couldn't see, and once or twice my voice broke. I was furious when Dan said, "Tailspin Annie. I'm not going to put you on. You're nothing but a cry-baby."

"Like hell, I am," I said. "I'm going on. How dare you talk like that?"

Afterwards, when I had given the broadcast in a steady voice, I brushed past him in the corridor without speaking. He followed me and said, "I had to do that. I knew if I made you mad you'd be O.K. That was a swell show."

Although some of my friends knew Florence Bird wrote under the name of Anne Francis, most people did not. Often people, unaware that I was Anne Francis, would talk to me about the *Tribune's* column on women's war work on the homefront, or about the *Behind the Headlines* broadcasts while I sat silent, listening with amusement to their comments. Sometimes I would defend Anne Francis in an objective, unemotional way when people disagreed with her opinions. Other times I would grin from ear to ear inside myself when they praised her work.

One morning J.B.'s secretary, Gwen Amos, his right hand and loyal friend, telephoned me. She was laughing so hard she could hardly speak. She told me that on the previous evening a matron in the circulation department of *The Winnipeg Tribune* had telephoned and asked if she might step upstairs for a few minutes. When she arrived, breathless with excitement, she said, "Miss Amos, Miss Amos! The editor is taking her out. Isn't it awful?"

She went on to say that her daughters had been at the St. Charles Country Club to dance two Saturday nights in succession, and each time they had seen John Bird dancing and drinking and having a great time with the same woman.

"And guess what, Miss Amos! The girls asked around and found out who she is. She's that Anne Francis who broadcasts for the CBC! He's carrying on with her, Miss Amos. Mark my word, he's carrying on with her."

I was highly amused, and so was J.B. He said, "Next time she mentions it, tell her the editor not only dances with Anne Francis, but takes her home and spends the night with her."

By the summer of 1944, we began to believe that victory was in sight for the allies. Charles Croft, after having been evacuated from Greece and Crete when German troops poured down into the Balkans in 1941, had been made head of Mobile Hospital No. 1 and had gone through the whole North African campaign wheeling back and forth across the desert as Montgomery and Rommel played their deadly game of tag. After Alamein his hospital had gone to Sicily with the 8th Army and was by then moving up the boot of Italy as the German Army retreated after Italy surrendered. He wrote to us frequently, saying he was worried about the schooling at a little place like Stonewall, and that the two older boys were reaching the age when he thought they should be sent to boarding school when they returned to England. J.B. was also worried—about Desmond in particular, since at fourteen he was not getting the tuition in Latin and French he would need to enter an English Public School. After talking the matter over with Phyllis, we arranged to send him to St. John's College School in Winnipeg as a five-day pupil. That was fortunate for us because he spent many week-ends at our place.

Although the war years in Winnipeg were a time of worry and strain, they were also immensely satisfying years for me because I was doing work I found fascinating and absorbing. I felt I was making a useful contribution to the war effort as well as learning a great deal about international affairs.

As time went on I did all sorts of radio programs. Once, during the summer months, I wrote twenty-one five-minute dramas as a volunteer effort for the War Savings Bond drive. The corny little spots concerned a bond salesman, Joe Victory Man, who told his wife, when he came home in the evening, why various people had bought bonds that day. A professional actor and actress did the show free of charge and Esse Ljungh produced it at seven o'clock in the evening on a local station owned by *The Winnipeg Free Press*. At first I worked with Esse at the studio, but when the show was going well I listened at home to see how it sounded in a normal listening atmosphere. One night I was astonished to hear that Joe Victory Man had developed a strong Swedish accent remarkably like that of Esse Ljungh. When the show was over, I telephoned Esse who told me Joe had not turned up so he'd had to read the script himself. While he was on the air he had seen the missing man looking through the control room glass with a pale and anguished face. It turned out that the unhappy actor had gone to the lavatory in the *Free Press* building on his way to the studio and had locked himself in. He had banged on the door and yelled for half an hour before the janitor had heard him and forced the door open but by then the show was on the air.

J.B. and I were young and strong during the war years, so that although we both worked very hard during the day and long into the night, we found time to lead a varied social life. We tried to spend the week-ends together, riding horseback and having people in for meals or going to the houses of friends.

Winnipeg is Canada's navel, one of the transit centres of the world. Many people used to break their train journeys there on their way east and west. If they were politicians or civil servants, they usually dropped in to see the editor of *The Winnipeg Tribune,* and J.B. often asked them to come to our house for a drink or a meal if he thought they were interesting.

One day J.B. brought John Grierson, the Film Commissioner, for dinner. Grierson came often after that and became a valued friend. He was short and stocky, a man whose soul was too big for his body. I always thought of him as a great towering figure because he was intellectually a giant and was constantly surprised when I noticed how small he looked beside J.B. who is six foot one. He had remarkably alive penetrating eyes, greatly magnified behind thick-lensed glasses, which dominated his face. The son of a Scottish Presbyterian school master, he had an evangelical approach toward film-making and the profound belief that God had touched him on the shoulder. He liked to pose as a tough guy, and expressed his idealism and sophisticated theories in a fruity American vernacular that sounded very odd when delivered with a strong Scottish accent.

Grierson was a man of great personal integrity as well as an innovative genius. He had a gift for finding young men and women with creative talent. When he met someone who impressed him as having unusual intelligence or fresh ideas he would hire him or her at once and then create a job to fit the person instead of following the usual procedure of finding the person to fit the job. Under his leadership, during the war, the Film Board made a vital contribution to Canadian life.

At that time there was a considerable number of first-class women in the production as well as the administration side of the organization. Twenty-five years later that had changed; a study made for the Royal Commission on the Status of Women in Canada revealed that women have been practically phased out of the top managerial and production jobs in the Film Board. In 1970, when he was in Canada lecturing at McGill University, I asked Grierson if women had been satisfactory in his day. He told me that they had turned out to be just as good as the men, although he had originally hired a great many women at all levels because he thought young men would be called up for military service and he wanted to build an operation capable of carrying on successfully when they left.

Occasionally Malcolm MacDonald, the British High Commissioner in Ottawa, would come to see us in Winnipeg when he was making official tours of Canada. He used to tell his staff he had to see J.B. on important business, implying a hush-hush conference on the conduct of the war, but on arrival at our house would talk to J.B. as much about birds as about politics. At that time he was engaged in writing his delightful book *The Birds of Brewery Creek,* now a sort of almanac for Ottawa bird-watchers. He used to get up at dawn on spring and summer mornings and paddle his canoe across the Ottawa River to the estuary of Brewery Creek where he observed a great variety of birds. During three months of winter he went across the ice on skis. Somehow he found time to write about his bird-watching in spite of the pressure of wartime responsibility and the demanding social life of a chief of mission.

Once a Member of Parliament from Saskatchewan, a tall back-bencher named John Diefenbaker, came to Elm Street with his adoring wife Edna. He had a pompadour of curly hair and looked like an intelligent parakeet. He quite evidently dramatized himself as the defender of the underdog. He had a large repertoire of anecdotes which he related in a carefully calculated, cracker-barrel style, and he told us several which we thought were extremely funny. But if anyone had told me then that John Diefenbaker would one day be Prime Minister of Canada, I would have laughed even louder than I did at his jokes. I thought Dief was a simple, corny guy, and had no idea that he was a gifted politician, a fantastically versatile orator, and a man with a consuming desire for power, a combination which was to carry him to the top, even though he lacked the intellectual flexibility and the understanding of French Canada so essential for the Prime Minister of our fragmented country.

In 1945, after he became Minister of National Health and Welfare, Brooke Claxton came to stay for a couple of nights. He was touring the country to sell the idea of Family Allowances (regarded by many as an outrageous form of political bribery), and he had three speeches to make in one day. As he was usually drenched with sweat after a speech, I took a suitcase with a couple of clean shirts up to a suite in the Fort Garry Hotel where Carl Goldenberg was staying while conducting one of the many royal commissions of which he has been chairman. Between speeches Brooke rushed up to Carl's room and changed his shirt. He was glad, he said, that he didn't have to appear on the platform looking like a wilted lettuce leaf.

After Brooke's last speech we went to a party at the house of Phil Chester, the manager of the Hudson's Bay Company. J.B. went home early but Brooke and I stayed on until after midnight, as there was plenty of good food and drink and much good conversation. When we got back to Elm Street, Brooke announced that he was hungry. He said he could never eat when he was lecturing and had been too keyed up to be able to touch food while he was at the Chesters. I cooked large quantities of bacon and eggs and made toast and coffee which he consumed with good appetite. Then we sat by the fire and talked until around 2 a.m., when I went up to bed.

During the night I was wakened by someone moving around the house. I looked out of my door and saw a slit of light under the door of the spare room. It was then five o'clock in the morning. I hoped our guest was not ill but decided to leave him be. At seven o'clock Louise brought me breakfast on a tray, and a minute later Brooke Claxton arrived, barefoot and wearing a dressing-gown over his pyjamas.

"I've been up all night," he said. "I've been making corrections on a final draft of a treatise on military law. Do you mind if I phone my secretary and dictate them to her?"

I said I didn't mind, whereupon he sat cross-legged on the bedroom floor, carefully and patiently dictating changes in the typescript over the phone.

Brooke was a compulsive worker. Though he was deeply disappointed that he never became prime minister, he always dreamed great dreams for Canada. For a time the shine of his idealism was dulled by the demands of political expediency, as is almost always the case with cabinet ministers, but later, when he became chairman of the Canada Council, he found himself again. More than anyone I have ever known, he had a passionate love of his country.

When Ruth Draper, the diseuse, came to Winnipeg for a performance, she stayed at Government House with the Lieutenant Governor and Mrs. McWilliams. I invited her for an early family dinner before her show because the Drapers had been close friends of Cousin Flos La-Farge in New York. It began to snow during the afternoon, and when Ruth Draper arrived on our doorstep she was in a sizzling fury; she had not worn overshoes and her feet were soaking wet. We did our best to appease her by sitting her by the fire, putting a glass of sherry into her hand, and hanging her fragile, high-heeled slippers on the fender to dry. J.B. rushed upstairs to get her my warm slippers.

She kept saying, "I know I'll catch cold. I know I'll get laryngitis and lose my voice. I always catch cold when I get my feet wet. . . ."

When J.B. knelt at her feet to put on the slippers for her, he said, "You have such tiny feet. I'm afraid these are much too big for you."

She cheered up after that and I thought now all would be well. It wasn't, because at dinner J.B. asked her why she had not written any new sketches for years. She replied that people loved the old ones, and as not everyone had heard them all she thought it unnecessary to write any new ones. He urged her to go to England and spend several nights listening to people talk in the air raid shelters in the Underground and then write about the courageous people of the blitz. He kept saying he thought she could do a wonderful job and help the war effort. Ruth Draper kept saying it was quite impossible for her to do it. We left for the theatre after dinner in an atmosphere of polite antagonism.

Afterwards I was told by a close friend of hers that Ruth's creative talent and dried up after Lauro de Bosis, her fiancé, had disappeared several years before. De Bosis was a brilliant young Italian, much younger than Ruth Draper, who detested Mussolini and all his works. One day, in a gallant and futile effort to upset the regime, he flew a single-engine plane over Rome in order to distribute anti-Fascist leaflets. Italian military planes pursued him out over the sea and that was the last that was heard of him. Ruth did not hesitate to use all her considerable influence in efforts to persuade the Italian government to tell her whether he had been shot down to his death or had bailed out and been taken prisoner. She even had an audience with Mussolini, who praised her talent but told her nothing about de Bosis. After Italy came into the war she realized there was no more hope that she would ever know what had happened to him.

In July 1945, after the end of the war in Europe, Charles Croft was given leave to come to Canada so that he might take his family back to England. He spent a month in Stonewall getting to know his wife and children again, and then the Crofts spent a week with us at a camp on the Lake of the Woods. It was a wonderful week, the kind we had dreamed of having when the war was over.

J.B. was tremendously moved by the reunion with his old friend and by finding a new dimension of friendship very different from the light-hearted relationship of their college days. Both J.B. and I had a feeling of relief, of gratitude, of deep inner happiness, that Charles had survived the terrible danger and privations of nearly five years of active service— two years of it in the desert—and was now miraculously reunited with his family in Canada. We found it unbelievably good that the story had a happy ending. We were particularly thankful when Charles told us the house at Plymouth had been damaged by a bomb. But though we had a good feeling about it all, we were also sad, and had a sense of loss because the boys were going out of our lives.

August 14th was to be the Croft family's last day in Winnipeg, and we had arranged to give them dinner at the Manitoba Club before putting them on the boat-train.

When the day arrived our minds were in the Pacific. Hourly we awaited the news that VJ Day had come at last. I drove Desmond and Jonny to join the others at the club just before dinner-time, and when I arrived there was a call from J.B. saying he couldn't possibly leave the office; he was waiting to bring out an "extra" and had to be there to give the go-ahead signal. He said he was not taking any chances about jumping the gun and letting the presses roll prematurely. (Two days before, the CBC had goofed, acting on a false report that Japan had surrendered, by playing a pre-recorded message from Mackenzie King to the Canadian people announcing the end of the war.) J.B. told me to give the Crofts his love and to come to the office as soon as possible. He wanted me to be ready to produce broadcasts by him and four other members of the editorial staff when Japan's capitulation became official.

After a subdued dinner-party the Crofts and I walked over to the CNR station. As we stepped onto the train platform a siren on top of the *Free Press* building went off and a few seconds later bedlam broke loose, as every car horn in Winnipeg began to hoot and people began to shout, "It's all over!"

As we walked beside the train, people who had obviously never met before beat one another on the back, kissed and hugged one another, or laughed and cried hysterically. Desmond kept bouncing along beside me, saying over and over again, in great excitement, "Aunt Bird, Aunt Bird, now you can start smoking again. Now you can have a cigarette again." I had given up smoking for the duration when the Crofts arrived, in order to save money.

Charles, Phyllis and I were too full of emotion to be able to say more than good-bye. There was really nothing left for us to say. They climbed up the Pullman steps, turned to wave a silent farewell from the platform, and then went into the car, herding the four children ahead of them. I waved, hurried back to the car and then drove to the *Tribune*.

I was very busy for a couple of hours after that, entirely forgetting the Crofts as I timed the *Tribune* commentators and gave them the cue to go on the air when I heard the announcer introduce them from the studio. At some point or other I also delivered a short broadcast about Women's Voluntary Services in Winnipeg since I was a columnist of the *Tribune*.

Once the "extra" was out on the street, the presses came to rest and the "hell-pot," in which used type is tossed to be melted down for future use, stopped boiling. The newsroom, earlier so full of noise and activity, was silent, a derelict place. The floor was covered with scraps of paper torn off the teletype machines. Huge wire waste-baskets belched paper, and typewriting tables were crowded with empty coke bottles and ash-trays full of cigarette stubs. After the broadcasters had signed off and gone home, the building had a curious lifeless feeling. J.B. and I were the last to leave. Frenchie, the night elevator man, seemed lonely and remote, somehow unfamiliar. His voice sounded hollow and ghostly as he said good-night and clanged the door shut behind us.

As we drove home the streets were empty except for a few groups of people on Portage Avenue singing "There'll always be an England" in lugubrious, drunken disharmony. When we passed a friend's house we saw a number of cars parked outside and debated whether we would join what was obviously a victory celebration party. But we decided to go home because neither of us was in the mood for revelry. Too much had happened.

J.B. had bought a bottle of champagne a month or so earlier for us to drink a toast to victory but that night we both felt that victory was a dead thing after so much death. We found we were utterly exhausted. We sat by the fire for a while and talked. I smoked a cigarette. It tasted like what I imagine wormwood tastes like, and made me feel sick in my stomach.

When we went upstairs we found a child's sock lying in the hall. It was only then that complete realization came through to us: the Crofts, such an integral part of our lives for five years, had gone away. It seemed symbolic that they had departed at the exact moment the war came to an end.

In the winter of 1946 I gave only two, instead of three *Headline History* broadcasts a week on the Western Network because the pressure of war had been lifted. However, I was broadcasting more than ever before because Bessy Long, the director of Women's Interests for the CBC in Toronto, asked me to do a series of afternoon broadcasts entitled *Blue-Print for Peace* on the National Network. Week after week I told the women of Canada about UNRRA, the UN Charter, Bretton

Woods, UNESCO, and the other UN government agencies then being set up. I also was asked to give a few talks on *Mid-Week Review,* an evening program analyzing either national or international news.

It was not a good year for J.B. He had been drained dry physically and emotionally by the war, and when he should have been able to let up and recharge his batteries, he found himself the reluctant editor of a joint operation of *The Winnipeg Free Press* and *The Winnipeg Tribune* as a result of a strike by the International Typographers' Union. He called it the *Free Tribulation.*

When we left Montreal, J.B. made a promise that we would only stay in Winnipeg for five years. We had stayed for nine, so by then both of us felt that phase of our life was over and that we must move on. When the Southam Company offered him a transfer to Ottawa as chief of the Southam News Services, we were both delighted.

Unfortunately J.B. was not well and needed a long holiday before taking over the new job. Accordingly, we went to stay with John Monks and his wife Anne, at Roque Island, off the coast of Maine, before going to Saunderstown. While we were there, Mother became seriously ill and I had to fly to Rhode Island in a hurry. She obviously had not long to live, and I felt I must stay near the hospital so that I could be with her every day until she died. J.B. went on to Ottawa, to try to find a place to live while I stayed on alone in the big cottage so full of memories of my girlhood.

Mother's death was a major amputation, bringing with it the awful knowledge that I was now a member of the older generation.

When I had attended to all the heart-breaking details accompanying the death of the head of a family, Ben Bush helped me close the house. Many years before, when Mother was first stricken with Parkinson's Disease, he had promised to stay with her until she died. He had kept his promise and had remained in her employ for twenty years. His kindness to her was remarkable. Once I apologized to him after Mother had been rude to him in a most uncharacteristic way. He then said something which helped me at the time and many times since. He said, "Don't worry, Miss Florence. I understand. I just remembers her the way she used to be." It is something all of us need to be able to do for people we love.

When Mother died, an important time capsule was completed for Ben as well as for me.

My brother Shan had inherited mother's bright green Ford touring car which we had run around in during many happy holidays in Rhode

Island. He gave it to Ben Bush, and Ben drove me in it to the country railway station where I was to take the train northward. Mother had always come to see me off at the station when I was a girl going to camp or to college, and when I was a young married woman returning to my own home in New York, Washington, Montreal or Winnipeg. She had always stood on the platform and waved, and I had always pressed my face close to the car window and waved as the train pulled out, until she was out of sight. It seemed strange to see Ben Bush standing alone beside the little green car, waving me farewell as the train moved off. Yesterday was gone forever and today was moving into tomorrow for both of us.

Ottawa

When I arrived in Ottawa I found J.B. in a state of profound gloom because he had not been able to find an apartment. Ottawa had undergone a population explosion during the war. Government departments and agencies, such as National Defence and the Wartime Prices and Trade Board, had expanded rapidly year after year. At the same time there had been little or no building, due to the shortage of materials and construction workers. It might have been possible to buy a house of some kind but we didn't have enough capital.

J.B. had been living at the Chateau Laurier Hotel for a month and was depressed by the interior décor. It had been ugly to begin with, but by the end of the war was grubby, like an old woman who has gone to bed with her make-up on.

"If I have to look at another potted fern," he said, "I think I'll shoot it."

Consequently, after I had unpacked I decided I had better go out and look for a place to live. As I wandered through the hotel lobby in a state of vague indecision, I ran into our old friend John Grierson.

"Come for lunch," he said.

Over a Dubonnet-on-the-rocks I told him about J.B.'s frustration.

"Maybe I can help," he said.

He went on to say bitterly that he was leaving Canada because the government had failed to back him up after the Gouzenko affair. One of Grierson's private secretaries, supplied by the government stenographic pool, had come under suspicion and Grierson's reputation had suffered because of "guilt by association."

A man of integrity with great pride in his own incorruptibility as a civil servant and in the way he had built up the National Film Board as part of the war effort, Grierson found intolerable the distrust and rejection he was encountering among officials he had regarded as friends. He felt he had been treated unjustly, and concluded that there was no place for him in Canada at that time.

(During the next twenty years John Grierson found himself a new career as a television personality with his own program. Life was not easy for him, however. He contracted tuberculosis and recovered from it. He nearly drank himself to death but eventually went on the wagon for good, and lived to see his reputation gleam again. In the late sixties the British government presented him with a C.B.E. and Canada welcomed him back, a man in his seventies, to inspire the young at McGill University, as he had an earlier generation when he was Film Commissioner.)

That day at lunch in the Chateau Laurier Grill, he was angry and disillusioned, appalled by the way his world had collapsed around him and yet, characteristically, he put the problems of a friend ahead of his own.

"Margaret and I have a small apartment here," he said. "We were planning to keep it on as a *pied à terre* in case they want me to come back. But I think you and John need it more than we do. I'll speak to the landlord about it. There's a waiting list a mile long for every apartment in town but he's a good friend of mine so I think he'll let you take over."

A fortnight later we were installed in Grierson's flat on the ground floor of 30 Cooper Street. It was one of six apartments in the old Fraser mansion built in a more expansive era by an Ottawa lumber king. A huge living room with a wood-burning fireplace flanked by window seats, was joined to a large dining room by a wide arch to form a sort of baronial hall. A screened porch opened off the dining room and beyond it was an enormous lawn surrounded by flower beds. One of our friends once described the 30 Cooper Street apartment as being Queen Anne in front and Sally Anne in the back because though the two front rooms were very grand the single bedroom at the rear was so small that there was just enough room to get around the two beds and a bureau; we had to take turns getting dressed in order to avoid collisions.

The communications media were well represented in the house. The Davidson Duntons had one of the top floor apartments and the Sydney Newmans the other. Davey Dunton, our old friend from Montreal, was then president of the Canadian Broadcasting Corporation, and Syd

Newman, a much younger man, was editing film for the National Film Board. (Twenty-six years later he would come back to Canada, after a career in broadcasting in England, to become National Film Commissioner.) Syd and Betty Newman became good friends and we spent many stimulating hours settling the affairs of the nation in uninhibited conversation, as we still do whenever we have a chance to get together.

Our neighbours on the ground floor were Mr. and Mrs. Godfroy Patteson, an aged couple who were Mackenzie King's closest personal friends. Joan Patteson, a woman of great charm and dignity as well as beauty even when in her seventies, often acted as hostess at the bachelor Prime Minister's dinner parties.

Mr. King frequently had dinner with the Pattesons on Sunday nights and afterwards sang hymns with them, while Mrs. Patteson played the accompaniments on the piano. The old upright piano stood against the back of one of our dining-room walls, so we were right in on the sing-song. The Prime Minister did not have as fine a voice as the cantor in the synagogue next door to our apartment in New York, but the hymns had a familiar, homey sound and reminded me of the Sunday nights when we all used to sing songs from the *Scottish Students Song Book,* gathered around the upright piano in the Saunderstown house while Mother was alive.

During the five years we lived at 30 Cooper Street, J.B. and I became friends of the Pattesons through a shared interest in gardening and birds. It is impossible for J.B. to exist close to any bit of earth no matter how small, without planting seeds in it. He gave the apartment-house superintendent a hand with the flower beds to make them bloom georgeously, and planted a vegetable garden for us. He raised sweet corn and used to lead our dinner guests ceremoniously out to the garden to choose the ears of corn for their dinner. He planted a small flower garden for the Pattesons when he found out they loved to putter in a garden but had become too old and arthritic to do the hard work.

Dressed in his gardening clothes, with his hands and shoes covered with earth, J.B. would stroll around to their back door to take them flowers or to find out what seedlings they would like him to buy in the market. Occasionally the Prime Minister was there, and would sit on a kitchen chair on the back stoop while J.B. sat smoking on the steps. They discussed gardening and birds, since Mackenzie King fancied himself as a bird-watcher. J.B. was disconcerted when he walked us around Kingsmere one day and proudly pointed to three bluebird boxes

all on the same telegraph pole. Evidently the Prime Minister was unaware that bluebirds are jealous of their territory and will drive away
others of their own species from the nesting area.

At that time I was making frequent afternoon news commentaries
for *Trans-Canada Matinée* at two o'clock in the afternoon, as well as for
Capital Report about once a month on Sunday afternoon. Mackenzie
King had a radio in his office and often listened to me before he went
into the House of Commons and from time to time would telephone me
either to congratulate me or to put me right. I was on *Trans-Canada
Matinée* the day in 1948 when he announced his retirement, and wrote
a sympathetic script about the Prime Minister, saying the captain of
the ship of state was by definition a lonely man, but would be even
lonelier when he retired from public life. After I got home from the
studio, Mrs. Patteson telephoned me to say the Prime Minister had
heard my broadcast and wanted to talk to me about it. He was coming
to call on her that evening, she said, and wanted J.B. and me to step
across the hall around nine o'clock.

I was rather nervous about the confrontation, but King put me at my
ease with all the skill of an accomplished host. He asked me to sit beside
him on a love-seat and, in spite of looking like a cross between a small
china Buddha and Puck, exerted a strange sort of female charm that
made me realize that he was a master manipulator. After a while he
said, "That was a very good broadcast this afternoon, but there's one
thing you have all wrong. I won't be lonely when I retire. I have
hundreds of friends. People write to me all the time."

I found it pathetic that the old man should think all the people who
wrote laudatory letters to the Prime Minister were his friends.

At ten o'clock he asked Mrs. Patteson to turn on the CBC national
news. When the announcer said there was much speculation in the press
about whether the Prime Minister really did intend to retire or was
just being devious as usual, King rubbed his hands together and literally
bounced up and down, laughing and saying several times, "I don't see
how I could have made it any clearer than I did. Strange that they don't
believe me. How could I have made it any clearer?"

While pretending to be annoyed by the confusion of the press he was
obviously delighted by it.

After the broadcast was over he said, "I don't see how I could have
made it any clearer, do you?"

"However," he said portentously after a pause, "the Berlin Blockade has created a very dangerous situation and if it leads to war, which is quite possible, and the people of Canada need me in a national emergency, then I would have to reconsider my decision."

He went on to say the press was obtuse in failing to understand that he could only present his resignation as Prime Minister to the Crown, whereas, of course, he could quite easily resign as party leader.

Two years later, in July 1950, on a Saturday, when we were getting ready to drive to our camp in the Gatineau Hills we heard a news bulletin on the radio announcing that Mackenzie King was lying seriously ill in his house in Kingsmere. I was scheduled to be on *Capital Report* the next day, had already written my broadcast, and was planning to come down to Ottawa on the Sunday morning in order to deliver it right after lunch. It was obvious I would have to write a new script when, late that afternoon, after we had reached camp, there was another bulletin saying the former Prime Minister was sinking fast.

J.B. and I sat on our front verandah, looking out at our tranquil little lake, and talked about the best approach toward writing an obituary broadcast about such a complex, many-faceted, controversial character. After an early dinner I left J.B. and drove back to town. As I emerged from the Precambrian Shield and drove down into the Ottawa Valley, the sun was setting, and Kingsmere Mountain looked purple against the pale summer sky. It gave me a strangely sad feeling because I knew that under its shadow a lonely old man lay dying.

By coincidence, Raymond Gram Swing, one of the best American broadcasters of the period whom I admired tremendously, happened to be tuned in on the CBC shortwave while he was staying in Jamaica and heard my piece on King on *Capital Report*. The following autumn Swing came to Ottawa on an assignment for *The Voice of America* and looked me up. I had lunch with him and we talked about international affairs, finding we saw eye-to-eye about a great many things. He came to our apartment for dinner the next night and there was more good conversation. When he went back to Washington he sent me flowers with a note: "In memory of a friendship born full grown as if from the head of Zeus."

Before the days of television, *Capital Report* was a prestigious program. When I first started broadcasting on it people often asked me if J.B. wrote my broadcasts. This bland assumption of female incompetence used to make me furious. It made J.B. mad too; he often timed my scripts for me with our stop watch and helped me with the cutting, as I helped him when he was preparing a broadcast, but he would no more have told me what to say than I would have told him. People stopped asking me these patronizing questions after I gave a number of tough broadcasts while he was known to be out of the country.

It gave us both considerable satisfaction when in the same year J.B. won a National Press Club award for an article on Nye Bevan and I won a Women's National Press Club award for an article on Ukrainian culture. They were written at the same time while we were 3,000 miles apart, so that collusion would have been impossible.

As professional writers and broadcasters, J.B. and I have shared an abiding involvement in public affairs and have participated in the process of democracy. Each of us has always been involved in the other's work. We have spent many hours working together, reading each other's copy if there was time, and saying candidly what we thought of it. Often we disagree about interpretations of a political situation. Often we argue. But disagreements and arguments are stimulating and clarifying because there has never been any jealousy between us. We have always worked in the same fields of interest but never in competition, and that has helped us to grow together instead of apart.

I think the fact that we both have had to write against deadlines has taken some of the pressure off our marriage. We understand the demands of our profession. We know what it feels like to be drained and depressed when we have finally put "30" at the end of a long story. We know about the need to unwind and talk and talk, sometimes for hours, when a broadcasting stint is over, even if it is late at night. Over the years we have understood each other's needs because we shared them.

Another tremendous bond between us is our shared love of earth, rock, and water, and our pleasure in observing birds, beasts, flowers, trees and the whole process of natural history. My interest in birds, beasts and flowers goes back a long way; Mother encouraged me and my brother John to make bird lists, and to collect and identify wild flowers as she did.

J.B. is an ardent, unusually well-informed bird-watcher; for over twenty years he has written a column, "Bird's Eye View" about birds and natural history for *The Ottawa Journal,* and in order to develop an expertise of my own I have learned quite a bit about wild flowers. I know something about birds too and have occasionally pinch-hit as a "Bird's Eye View" columnist when J.B. has been away on assignments or swamped by the Budget or some other commotion on Parliament Hill.

When we are at our little lake in the Gatineau, I know where to look for blue hepaticas, red wild ginger and the first shoots of trilliums under brown leaves in early spring. I know where the wild red columbine grows out of bits of earth in the cracks of a large rock, where the yellow ladyslippers can be found on a path through the woods, and where the showy orchis hides near the old ice-house. I've identified one hundred and thirty-four varieties of wild flowers on our own land. They give us moments of pure joy when we visit them every spring and summer.

As far as I am concerned winter and city are synonymous as are summer and country. I am half town mouse, half country mouse, but in no way a suburban mouse, this being one of the reasons why I disliked our house in River Heights in Winnipeg. For me, the best thing about Ottawa is that it is close to the beautiful Gatineau Hills and is so easy to get out of. The autumn we arrived in Ottawa, J.B. and I began looking for a bit of land beside a lake where we could build a weekend shack. When we were in Winnipeg I had refused to give in to J.B.'s pleas to buy a lot at the Lake of the Woods: I had thought we would only be in Manitoba for five years and did not want to put down roots which would have to be pulled up again. But we planned to stay in Ottawa, and since both of us felt city-pent in an apartment, we wanted a little place of our own in the country. We wanted to own a tiny piece of Canada again.

After driving around for a month or so exploring the surrounding country with the aid of a topographical map, we bought a half-built cottage on a small lake sixteen miles from Parliament Hill. A local farmer finished building the shack for us so that we were able to spend every weekend there when summer came. It was a beautiful little lake and the neighbours, French Canadians from Hull and Gatineau, made us feel at home, allowing us to speak French and putting up with our un-grammatical language.

We liked the place but found it too heavily built up and our lot much too small to provide the territory needed to attract a variety of birds so that J.B. could observe their behaviour. It was, in fact, too suburban for us. Both of us dreamed of finding a lonely lake, a Walden Pond, close enough to town to enable us to avoid a long motor trip every weekend. That summer once we were installed, we used our camp as a jumping-off place and went on looking. But without success; we found several lakes near us, but the lonely ones without a row of cottages standing cheek by jowl every hundred feet were so far from the highway that it would have cost a fortune to make a road into any of of them.

During the summer our next-door neighbour at the lake invited J.B. to go fishing with him to "a secret lake," where, he said, there were huge bass. He made it a point that they should go in J.B.'s car, the Studebaker roadster we had brought from Winnipeg. His insistence made us suspect that the road was not of the best, and how right we were. J.B. departed early in the morning and returned late in the day without any bass but with shining eyes. "I've found it," he said. "It's only about three miles from here. It's rather a bad road, I'm afraid, but that doesn't matter."

The next day I packed a picnic lunch in a knapsack and we set off, with me at the wheel. For the first mile the road was rough but passable. For the next two miles it was the "rocky road to Dublin" with a vengeance, a wood path full of boulders with deep ruts. The rocks kept scraping against the underpart of the car no matter how carefully I manoeuvred, and I was sure that its vitals were being torn out. I began to panic as the road got narrower and rougher, but I had to go on because there was no way to turn the car around and go back. I was furious at J.B. for bringing me and the car there, and he was distressed because I was in such a flap. But at the same time he was determined to do what he intended to do. He kept saying, "We're almost there now. Just keep your nerve. There's a place a little further on where you can turn around and everything."

I was even more furious, after we had parked in a lumber trail forking off the road, when J.B. led the way into a jungle of brambles and thick second growth, saying, "There ought to be a path somewhere here. Anyway it's not very far to the lake."

He couldn't find the path, and we struggled through the bush, our arms and legs scratched by thorns and the branches of small trees. We were in an old meadow, cleared of rock and trees about the time of Confederation, but now completely overgrown, which had been fenced by barbed wire to keep cattle from straying. The fence posts had long since become rotten and fallen over, but the wire was still strong and I walked into a strand of it and cut a deep scratch in my leg. I was sure I would die of lockjaw and swore and wept and made one hell of a row. J.B. said, "I'm sorry. I'm terribly sorry, what rotten luck," and plunged ahead, and I followed him since I didn't want to be left alone and bleeding in the middle of nowhere.

J.B. kept saying, "The lake can't be far now."

After a long time we found it. I had stopped making a hullabaloo by then but was so mad I wouldn't speak to him.

There was a footpath, cut by generations of poachers, leading around the edge of the lake, and we followed it until we came to a big rock in the sun beside the water. There we sat down to rest. J.B. opened the knapsack and gave me a bottle of beer and a roast beef sandwich. I sat with my back to him, silent, sulking, ashamed of having behaved so badly.

I found myself looking at a lake about a third of a mile long, fringed by tall dark cedars, slim white birches, and poplars whose leaves trembled in a silver-and-green dance as a light wind touched them. At the far end, near the small creek that acted as an outlet, there was a marsh with a stand of tamarack, their feathery needles pale green in contrast to the dark green of maple and pine on the hill rising steeply behind the low-lying land. The water beside me was very clear and obviously very deep and, as I looked into it, a school of half a dozen large bass sailed past.

It was silent there until a kingfisher, annoyed by our presence, made its angry, rattling call. A pair of painted turtles sunned themselves on a log a few feet from us. It was hot in the sun and the air smelt of sun-warmed pine needles. I dropped a pebble into the water and watched it sink into the darkness below as tiny bubbles followed its course. I scanned the shore appraisingly, thoughtfully. "Where shall we put the shack?" I said.

It required long and elaborate negotiations before we bought nine acres at the head of the lake, which, because of a curve in the road, turned out to be only about a hundred and twenty-five yards from the road instead of the half mile it had seemed when I struggled through the bush the first day I saw it.

A couple of farmers, Paul-Emile Rainville and Joe Prudhomme, helped us clear the old meadow and built us a small cabin which I had spent the winter designing. Building materials were in short supply so I had to buy nails half-a-pound at a time from different hardware stores. I supervised the building, an exercise which improved my French, since the farmers spoke only a few words of English. There were, from time to time, problems of communication, as when I kept talking to Paul-Emile Rainville about *plafond* (ceiling), when I meant *plancher* (floor), and when I insisted that the doors would not need any hinges because he called them *pentures,* and I thought he meant *peinture* (paint).

The shack has two small bedrooms looking out on the lake, a living-room and a large kitchen, a front porch, screened-in to protect us from black flies and mosquitoes, and a lean-to shed in the back to keep the firewood dry. I bought a wood-burning cooking stove for five dollars at a second-hand store in the market in Ottawa and a big box stove to keep the place warm in all weathers.

At that time there was no plumbing. J.B. carried buckets of water up the hill from the lake forty feet away. We found a spring for drinking water, and Rainville built us a splendid privy. We had oil lamps which gave a warm light but were bad for reading in bed and a nuisance to fill and trim. The farmer built us an icehouse which he filled with fifty-pound chunks of ice, cut from the lake in winter and packed in sawdust. J.B. used to dig them out with a shovel and pickaxe, take them to the lake to wash on a wheelbarrow and then heave them into the icebox, a strenuous operation.

Bit by bit, every few years after that, we bought a little more land until, after twenty-two years, we owned all the land around the lake, about seventy-five acres of woodland in all.

After sixteen years we began to feel the need for a few more creature comforts and had a propane stove and refrigerator installed and put in a gasoline pump to bring water from the lake to a tank to supply the kitchen sink with running water. When the Quebec Hydro finally came our way, we became very grand and added a "wart" to the house; a full bathroom with hot-and-cold running water. We now have a telephone as well as electric lights. In fact, the little shack now has what *Le Guide Michelin* calls *"tous conforts."*

"The Frogpond," which J.B. has written so much about in his weekly column on birds, is a good place for writing, reading and thinking, a good place to talk with friends. Each year we spend more time there since we need, as we grow older, the healing sense of peace it gives us. It is peaceful there but not dull. There is always something interesting going on, always birds to watch, chipmunks to feed by hand with peanuts, flowers to find in secret places. We swim a couple of times a day when the warm weather comes, walk on old trails through the woods in spring and autumn, and fish for big bass before sundown on summer evenings.

Every year the city grows closer as more people buy lots along the road which has been made into a rough but passable back-country highway. In recent years thieves have often broken into the cottage, stealing fishing rods, flashlights and blankets, and poachers often leave dead bait and sandwich droppings around the dock when we are not there. Some of the cottagers on a nearby lake drop their garbage on our land when they drive back to town on Sunday nights instead of burning it. Often now we hear motorcycles on the road. But the place has not yet lost its magic, its feeling of wildness.

Shortly after we moved to Ottawa, the CBC's Bessy Long, a grand old feminist, gave me a piece of sound advice. She said, "Get to be a specialist in something so that when producers are looking for a person to do a job in that area they automatically think of you. Why don't you become a specialist in the problems of working women? We've won the right to vote so we have our political rights, but working women are still discriminated against. The economic rights of women are what we must fight for now."

I spent a lot of time in the Parliamentary Library reading about the history of working women, and after considerable research I wrote and delivered thirteen ten-minute scripts in a series called *Women at Work*. I learned a great deal as a result of that effort. As a result of the *Women at Work* series, the Canadian Institute of International Affairs asked me to write a *Headline Book,* a pamphlet on the status of women. The research required for that made me aware of the many other ways in which women are second-class citizens.

One change in laws in regard to women was of particular personal interest to me. In 1947, the Canadian Citizenship Act, establishing a Canadian citizenship status, became law. Before that, people identified as Canadians were British subjects either by birth or by naturalization and an alien woman married to a British subject became a British subject automatically. It had always irked me that I was a Canadian only becuse I was married to J.B. I felt marriage and being a citizen of a country involved quite different intellectual and emotional commitments. To change one's nationality requires an act of faith in a community and identification with it. It is something one has to feel with an inner conviction. Otherwise it has no meaning except as a legality. By 1947 I knew for a certainty that I was Canadian, and I decided to apply for a certificate of citizenship to prove an act of faith. Walter Harris was the Minister of Citizenship and Immigration at that time. I sat beside him at dinner one evening and asked him if I needed to be sponsored after having been a British subject by marriage for nineteen years. He kidded me along for a few minutes rejecting the sponsors I suggested: Brooke Claxton, a Liberal Cabinet Minister; Jim Macdonnell, a Conservative M.P.; and Arnold Heeney, the Clerk of the Privy Council. I only became aware Harris was pulling my leg when he said, "I guess you really ought to find a communist to sponsor you because a communist would be the only person who could possibly object to your becoming a Canadian especially since you are one already."

A few weeks later Harris came to a dinner party in our apartment. Quite late in the evening during an argument (probably about Canadian identity, since that was an inevitable topic of conversation in those days), I made some statement which made J.B. burst out, "Woman, I could beat you for saying that."

Then Walter Harris spoke up. "You had better not beat her, John," he said, "because she is now a Canadian citizen in her own right, not because she married you. I have something here to prove it."

He put his hand in his pocket and drew out a Certificate of Citizenship signed by himself. He had been keeping it all evening until a suitable moment occurred for him to present it to me with fanfare.

That "scrap of paper" means a great deal of me; it is the symbol of a state of mind, an intellectual and emotional integration.

The forties and fifties in Ottawa were exciting years for me professionally. With the arrival of television I found myself taking part frequently in press conferences and panels on national and international affairs. During the 1953 national election, the first to be televised, Blair Fraser, Gordon Sinclair and I were commentators in the big TV election centre in Toronto. The whole operation was a shambles, incredibly amateurish compared with the smooth technical arrangements for the coverage of recent elections. The telephone lines to centres in other parts of the country did not work for most of the evening, so that Blair spent a lot of time saying, "Are you there? Can you hear me? I can't hear you."

I was still so new to the game I didn't know that when the green light on top of the camera is on, the picture is still on the air even if the audio is off. At the end of my first broadcast of the evening I put my head on the shoulder of the announcer who had been interviewing me and groaned, "Oh God, wasn't that awful?" while the entire country watched me. Fortunately they couldn't hear me.

As election night wore on I could feel my pancake make-up beginning to crack like the top of a badly baked cake every time I smiled or said anything, and I developed a searing headache from the lights. After the Liberal victory was obvious and Louis St. Laurent had gone on the air, Ross McLean, the producer, came over to me and said, "I want you to introduce the defeated party leaders. Talk about the importance of the Opposition in parliamentary government—that sort of thing—before you introduce them."

Moving toward my typewriter to write a few notes, I asked, "When will I be going on?"

Ross looked at his watch. "Let me see," he said, "in just about a minute from now. I guess we'd better be walking over to the camera right away."

"Where are they talking from?" I asked as we sprinted across the huge studio.

"George Drew is in Ottawa. I don't know where the others are but I'll find out and send you a note when the time comes."

I sat down and the camera, leering with its Cyclops' eye, began to move toward me. The floor director said, "Look plenty interested, Anne. I'm going to put the camera on you from time to time while they're talking."

I had often written about the role of the Opposition, so I spouted forth a short rehash of old broadcasts in a few sentences. Looking "plenty interested" was a different matter. I had no earphones to give me an audio-feedback so I hadn't the slightest idea what the party leaders were saying. I didn't know whether to look sad or amused, horrified or approving. I could see the screen but it was not carrying a live picture of the defeated leaders, only photographs of them while they were speaking. I sat there presenting a face which I hoped showed deep thought, a poker face because I didn't know whether George Drew was making gracious remarks or claiming "we was robbed," whether M.J. Coldwell was elated or downcast by the CCF showing, whether Solon Low was being belligerent or philosophical.

As far as my career as a writer and broadcaster was concerned, my life in Ottawa at that time was all I could ask for. I was busy, interested in my work, and I greatly enjoyed the satisfaction of proving that a woman could take her place in the big league of broadcasters on national and international affairs, something no woman had done before in Canada. I worked very hard and felt it worthwhile because of the respect and recognition I was receiving. But at the same time, I was deeply unhappy.

J.B. was ill. He had started drinking heavily while we were in Winnipeg, using alcohol to keep himself going. It only added to his exhaustion and nervous strain. After we moved to Ottawa he began to lose his tolerance for alcohol, as so many people do as they grow older. By the time he realized he had an alcohol problem he could not stop drinking in spite of desperate efforts which went on for years.

It was a dreadful period for both of us. We were constantly in despair. All I could do was stand and wait, never losing confidence and always trying to make J.B. know I loved him and would go on loving him whatever happened. It was terrible not to be able to do more than that, but I knew that J.B. had to find the help he needed himself and to find the strength to heal himself in his own way.

In 1953, when he was fifty-one years old, he found the way. Since August of that year he has not taken an alcoholic drink of any kind. That August we came out of the tunnel. The twenty years since then have been the happiest of all our happy years together.

The Levant

In 1955, nine years after we moved to Ottawa, I began to feel that I was in a rut professionally. The CBC had sent me to New York for a fortnight to cover the United Nations and I had gone to Toronto and Montreal to take part in TV shows a number of times, but I had not been to Europe since 1936. I felt I was badly out of touch with what was happening there and did not want to go on writing commentaries on international affairs based entirely on information gained at second hand from other people or from books. I felt that, at the age of forty-seven, I was not developing into the sort of person I wanted to be. During the war I had had no choice but to stay in Winnipeg because I had so many responsibilities there. And while J.B. was ill I wanted to be on hand in case he needed me. But now I was determined to lead a more interesting, less restricted life, and to widen my horizons.

Since I was a freelance writer and broadcaster, I did not have a big newspaper to send me overseas, as J.B. had always had, and I didn't want to try to persuade the CBC to give me an overseas assignment until I knew more about post-war Europe at first hand. About that time I heard that NATO arranged tours for journalists who had been recommended by the governments of their respective countries. I did not see why only men should go on such tours and mentioned the matter to John Holmes, then Assistant Under Secretary of State for External Affairs. He said he saw no reason why a woman should not go, and recommended me for a tour of Greece and Turkey that was coming up in the spring.

Cyprus, then a British colony, was just emerging as a bone of serious contention between Greece and Turkey. The government of Greece was openly supporting the group of Cypriots who were agitating for Enosis, that is union between Cyprus and Greece. On the other hand, the government of Turkey was adamant about refusing to allow Cyprus to become part of Greece not only because it wanted to protect the rights of the Turkish minority on the island but also because Cyprus is only forty miles off the Turkish coast. Turkey was satisfied with the status quo, since Britain did not threaten her, but would not tolerate having Greece in such a strategic position so close to the mainland. The Turks and the Greeks are hereditary enemies and are always on guard against each other.

Since Greece and Turkey are both members of NATO, the tension between them over Cyprus was of considerable interest to Canadians, as it obviously weakened the eastern flank of the defence alliance to which Canada also belongs. I had been broadcasting about the situation, basing my opinions on books, and magazine and newspaper articles, and was delighted at the opportunity to be able to study and broadcast about it from information gained at first hand.

When a good friend, Michael Comay, the Israeli Ambassador in Ottawa, heard I was going to the Levant, he invited me to go on from Turkey to Israel for a fortnight as the guest of his government. I was excited by his invitation because I knew that Israel is the most fascinating social experiment of our time and I wanted to know more about it. A Canadian, Lieutenant-General E.L.M. "Tommy" Burns, was then the Commander of the UN Truce Observation Team which had the job of reporting violations of the cease-fire between the Israelis and the Arabs. I felt sure there was a good story in their work and I told Michael Comay I would accept the invitation of the Israeli government with the greatest of enthusiasm, provided I would be allowed to go anywhere I wanted to go and write the truth as I found it, without obligation either to him or to his government. (This is the arrangement I have made ever since, when I have been invited to a country as the guest of its government. It is essential not to allow one's judgement to be influenced by favours.)

To make the most of the opportunity, I decided to spend a fortnight in England, a week or so in Paris where the tour started, and to go back to England for about ten days on the way home from the Middle East.

For a couple of months before I left, when I was not working on broadcasts, I did my homework. I had been given permission to use the library of the Department of External Affairs and I also talked to several people in the Department who had either been stationed in

Greece, Turkey or Israel, or who were in the section responsible for recommendations concerning Canada's policy toward these countries. I always find the preparation for an assignment abroad almost as interesting, though not as stimulating, as the trip itself.

In May I flew to London on a two-storey BOAC plane which had a bar on the ground floor. The passengers moved around and fraternized over drinks, and there was much of the cheery atmosphere of a transatlantic crossing by ship. It took eleven hours to get to London, so we were able to get a night's sleep and a leisurely breakfast. These days, every time a stewardess shoves a cold box-breakfast at me a few hours after I've eaten a huge dinner I think nostalgically of the breakfast on my first transatlantic flight—grilled sausages, tomatoes and mushrooms, and fried eggs. And I was in economy-class.

It's sad that travel comfort has deteriorated in recent years. Speed in the air does not compensate for lack of leg-room between seats, overcrowded planes and airports, and the long waits entailed by huge planes. I have crossed the Atlantic by air sixteen times since 1955 and each year the flight becomes more uncomfortable. I've also crossed by ship half a dozen times during the same period and find myself hankering after the little Cunarders that were much more relaxed and simple, more like ships than the present-day floating hotels with their fancy menus and night-clubs, designed to make every traveller feel for five days like a millionaire with dyspepsia.

Returning to London after so many years was sheer joy. Desmond Croft, then a medical student and living in London, came to the hotel soon after I arrived and took me to a Soho restaurant for dinner. I had not seen him since he visited us for a summer, the year before he went up to Oxford, and was happy to find he had matured into a delightful young man. Still thinking of him as the round-faced little boy he had been in Winnipeg, I was quite startled when he picked up the wine card after we had ordered our dinner and carried on a knowledgeable discussion with the wine waiter.

While I was in London, I wrote and delivered a few broadcasts for the BBC and undertook to do others when I got back from Israel six weeks later. A Canadian friend, Jean Gow, taught me the trick of going to the City of London on a Sunday when there is no traffic and one can see the old town without being jostled on the pavements. The two of us spent a couple of mornings admiring the Christopher Wren churches and looking sadly at the piles of rubble not yet cleared away after the blitz, and at the empty lots which had been cleared, where wild flowers were growing.

In Paris the horse-chestnut trees were in bloom and the city was still as I remembered it. The NATO tour began with a day of lectures at SHAPE (Supreme Headquarters Allied Powers Europe), and there I met the other seven journalists who had come from Norway, Denmark, France, Luxembourg, Portugal, Italy and the Netherlands.

NATO had made reservations for us at the Hotel Brabançonne, near the Eiffel Tower, a part of Paris I had never stayed in before. I found it dull and bourgeois after L'Aiglon, on the Boulevard Raspail, where J.B. and I had stayed on the celebrated occasion when he won the bottles of champagne in the hoop-la game. However, I discovered the *esprit qaulois* had not been dimmed by the respectable surroundings. I had been given a double room and on the first morning after I ordered breakfast, two *cafés complets* arrived. I explained to the maid that my husband was in Canada and I was travelling alone. The next morning she again brought me two breakfasts and again I explained. On the third morning she came in with two breakfasts and said, conveying astonishment and disapproval in two words, "*Encore seule?*"

After that she gave me up; she had obviously written me off as a failure—a woman who spent the day in the company of nine men but couldn't find one man for the night.

Even before we took the plane for Athens, the NATO journalists had divided themselves up into a northern group and a southern group, something which happened on every tour. The Norwegian became ill with dysentery after drinking milk in Athens, but the Canadian, the Netherlander, the Dane and the Icelander shared the same chauffeur-driven limousine and went on expeditions together on days off. We had every third day off from lectures, press conferences with officials, and field trips to observe a fighter squadron practising manoeuvres and to watch guerrillas scale a mountainside and ambush a truck on a mountain road.

On one glorious day off, the northern group took an excursion steamer to Aegina, the nearest island to Piraeus, where we hired a horse and wagon and, happy and relaxed, drove at a snail's pace over the hills. At noon, the driver and, to my astonishment, the horse lay down in the shade and went to sleep. While they slept we went swimming in a deserted cove, putting our bathing-suits on behind the rocks, and then had lunch in a little hotel on a cliff looking down over the Aegean Sea.

We drank cool retsina and talked and talked. I was completely enchanted by the silhouette of the brown hills of the island and the extraordinary clear light. For me the scenery was even more satisfying than that of Italy, something I could never have believed possible, and the whole feeling of the place made me want to talk about philosophy rather than about politics as I usually did. As I sat, feeling the sun warm my skin still cold after the swim in chilly water, and feeling my insides warmed by the cool wine, I said I thought it was ridiculous to go back to the sort of life we all led. Er¹ing Bjol, the Dane, laughed and said, "If you stayed here you would start a clinic for sick children within three months and be up to your neck in good works before six months had gone by."

Erling Bjol and Edouard Messer, the Netherlander, soon became my friends. Erling, a slim, blond Dane, was in many ways like J.B. He was extremely intelligent, witty, a good raconteur, and a kind, decent man. He had brought a book of Greek poetry with him and was as much interested in the architecture and sculpture of ancient Greece as in the political and military affairs we were supposed to be studying. He spoke five languages, including Russian, and knew an impressive amount about European politics, so that talking to him day-in and day-out was an education for me. He was then working for *Information*, a former underground newspaper started during the Nazi occupation of Denmark, and since then has become a professor of political science at Aarhus University.

Edouard Messer, a tall, thin, rather stern, matter-of-fact Netherlander, was the editor of an Amsterdam daily newspaper, an extremely intelligent man, and also, like Erling, a kind and decent one. The two of them made the trip a delight for me when it could easily have been a misery. They made me feel they liked me, enjoyed my company and respected my opinions, while several members of the southern group often made unpleasant remarks about women "of my kind," whatever that was, and oscillated between making unsuccessful passes at me, sneering at me, and providing me with phoney stories, which I knew too much to believe.

It was only on the last day of the trip that I understood their behaviour. When the Canadian ambassador to Turkey gave me a couple of bottles of Scotch, I invited both groups for a farewell drink, and when, for the first time, we were all getting along well together, I asked the Italian why he and the other Latins had given me such a rough time.

"We don't understand you at all," he said. "We simply can't figure you out. You ask questions like a man. You know a lot. You travel with all these men, and yet you are very feminine. And you write to your husband every day." Obviously they thought in terms of stereotypes, and because I didn't fit the pattern they resented me.

Erling Bjol and Edouard Messer took me to see the night life of Athens and Istanbul, something I could not have done on my own in that part of the world. They also acted as rather solemn chaperones. They worried because, since I was the only woman, officials always gave me the seat of honour at meals, and rather maliciously plied me with drink by catching my eye for a succession of toasts. When at dinner my voice became a bit too high or my laugh too loud, my duennas would put their hands over their glasses and make fierce faces at me as a signal that I had had enough wine. And I, obediently, would put my hand over my own glass when the waiter came around again, praying silently that the Canadian wouldn't get tight and pass out, thereby disgracing her sex and her country. Several of the men got drunk on a number of occasions, and they were just kidded about their hangovers the next morning. But if I had drunk more than I could handle, it would have been a disgraceful affair and proved, to those who wanted proof, that women should not be allowed to go on strenuous trips designed for tough members of the newspaper fraternity.

One day, after we landed at a Turkish Air Force base in Anatolia, I asked the Dane and the Netherlander if they had found the way to the W.C. (We had been flying with the Air Force in a DC-3 without a toilet since six in the morning and it was then noon.) They shook their heads.

"You can't go there," Messer said.

"Out of the question," said Erling. "We've just been there. You can't use it. It defies description, it's so filthy. And to get to it you'd have to go through a room full of Turkish soldiers who are drinking. They'd embarrass you very much."

"That's all very well," I said, "but what am I going to do?"

"We will find a way," said Erling. "Messer and I will find a place for you to go."

They wandered off around the corner of the barracks and came back soon after.

"We've found a stone wall," Erling said. "If you can climb over it, there's a pasture on the other side and you'll be quite private. Messer and I will stand guard and keep anyone from disturbing you."

It was characteristic of the cultural difference between the two groups of NATO journalists that when the tour broke up in Istanbul all the members of the southern group went back to Paris on the round-trip ticket supplied by NATO, while the Dane went to Yugoslavia, the Netherlander to Vienna, the Icelander to Saudi Arabia, and the Canadian to Israel.

Erling Bjol put me on the plane for Tel Aviv at two in the morning after one of those bitter-sweet, festive dinners when two people who like each other know they will probably never see each other again. I wanted Erling and J.B. to meet, and the three of us tried to get together for a number of years without success. When we went to Copenhagen, Erling was in Paris; when we went to Paris, Erling was transferred back to Copenhagen; and when we went to Berlin, Erling's paper sent him to Brussels the day before we arrived. Once he sent me a Christmas card saying, "In what capital of Europe will we miss each other this year?"

In 1966, when I was in the airport in Vienna on my way to Milan from Budapest, I heard a voice call, "Mrs. Bird, Mrs. Bird!" And there was Erling on his way to Copenhagen from Bucharest. We had an hour before our planes left and talked about the *détente* in East-West relations as if we had seen each other the day before instead of for the first time in eleven years. As he left me at the gate to board my plane, he said, "I seem to make a habit of putting you on planes."

The plane Erling put me on in Istanbul landed, unexpectedly, in Cyprus. We were told there was fog over Tel Aviv for the first time in six years and since it was an El Al airliner it could not land in Lebanon or Syria without being confiscated. I was delighted to find myself in Cyprus, having spent the past three weeks listening to Greeks and Turks put forward their points of view about the island.

All the other passengers were either Americans or Israelis and were herded into the airport, but I, having a Canadian passport, was a British subject and allowed to go out and around. I had an instructive time talking to the Cypriot soldiers guarding the airport who spoke enough English to assure me they were all for Enosis.

At dawn, with that intensity of perception that comes from being very tired I was thrilled by "the hidden sun that rings black Cyprus with a lake of fire." Then at eight o'clock in the morning, the plane took off for Israel. As it rose into the air, I fainted, to the dismay of the stewardess and the man sitting beside me. I had been up all night and had had only four hours' sleep the night before after flying from Izmir to Istanbul, so all I needed was rest.

I slept from ten that morning until four o'clock in the afternoon in a little hotel in Tel Aviv and then drove to Jerusalem with a guide in a car supplied by the government of Israel. The guide, Dave Solomon, an intelligent, sensitive man, was a former New Yorker who had fought against the British during the days of the Palestine protectorate. The chauffeur, Nissim, was an Iraqi who had been in the British Army during the Second World War. The car was a Chevrolet which had gone 250,000 miles. The four of us got along together famously.

Israel was a revelation. Although the scenery is characteristic of the dry, semi-desert terrain of that part of the Mediterranean Littoral, the people are European in their outlook, and in the energetic way they have tackled the problems of their new country. There are probably more intelligent, interesting people to the square inch in that narrow strip of land than in any other country in the world.

In 1955 the desert was beginning to bloom under the passionate care of the men and women I met in the kibbutzim as I was driven around the country, the people who were making dreams come true after two thousand years. I was delighted by the healthy children I saw everywhere, children straight of bone, well-nourished, bronzed by the sun, luxuriating under a shower, playing games, going to school in clean clothing with shoes on their feet. They looked healthy and active in contrast to the thin, often rickety and shoeless children I had just been seeing in Greece and Turkey.

I approved of the way the women worked on an equal footing with the men in the kibbutzim. I considered it an amazing *tour de force* the way immigrants, from Iraq and North Africa, many of whom were illiterate, were being provided with housing, jobs and education. I thought it was brilliant to have made Hebrew the *lingua franca* of Israel in order to unite the people of the Diaspora then pouring into the country from all over the world. The people coming to Israel because of a shared religion and history were from different cultural backgrounds and spoke many different tongues. The small country would have been turned into a Tower of Babel if they had not been required to learn a common language. Once I asked Dave Solomon who were the best immigrants, and he made me laugh when he said, "the Anglo-Saxons," meaning, of course, Jews who had come from Britain and the older Commonwealth countries.

It was impossible not to be moved by the resilience and courage of the Jews from Germany and Poland who were the survivors of Hitler's nearly successful genocide. I understood why they did not want anyone to forget the crimes against them and their people. And yet I could not believe there was virtue in the museum given over to the records of the atrocities committed at Buchenwald, Belsen and the other extermination factories. The museum was not designed just to educate tourists. As my guides said, it was there because "We do not want our children or their children after them ever to forget what happened to their people." It seemed to me then, and still does, that the perpetuation of hatred and resentment by a group of people is as destructive to them as it is to an individual.

I also deplored the way Israel had been forced to become a military nation. When I was there I felt my usual, immediate reaction to geography and shared with the Israelis their feeling of vulnerability which was due to the fact that they were in a small enclave in enemy territory and were constantly menaced on all sides by a vast horde of understandably vindictive people dedicated to driving them into the sea. I watched air-raid shelters being built in the frontier settlements and was told about the incursions of Arab "apple pickers" who planted land mines and often killed the Israelis occupying their former homes.

Driving down through the narrow wasp-waist of Israel I had realized the ever-present pressure, the desperate need for more living space. It was easy to understand why the government of Israel was convinced that, in order to survive, it had to conscript men and women for military service and build up a deadly, efficient defensive and offensive military establishment. At the same time I could not help but be shocked by the extent and the ruthlessness of the retaliation raids by the Israelis on the Arab "apple pickers." I also detected a determination to increase Israeli territory bit by bit by the use of force, a policy which could not be a basis for peace.

The tragedy of the terrible, continuing Israeli-Arab feud is that no objective person can help having sympathy for both sides. I understand Arab hatred and resentment after being betrayed by the British when the First World War was over, and again by the United Nations when it created the State of Israel in what they regarded as their territory. But although I sympathized with the Arabs, I felt that for their own sake and for the sake of world peace they should accept the fact of Israel and work toward peaceful co-existence with her.

While I was in Jerusalem, I had a 7:30 breakfast with General Burns, and learned a great deal about the problems involved in peacekeeping as well as about the grim future for Israeli and Egyptian relations which he foresaw prophetically in his book *Between Arab and Israeli*.

I suppose that people can become adjusted to living on a time bomb but for the Israeli life was very tense, very real and very earnest then, as it is today. An incident brought that home to me rather poignantly. Late one afternoon Dave Solomon, Nissim, the Chevrolet and I arrived in Nahariya, a village on the Mediterranean. We had had a long hot drive and were tired. When I asked Dave and Nissim if they would like to take a walk with me on the seashore, they said, "Why? Why do you want to do that?"

"Because I love to walk on beaches, don't you?"

They said they had never walked on a beach.

"Then you had better come with me," I said.

It was a cloudy, windy afternoon. The beach was long and shallow, covered with a variety of seashells and tiny stones. I walked slowly, thinking that perhaps Christ and the disciples had once walked there or beached their fishing boats on the sand. From time to time I stooped to pick up a shell or a stone.

"Are they valuable?" Nissim asked.

"No," I said, "they aren't worth any money at all but they are beautiful and that's why I like them."

I told him how I had walked and gathered shells on lonely Wesquag Beach in Rhode Island when I was a child, and later on many beaches in Maine and the Caribbean, loving the feeling of sand under my bare feet and the sea air in my lungs.

"It's good to feel the rhythm of the waves," I said.

It wasn't long before Solomon and Nissim began to wander off, finding seashells and stones and, like children, bringing them to me for approval. Nissim would bring me a handful of shells which he would examine thoughtfully as I held them on the flattened palms of my extended hands.

"This one is ugly," he would say and throw it away. "And this one is beautiful. It we will keep."

We walked for an hour or so until the wind dropped and the sun began to go down behind the sea. The waves made a gentle lapping sound and the air was soft and moist after the dry heat of the day. We hardly talked, walking slowly, absorbing the evening calm. I had tied my shells and stones into a handkerchief which Nissim insisted upon carrying. He was a tall, heavily-built man but he walked lightly, carrying the little bundle with care.

That evening before dinner the two of them invited me to be their guest over a bottle of wine.

"We want to thank you for this afternoon," Dave Solomon said, lifting his glass in a toast, "that was a new and wonderful experience for us."

After I got home Solomon wrote me a short letter. It said, "It was wonderful to walk upon the shore and listen to the immemorial sound of the waves, for a brief time not needing to talk about politics and forgetting about fighting and the threat of war."

When I arrived in London a week later, after a tiring flight from Tel Aviv, I felt as if I had come home. The next morning I unpacked the suitcase of warm clothes I had left stored in the hotel. They were in need of pressing so I gave them all to the hotel valet, keeping back only a suit coat which didn't happen to be creased. They had just gone when Stuart Legge, one of the brightest of John Grierson's hand-fed film-makers, asked me for lunch. He was going abroad in the afternoon so it was our only chance of seeing each other. I accepted his invitation and then telephoned the valet to have my suit skirt sent up right away.

He said, all in one breath, "That will not be possible, Madam, because all our pressing is done in an establishment in quite a different part of London and the clothes are on their way there in a van—and God knows where it is now—and it will not be back until six o'clock this evening. I am very sorry, Madam, but there's nothing I can do about it."

The drip-dry cottons I had washed every night for six weeks while on the tour were too disreputable as well as too summery to wear for lunch at Wheeler's. But I was not going to let myself be deprived of my fillet of sole, my glass of Chablis, and a long talk with Stuart Legge—a clever, cynical, witty man, for whom I have great affection—especially as I was bursting with a story to tell about Israel and needed an audience. (The impact of Israel, so modern, so dynamic and exciting, had to a considerable extent driven out my impressions of Greece and Turkey. In later years I did not attempt to report on more than two countries, and preferably on only one, on a single trip abroad.)

After much thought I put on a black satin slip with lace around the bottom and topped it with my dark blue suit-coat, an odd-looking costume for a Mayfair luncheon engagement. Then I put my raincoat on, so that nobody was the wiser when I was out of doors. At lunch time I refused to check my raincoat, sliding it off my shoulders when I sat down, but keeping it buttoned below the waist. I wondered what "they" would have said if they knew I had no skirt on. Girls of my generation were always told by their mothers to wear clean underwear "in case you are knocked down in the traffic," but it was never considered necessary to admonish us not to go out without a skirt. Anyway it was a pleasant luncheon and over the top of the table I had the well-tailored look I always try to present when I am in London.

The BBC liked my broadcasts about Israel, and asked me to take part in a panel discussion about the forthcoming election in Britain. The chairman was Robert MacKenzie, a Canadian on the faculty of the London School of Economics who has written and broadcast a great deal about British politics and is, in fact, a leading authority on the subject. I had met him in Winnipeg when, as a young man, he took part in the first broadcast of a famous old radio program called *Citizens' Forum,* which went on for years.

I was surprised to find that because there was an election campaign going on the BBC producer insisted upon rehearsing the show in order to know exactly what we were going to say, something that had never happened to me in Canada. Before the rehearsal Bob MacKenzie took me aside and told me not to say all that I was going to say but save my tough stuff and best cracks for the live show when it would be impossible to censor me without taking the show off the air.

After the show was over, the BBC, more civilized about such things than the CBC, provided us with good drinks and excellent little sandwiches. A young Canadian, a member of the CBC London Bureau, was there. We were all relaxing and I was telling them about our NATO tour when suddenly he turned to me and said in a low voice, almost snarling, "Go home and cook your husband's breakfast."

I thought I must have misunderstood him. "What did you say?" I asked.

"Go home and cook your husband's breakfast," he repeated.

I decided that he had had too much to drink, and moved away to talk to someone else. That was the only time anyone in the CBC ever tried to make me feel I was not acceptable as a colleague and a commentator because I was a married woman.

That trip made me aware of how much I needed to widen my horizons, and I was determined never to let myself get stuck in a professional rut again. I kept on broadcasting regularly on national and international affairs from Ottawa, but during the next eleven years I went abroad on assignments every year and led a stimulating, often exciting life. I loved the travel years.

My next assignment came out of the blue. In the summer of 1956, I received a letter from "Mike" Pearson, then the Minister for External Affairs, inviting me to be a member of the delegation the Canadian government was sending to the UNESCO general conference being held in New Delhi the following autumn.

India

I have long believed that if the human race is to survive the nations of the world must be willing to hand over much of their national sovereignty to an international authority. An organization such as the United Nations, wholeheartedly supported by all its members, seems to me to be a necessity in order to prevent another world war in which, inevitably, nuclear weapons will be used. I have also always been interested in the work of UNESCO because its philosophy is based on the premise that war takes place in the minds of men and so the minds of men must be changed by means of international action. Consequently, I was greatly pleased to be asked to be a member of the Canadian delegation to the first UNESCO conference to be held in Asia. I was also delighted to have the opportunity of seeing something of India, a fabulous land I had wanted to visit ever since I was a child and Aunt Folly had read me Kipling's *Just So Stories,* the *Jungle Books,* and *Kim*—especially *Kim,* with its descriptions of life in the bazaars and villages.

I spent the rest of the summer reading about India and trying to absorb the huge number of UNESCO documents that the Department of External Affairs kept sending me. In October, the members of the delegation assembled in Ottawa for three days of briefing so that we would be familiar with the position of the Canadian government on the various projects on the agenda of the conference. We were also briefed on the historical, cultural and political background of India. The delegation was an interesting mixed bag, consisting of a senator, a couple of members of Parliament, a provincial civil servant in the field of education, an architect, and a couple of university professors. I was the token woman. Leonard Brockington was the chairman.

226

Brock had become a well-known national figure in the years that had passed since that afternoon, so charged with emotion, when he read poetry to us in the little house in Winnipeg on the day Britain declared war on Germany. He had a great gift for broadcasting because of his remarkable voice, and during the war had made a number of moving speeches on the air. On D-Day he had eloquently and movingly broadcast from a warship taking part in the operation in the English Channel. (Because he was bent double with arthritis, he had had to be slung aboard in one of the nets used to load baggage into the hold.) He had also, for a short time, written speeches for Prime Minister Mackenzie King, an assignment which was doomed to failure in advance since, as J.B. remarked, "Brock had a tongue of gold and King had the philosopher's stone in reverse turning all Brock's gold into lead."

The UNESCO conference was to open on November 7th. I decided to leave Canada well ahead of that date. Having been in Israel the year before, I wanted to know more about Arab countries, and so I planned to go to Lebanon via London for a few days, and to stop off in Baghdad and Egypt on the way home. For weeks we had been getting reports that tension was building up in the Middle East and naturally I wanted to go where the action was. If I had known I was heading into the Suez crisis of 1956, I would have been even more eager to go; I had a thirst for adventure which time has not yet slaked.

I was due to leave London for Beirut on October 30th. On the morning of October 29th, I heard on the BBC news that Israeli troops had entered the Sinai Peninsula and were moving toward the Suez Canal. Later I heard that Prime Minister Anthony Eden had issued an ultimatum to Israel and Egypt demanding an immediate cease-fire. I wondered how this would affect my plans to go to Beirut, and went to Canada House to ask Norman Robertson, the Canadian High Commissioner in London, for instructions. He told me the Americans were evacuating civilians from the Middle East but that Canada did not think it necessary to do that. While we were talking his telephone rang with a call from one of the members of our delegation who was taking his wife with him to India.

Robertson said, "If you are nervous about taking your wife I advise you not to go to Beirut."

When he hung up I asked him if he were going to advise me not to go, but he said, "No. You haven't asked my advice about that. You're a professional journalist. You can perform a useful function. It should be an interesting experience."

After I left him I got in touch with the BBC and asked the foreign news editor if he had a correspondent in Lebanon. He said he hadn't, and would be glad if I would send tapes to London during the week I was in Beirut.

Early in the morning of October 30th, I was all packed and ready to go to the airport when I received a message from Canada House saying the Department of External Affairs in Ottawa had sent instructions for me to proceed to Lebanon as planned and to give Leonard Brockington the same message when he joined my plane in Rome.

On the plane, a BOAC liner going from London to Karachi by way of Rome, Athens and Beirut, I found myself sitting beside a young man who was reading Rousseau while I devoured a "whodunit," my usual Pablum when I fly. We began to converse when our lunches arrived. He turned out to be a pilot on his way to Lebanon to pick up a plane. He was intelligent and amusing and knew a great deal about the Middle East. During the afternoon he went up to the cockpit to talk to the pilot.

When he came back, he said, "I'm not supposed to tell the passengers because they'll get upset but you're a journalist, so I guess it's all right to tell you. Anyway the pilot says he's had a message from London saying Egypt has refused to agree to a cease-fire and that means the English and the French will intervene. He says that from now on British planes are not going to be allowed to fly over Syria and Jordan, so this plane won't be able to go on to Karachi."

"I'm supposed to take this same flight from Beirut to Karachi next week," I said.

"Well, you won't be able to. No British plane will be allowed in or out of Lebanon after tonight."

"How on earth will I get out?"

"Maybe you could get to Istanbul. But it won't be easy because a lot of other people will have the same idea. By the way, I hope you don't mind my saying this, but I don't think you ought to walk around the streets alone tomorrow. The English aren't very popular with the Arabs right now."

"But I'm not English," I said, "and I am wearing a maple leaf pin on my lapel."

"You look English to them and you sound English. And nobody would know what the maple leaf means even if they noticed it. You'd have to wear your passport on your shoulder and even then most people wouldn't know what it was. I really do advise you not to go out alone."

It was after midnight when we landed at Beirut. Brock and I were met by the Canadian Minister to Lebanon with the same news the pilot had already given me. The passengers bound for the Far East by way of Karachi, were told that the plane was not going on and took the news philosophically and calmly as tired people often do. I admired a young couple en route to Tokyo with two small children and a baby, who walked off quite cheerfully in search of a hotel, carrying the baby in a Moses basket slung between them and each of them holding a toddler by the hand. Although I was calm on the surface like everyone else, I was tense and worried and, in spite of the soft, relaxing sea air, it took me a long time to get to sleep when at two in the morning I fell into bed in the Hotel St. Georges.

In the morning I sat on the balcony of my room eating breakfast and watching bronzed young men water-skiing and girls in bikinis going into the sea for an early dip. I was reminded of the stories about the exhausted soldiers rescued from the beaches of Dunkirk, who, after they were landed in England, looked out of the train windows on their way to camp or hospital and saw men in white flannels playing tennis and cricket in the peaceful, green countryside.

That day I found it difficult to get a substantiated story for my broadcast to the BBC. I had no hard news to go by, only rumours. The Canadian Legation was monitoring jubilant broadcasts from Israel announcing that the Israeli forces had swept across the Sinai Peninsula and were close to the canal, having destroyed large numbers of Egyptian tanks and guns and taking many prisoners on their way. However, nobody knew if this was accurate reporting (as it turned out to be) or propaganda for home consumption. In Beirut there was a growing atmosphere of tension. Troops in battle-dress were patrolling the streets and anti-aircraft gun emplacements were being set up here and there.

Car-loads and bus-loads of Europeans were pouring into the city, and since the hotels were full they camped in the lobbies or in the airport, waiting nervously in the hope of being evacuated, for though planes belonging to airlines other than the British or French were coming in and going out, they were full up. In the restaurant at lunch there was much angry talk by Lebanese loudly bringing down imprecations on the heads of the British and French in general and Anthony Eden in particular. The Europeans were very quiet and withdrawn, trying not to draw attention to themselves.

I wrote a broadcast about Beirut being a cave of winds of rumour and

got through to London after a long wait during which the Beirut oper-
ator kept saying *"un moment, s'il-vous plaît"* over and over again for
half an hour.

It was a comfort to hear a quiet English voice say, "Good to hear
you, Miss Francis. We're putting a tape recorder in at this end so just
talk naturally."

After that I talked into the telephone as if it were a mike and the tape
was twirling around in the studio next door instead of on the other side
of the Continent of Europe. I got quite a kick out of saying at the end,
"This is Anne Francis speaking from Beirut."

Later that night of October 31st, at a dinner party in the Canadian
Legation, we heard that Britain and France had begun to bomb Egypt.
The Canadians were shocked and strongly disapproving of the use of
force to bring about a cease-fire between Israel and Egypt, and we were
a bit smug and holier-than-thou about it.

I was proud of my country when, later in the week, at the United
Nations, "Mike" Pearson aligned Canada with the United States in con-
demning the French and British action. That was an unprecedented
move for an old Commonwealth country, but it seemed wise and states-
manlike from where I was sitting. I was astonished to hear that the
Conservative Opposition, as well as a great many Canadians, believed
we should have supported Britain, blindly, for the sake of the old
imperial ties. This feeling of blood loyalty to Britain seemed also to have
made them belittle Pearson's role in the UN decision to send a peacekeeping force into the Suez Canal zone. It has always seemed to me
to be a pity that the Canadian public as a whole does not, even yet,
seem to fully appreciate the importance of Pearson's contribution to
their security at that time, or were as proud as they should have been
when he was given the Nobel prize for his innovative and successful
effort to prevent what might have been the beginning of World War III.

The next day, I received a message from External Affairs in Ottawa
instructing me to get out of Lebanon at once and to proceed to New
Delhi as best I could. Brock had received the same message and told me
he was sure he would have enough pull to get out of the country somehow, pointing out that since he was the leader of the Canadian delegation
to UNESCO, it was more important for him to get to India than for me.
I agreed, feeling rather small and lonely, and spent the morning asking
all-and-sundry if they could help me on my way. Nobody seemed to
know anything about anything except that the Middle East was full of
Europeans and Americans who wanted out.

At noon, I went to a luncheon of a dozen Lebanese women given in my honour by the Canadian Minister. It was a strange meal. As we sat eating delicious food, we could hear the incessant sound of planes overhead, probably planes evacuating people, since the bombers taking off from Cyprus were certainly out of earshot. But that sound was like war-drums in my ears. Naturally all of us were thinking about the people only a few miles away who were being killed or wounded by the bombing, but nobody mentioned it.

A pediatrician told me about the Lebanese babies who died of dysentry because the water supply and the milk were not safe; she said she knew how to save the infants' lives but too often could not because of the conditions of life in the country. The principal of a school told me about her success with the eight hundred girls who were her pupils. A lawyer discussed the need for prison reform, especially for women. They were intelligent, fine women and I felt a strong bond with them. Fortunately, we were able to communicate easily in French. Yet we were all listening to the planes overhead and not one of us ever mentioned them or the war next door.

That evening I broadcast again to London.

The next day, November 2nd, I spent gathering material for another broadcast and badgering every airline office to make sure my name was on its waiting lists. Just before 6:30, when I was getting ready to ask for my line through to London, the telephone rang and a man's voice said, "I'm not responsible for this but there's a planeful of refugees coming up from Saudi Arabia on its way to Rome at seven o'clock and you may be able to get a seat on it. Better go out to the airport right away."

He hung up before I had time to thank him. I telephoned Brock's hotel and was told he had gone out. When I tried to get through to London I was told sharply that I would not be given a line any more, which I took to mean that censorship, imposed on telegraphs a couple of days before, had caught up with me.

I had packed in order to be ready to leave at a moment's notice so I closed my suitcases, checked out within ten minutes, and took a taxi to the airport. When I went to a wicket and asked about the plane coming up from Saudi Arabia the clerk laughed and said, "It's full up. You can't get on that."

"But what can I do?" I said. "I've given up my hotel room and there's not another room to be had in Beirut. Look at my white hair! A woman of my age can't sleep in the street."

I had never pulled that white hair gag before—nor since then. I felt ashamed at doing it but I had been told to go to New Delhi and was going to do my darnedest to get there. While I was pulling out the sob stops a handsome Lebanese, obviously a man of some importance judging by the way he carried himself, came over and looked at my passport.

"I see you are a Canadian," he said in French. "I've been to Canada. Do you know Granby?"

I said sure I knew Granby, which was true, as I had lunched there once on my way from Montreal to North Hatley by automobile.

"Do you know the mayor of Granby?"

"Oh yes, indeed," said I, which wasn't exactly true although I had heard about the zoo he had started in Granby and the way he went around the world collecting animals for it.

"He is a friend of mine," said the Arab. "Come in here."

He picked up my luggage and I followed him into a small office occupied by half a dozen Arabs. He sat down at a desk while the others sat around it on kitchen chairs. I sat on a tall stool of the kind clerks used in Charles Dickens' novels while the men talked in Arabic, wrote figures on paper, counted on their fingers, telephoned and argued.

It was very hot and stuffy and the stool was uncomfortable. After about five minutes I said in French, "What is happening? I don't understand a word anybody is saying."

"A plane with Danish refugees from an oil company in Saudi Arabia has just landed," the friend of the mayor of Granby said. "We're trying to figure out if it will be overweight if we put you on board."

A few minutes later he said, "You're on. It's going to Rome and you can probably get a plane to Karachi from there."

There was an explosion of pleasure from the men as well as from me. I shook hands with each of them and thanked them warmly, urging them to come and see me in Ottawa if ever they found their way to Canada.

"We will put you on board," someone said, and they picked up my suitcases and led me to the plane which had already been boarded. As I was half-way up the landing stairs, a man came running up with my dressing-case which had been left behind in the little room where all the calculations had been going on. I thanked everyone again, waved from the top of the stairs, went inside and sank into a seat with a great sense of relief.

Twenty minutes after we took off we landed in Beirut again because the plane had not been filled with gasoline.

We all trooped back to the airport to wait. Most of the passengers were Danish women and children. A number of the children had obviously been given to friends to take to Copenhagen by parents who were staying behind; some women seemed to be looking after half a dozen small, blond children close to the same age. One little girl in the waiting-room was very busy drawing on large sheets of paper with crayons: she was making a picture of the airport at night with the rows of blue lights along the runway.

While we were waiting, I telephoned the first secretary at the Canadian Legation to let him know I expected to be on my way shortly.

"Is Brockington with you?" he asked.

"No," I said. "I haven't seen him all day and he wasn't in his hotel when I phoned him just before leaving the St. Georges."

"Maybe he's gone already. He said he planned to leave by way of Istanbul so you probably won't see him until you get to New Delhi if you ever do."

We took off again at 8:30. At 10:30 we were given dinner and at one in the morning the plane landed in Rome. The children were asleep, some with encircling arms around them, others sitting on women's laps curled up like kittens in odd positions.

A Syrian and I were the only passengers to get off. The airport was deserted, very silent and very large. An agent glanced at our passports and put a chalk mark on our luggege in a perfunctory way.

As I was wondering how I would ever get all my luggage to a taxi, a man in uniform came running toward me. "Mrs. Bird," he called, "Mrs. Bird?"

I said, "Yes, I'm Mrs. Bird."

"What have you done with Mr. Brockington? Where is he?"

I said I hadn't done anything with Mr. Brockington and hadn't any idea where he was but I would be grateful if he would find me a taxi.

"The taxi will take you to the air terminal in Rome," he said, "and somebody there will find a hotel room for you. All the hotels are full but he will do what he can."

It was strange driving through the silent streets of Rome, past the Coliseum, stark and grey. I saw a couple of policemen in their grey-green capes walking slowly down the empty pavements which are so crowded in day-time. At the air terminal a man in uniform spent ten minutes telephoning and then gave the name of a hotel which still had a room. When the taxi took me there, the room clerk said he was sorry—

he had just given the room to someone else, but I could sleep in the lobby along with a great many other people. I insisted that I needed a room, however, so he gave me the name of another hotel.

After we had been on our way for ten minutes, the taxi driver said it would cost me another thousand lira. I didn't feel like arguing. I felt lonely and defenceless in the huge, empty city and very, very tired. After a long drive, we arrived at the Park Extension Hotel where I was given a room in a remote corner up many flights of stairs and down many corridors. The lobby was crowded with men in airforce uniforms who were sleeping on the floor with their heads on their duffel bags. Once in my room, I undressed and, without bothering to brush my teeth or take off my makeup, threw myself on the bed and fell asleep immediately.

At 8:30 the next morning I telephoned Norman Berlis, the first secretary at the Canadian Embassy.

"Thank God," he said. "We wondered where you were. John Bird has been taking the Department of External Affairs apart because he hasn't heard from you for four days. Where are you?"

"I don't know," I said. "I can't remember the name of the hotel and I have no idea where it is. I'll find out and let you know. I was so tired last night that I didn't know what part of Rome the taxi was taking me to."

"Come for dinner tonight," Berlis said. "I'll pick you up at eight o'clock. When you find out where you are, leave a message with my secretary."

I asked him to send a cable to Ottawa and dictated a short message in cablese which contained all the information I knew J.B. would want. It read as follows: "Out stop well stop Indiawarding soonest."

During the Suez crisis the embassy in Rome was having a hectic time trying to look after Canadian refugees from the Middle East who regarded our mission in Rome as a combination mother, banker, hotel and aeroplane booking agent, medical centre, counsellor and general accommodator. One Canadian woman had insisted that the embassy find a veterinarian to tend to her cat which had become indisposed after a succession of aeroplane flights—something which I gathered some of the diplomats felt was over and above the call of duty at a time when a full-scale war might erupt at any minute.

I spent the morning at the BOAC ticket office, most of the time waiting in a long line of worried, tired people. The agent said he would do what he could about getting me to New Delhi, but of course could make no commitment of any kind.

I slept most of the afternoon, after receiving a cable from J.B. which let me know he had received my cable and was no longer dismembering the Department of External Affairs in Ottawa now that he knew where I was and what I was up to.

When Berlis came for me in his car at eight o'clock that evening he said, "I realize you were exhausted and upset this morning or you wouldn't have sent such a strange cable. Do you think your husband could have made head or tail of it? Do you want me to send another for you?"

"Oh, he understood it perfectly," I said. "I've had an answer from him already. He sent it to the Embassy and one of your people telephoned it to me."

"What did it say?"

"It said, 'Hallelujah'."

Thérèse Casgrain was also a dinner guest that night. She had been stranded in Athens on her way to a socialist conference in Bombay, had somehow managed to get back to Rome, and like me, was trying to find her way to India. Madame Casgrain, one of the great Canadian women, has done more than any single person for the cause of women's rights in the Province of Quebec. Handsome, elegant in the way many French-Canadian women are elegant, she is also intelligent, witty and wise. It's a pity that she was not given official recognition sooner; she was only a senator for nine months before having to retire when she reached the age of seventy-five. In 1956 she was full of vigour—as she still is for that matter—and helped to make the dinner an amusing occasion instead of a depressing one.

The owner of the apartment house had turned off the central heating anticipating that no oil could be brought from the Middle East for some time to come. It was very cold in the big, high-ceilinged rooms with the marble floors, cold the way I remember it from the pensione we had stayed in on my first trip to Rome when I was nineteen. However, Mrs. Berlis had put a little electric stove under the table, which kept our feet warm, and I wore my trusty muskrat cape over my shoulders. After dinner we carried the stove with us and the four of us huddled around it, warming our outstretched hands the way, on cold days, the street chestnut-vendors in Paris warm their hands at their little charcoal stoves.

On November 5th, the day British and French troops landed in Egypt, I boarded the BOAC flight for Karachi which I had originally planned to take from Beirut; UNESCO had made a great effort to ensure that the refugees from the Middle East who had reached Rome would

be able to go on to India. Several other members of the Canadian delegation, the ones who had stayed in London, were on board, so I had
company. Brockington had turned up in Rome the morning before and
although he was not well, had gone ahead of us on an earlier plane.

Just before we took off the pilot told us he was flying a route he had
never taken before, by way of Athens, Istanbul, Baghdad and Abadan.
He said it was more than likely that the Iraqi might confiscate the plane
and intern the passengers because Arab feeling was very bitter against
the British. He said he had warned us and if anyone did not want to take
the flight, to please leave the plane immediately. No one left.

We put down at Athens and went into the airport for coffee. A few
minutes later a Russian plane full of athletes landed. The Olympics were
taking place in Australia that year and the Russians were on their way
there. The athletes, fine-looking men and women dressed in exercise
suits, came bouncing into the restaurant, waving their arms and spring-
ing into the air.

We put down again at Istanbul around midnight. Soon after the
Russian plane also came in, and while we were sitting—groggy, with
eyes like buttonholes—the athletes bounced in like ballet-dancers. They
made us feel very old and tired.

The next afternoon we landed in Abadan. Once again the Russian
plane followed us in, but this time the athletes straggled into the airport,
moving with heavy feet and looking as tired and worn as we did. We
felt kindly toward them; it was a relief to find they were human after all.

In Abadan, as I sat on a bench in the shade outside the airport, I saw
three women and a child who have always stayed in my mind as symbols
of what is happening in Asia. Two of the women were wearing the
burka, the black tent-like garment which completely conceals the face
and body of a Muslim woman in purdah. Only their hands were uncovered. Those work-worn hands, speckled like a toad with brown spots,
the fingers calloused, the nails broken, told me that the women were
old as clearly as if their faces and bodies had been visible. It was very
hot and I wondered how they could bear the heat without any air on
their bodies. They sat, talking little, not moving. I imagined they were
the wives of a desert Arab. With them was a young woman also wearing
the burka, who had thrown back the hood and veil so that her head
and face were bare. She had the full-blown beauty, the heavy, dark hair
and warm skin which make eastern women so alluring, and there was
something very alive and exciting about her as she stood scanning the
sky or walking up and down impatiently. In her arms she carried a baby

dressed in a blue knitted suit. It seemed to me that I was seeing the past symbolized by the old women; the present by the woman in transition, half emerging from the subjugation of purdah; and the future by the baby, who would demand the freedom that women in developed countries now have.

The plane reached Karachi around eleven that night. We were sent to the BOAC guest house where we had a few hours' sleep and a shower before taking the plane for New Delhi at two in the morning. While we were waiting, Brockington came stumping across the rotunda of the airport, leaning heavily on his cane. He and another member of the delegation sat in the seats behind me and talked for the rest of the night. He was in pain most of the time, a sick man suffering not only from arthritis, but also diabetes, and he slept little at a time. While we were in India, he would sit, smoking cigar after cigar, in the drawing-room reserved for the delegation, until his bearer helped him to bed at two or three in the morning.

I found India beautiful, fascinating, terrible and wonderful. There is so much beauty, so much colour; the blue sky, "a pale blue cup"; the green of the grass on the November and December mornings when I rose early to go into a village to make a film for the CBC; the rich red of the Red Fort and the warm ochre of the mosques and temples; the slim women moving gracefully in their bright-coloured, floating saris; the school-girls in their white trousers and pale-blue jackets; the leis of orange marigolds around the necks of the tawny oxen.

And there is so much that is terrible: the poverty, the tiny, sickly babies soon to die; the people sleeping on the streets because they have no other place to sleep; the lepers, shapeless figures in gray, with faces covered, sitting under the bridge between old Delhi and New Delhi; the sheer numbers of people living on a thin edge between life and death.

And there is much that is wonderful: the courage of the men and women trying to fight famine, poverty and the relentless pressure of the growing population; the intelligence and the pride of those people.

I do not see how any sensitive person can go to India without returning home a different person. It is only after you have seen India, smelled it, heard it, let it sink into the marrow of mind and senses, that you can fully understand the statistics which show that most of the people in the world are sick, hungry and poor. For me, in India, statistics became people.

By contrast with the poverty around us, as is always the way, the delegates to UNESCO lived in luxury and were wined and dined daily.

The conference opened in an atmosphere of bitterness and dissension. It was sad to find the Suez crisis tearing apart an organization dedicated to the preservation of peace by means of educational, cultural and scientific improvements. It was a gathering of high-minded, dedicated people from all the UN countries, but since each delegation had to put forward the policies of the country it represented, the conference was very little different from any other UN meeting—except perhaps that there were more documents. By the end of five weeks my small sitting room looked as if I had gone into the paper salvage business as we did for the Patriotic Salvage Corps during the war. At first I tried to read all the paper hand-outs, but gave up when I found other delegates were not, because there just wasn't time. As it was, we were on the go from 8:30 in the morning until after midnight.

The first few days of the conference were charged with emotion. The British, the French and the Israelis were regarded as the skunks at the party by the delegations from the Arab countries as well as by the Indians and Pakistanis, while the Americans and the Canadians were aces high with them. The newspapers in India were full of angry editorials about the war in "West Asia" and gave scant coverage to the revolution in Hungary and the way Russian tanks had put an end to the successful uprising of the Hungarian freedom fighters.

Nehru had been quick to condemn the British and French intervention in the Middle East but slow to raise his voice against Russia, probably because Russia and China seem very close when you are in India, something you feel in a different way when you are there than if you only look at a map.

I was given a revealing insight into the Indian attitude toward Britain when I had an argument with a Hindu who had been inveighing against the British action.

"Why," I asked, "are you so angry at the British and have so little to say about what the Russians are doing in Hungary?"

"Nobody," he replied, "expects anything different from Russia, but Britain is the mother country and we expect better of her."

I was on the UNESCO Communications Committee.

This involved voting on a long list of projects having to do with information about UNESCO and its work. It didn't require much expertise because Mary Dench, the delegation's adviser from the Department of External Affairs, sat beside me and made sure that I did not deviate from the government's official policy.

On one occasion, when Mary was ill, I happened to be half asleep; I had started the day at 6:30 in order to work in a village on the CBC film. My good friends in the Australian delegation insisted later that I voted For, and Against, and Abstained, on one of the motions—a gross exaggeration, of course.

As far as I was concerned, the impact of India far outweighed that of the UNESCO conference itself. However, I was very busy, because Brockington asked me to do a number of broadcasts for him on All India Radio. I also wrote several others for Canadian consumption which were put on tape and relayed to the CBC in London by air-freight.

Before I went to India, Sir Archibald Nye, the British High Commissioner in Ottawa, then about to retire, had given me a long and priceless briefing about the country. He and his wife Colleen had become valued friends, habitués of our little shack in the Gatineau Hills. Archie was a man of great intelligence and integrity, a warm person when you got to know him, although somewhat stiff and shy with acquaintances. He had a fine sense of humour and was an accomplished raconteur. He had a particularly rich fund of Churchill stories, since he had had a good deal to do with the Prime Minister while he was Vice-Chief of Imperial Staff, second to General Alanbrooke, during the war.

Later he was Governor-General of Madras, and after India became independent, went back as British High Commissioner to India at the request of Nehru.

Archie and Colleen loved India, had the greatest sympathy for her people, and had many friends there. Colleen also gave me a briefing on India and sent me off with letters of introduction to a number of outstanding women, such as Amrit Kaur, the Minister of Health and Welfare at that time.

These letters were an open sesame to a number of Indian households and Colleen's friends talked freely to me. I achieved a high regard for the women who had gone to prison with Gandhi and Nehru and, on the strength of their record, had been elected to the Indian Parliament. They worked hard, knew what they were doing, refused to be defeated by the monumental problems of the country, and generally had the self-confidence so many Canadian women lack.

There are two other reasons why Indian women have a much better political record than Canadian women. First: in India every intelligent, educated person is desperately needed, and women are not allowed to waste their ability, as often happens in Canada. Second: until recently it was always easy to get domestic servants for a small wage, so that women in public life were freed from the tiring, time-consuming demands of home and children which prevent many Canadian women from getting experience in politics or business while their children are young.

On the way home from New Delhi I stopped off in Karachi, to stay with Morley Scott, the Canadian High Commissioner to Pakistan. Thanks to him, during the next few days I met a number of remarkable women who were running APWA (All Pakistan Women's Association). Three of them arrived at the residence in a chauffeur-driven station wagon at eight in the morning and took me out for the day to show me what they had done to help the millions of refugees who had come across the border from India after the partition of the sub-continent in 1948.

They showed me refugee children at school under the arches of a bridge over a river. They explained that there were no schoolhouses for the refugee children who needed an education, and so they had decided to use the bridge because it provided protection from sun or rain. They said, "Teachers and pupils are more important than buildings."

They took me to a model village for refugees and showed me with pride that water was piped in and there was a tap in front of each little house so that the women did not have to carry water in buckets from the village well. That morning we also visited a clinic; a girls' high school; a handicraft centre; and a huge boarding school where girls were being taught home economics. It had been cool when we started out in the morning, but by noon the sun was hot and by mid-afternoon I was beginning to feel very tired. My fatigue surprised the begums who told me that when Eleanor Roosevelt had visited Karachi she had done twice as much in a day without showing any sign of flagging. When I had been in Israel the year before, "Eleanor" had just left. She had seen three schools to my one. I had become accustomed to explaining my comparative lassitude by saying that Mrs. Roosevelt was twenty years older than I, and I hoped to be more energetic by the time I was seventy.

The APWA women were obviously accomplished organizers. What they had achieved was impressive by any standard but was extraordinary considering that most of them had only recently emerged from purdah. It seems to me remarkable that they were able to adapt themselves so quickly and had become efficient executives after having been cut off from the outside world for such a large portion of their lives. One of them said she still found it very hard to discuss business matters with men after not having spoken to any men outside of her immediate family for forty years.

She said, "The first time I uncovered my face and went to the office of a businessman it was as dreadful for me as it would be for you to walk naked in the street. I could only do it because it was absolutely essential for us to help all the destitute refugees."

Those women reinforced my belief, gained during my experience with volunteers in Winnipeg during the war, that women are capable of doing anything they are convinced should be done, provided they are given the opportunity. It is a pity that it so often requires a war or other catastrophe to give them the motivation and the opportunity they need to make full use of their ability.

After I got back from India I wrote a number of broadcasts about life in that country. One of them received a first prize from the Women's National Press Club, along with one in another series on what was happening to Canadian women when they were found guilty of an offence and were sent to prison.

Women and the Law

The series of broadcasts about women and the law required a great deal of first-hand research that gave me a violent nervous headache for days on end. Two members of the Elizabeth Fry Society in Ottawa took me into the old Nicholas Street jail, only recently closed down after having been condemned for years as being unfit for use. The women prisoners were locked up at night, two or three in a cell, but during the day they were shut out of the cell blocks and had to sit on a backless bench in the corridor in front of the cells. Barred windows, high in the wall, showed only "that little patch of blue that prisoners call the sky." The women sat there all day long, talking, playing games such as checkers, leafing through magazines supplied by the Elizabeth Fry Society, or just sitting on their hands and staring off into space.

The afternoon I visited the jail, a number of old alcoholics were in the corridor, derelicts who had been arrested for being drunk in public as often as fifty times. There were also a couple of dreary-looking prostitutes, a petty thief and a sixteen-year old girl who had attempted to commit suicide. I was horrified to find a mentally ill girl in such a place and in such company. I was more horrified still when it was explained to me that there was no bed for her in the psychiatric ward of the Ottawa Civic Hospital, and she had been sent to the jail until a place could be found for her in the hospital for mentally ill and retarded people in Brockville.

I was unable to visit the prison for women in Montreal, a notorious hell-hole, because officials of the Duplessis regime refused to allow me to see for myself what went on there. However, I managed to get a great deal of convincing evidence for my broadcasts from the prison chaplain, several members of the staff, nuns who worked there and one of the former inmates. They all told the same stories about bad food, dirt, vermin, lack of exercise for the prisoners, no occupational therapy or psychiatric treatment, and overcrowding—twenty women in one small room so that they had to crawl over each other to get into their cots at night. It required a change of government before the iniquitous Montreal prison for women was closed and prison reform began to take place in the province of Quebec. While Maurice Duplessis was Premier, little was done to help the insane or to rehabilitate prisoners of either sex. I have been told that Duplessis once said in public that he was not interested in them because they did not have the right to vote.

Although I could not get into the prison I did succeed in seeing how the law sometimes treated women in Montreal. A young French-Canadian social worker took me into the "cow pen" of the city jail so I could talk to some of the women who had been brought in there the night before and were waiting to go into court. It was strange and rather frightening to hear the great barred door slam behind me and to find myself in a big room along with a dozen women who, because of an accident of birth, led lives so different from my own. Most of them were prostitutes or lushes.

The social worker told me that she had never seen a Jewish prostitute in the "cow pen" because the Jewish community, having a strong family feeling and a good system of social services, looked after its own.

That day, several of the prostitutes in the Montreal city jail told me that it was almost impossible for them to change their way of life even if they wanted to do so. They explained that after they had served a prison sentence they would have no place to go for the night when they were released. They would have only the clothes they stood up in, since their rooms would have been rented and their personal possessions would have disappeared. This often meant that if they were sent to prison in the summer, when they were wearing cotton dresses, they might come out to find themselves without warm clothing in freezing autumn or winter weather. When they were taken into custody by the police, they had usually little money in their pockets so when they came out of prison they knew of only one way to earn money to pay for meals or a room and that was to start soliciting again. They said that even if they were not soliciting they were often arrested since they were known to the police who, under the vagrancy clauses in the Criminal Code, could arrest them if they were in a public place and unable to give a satisfactory account of themselves.

Thirteen years later the Royal Commission on the Status of Women recommended that those vagrancy clauses be taken out of the Criminal Code. Parliament did so in 1972.

After I had talked to the women in the "cow pen," the social worker said, "I'm going to try to get you into Number 10 police station. There are half a dozen insane women there and I think you ought to see and write about them, if you have the courage."

When we reached the station she told the constable on duty I was a social worker because, she said, he would never let me in if he knew I was a reporter.

The policeman turned out to be eager to let us see the women, who were locked in cells at the rear of the building. He delivered a running commentary about them as he led us to the basement.

"They've been here for months," he said. "We're policemen; we aren't doctors and nurses and we don't know what to do for them. When they get covered with their own filth we hose them down but that's about the only treatment they get. They're not supposed to be here but there's no room for them in any of the mental hospitals. I certainly wish you would do something so that somebody takes them away."

It was cold in the basement. The cells in which the women were confined were bare of furnishings of any kind. Some of the women were naked, the others wore stained white cotton hospital-gowns. They sat or lay on the concrete floor or stood holding on to the bars.

When I said I thought they ought to have mattresses and blankets the policeman shook his head.

"We don't dare to give them anything. They tear everything to pieces and besides they might hang themselves with the blankets. They're violent. They don't know what they're doing. Anyway there's no way of keeping their bedding clean. They just let go like animals so we have to clean it up with the hose."

The women holding on to the bars kept reaching out at us with bony hands at the end of bony arms.

"Be careful," the policeman warned. "They'll grab you and hurt you if you get too close."

The place smelt of urine and excrement and echoed with the sound of animal cries and groans.

I wrote, in anger and in pity, about the barbaric treatment those sick women were receiving. I was told that the women had been moved after the broadcasts went on the air, but I don't know if they were sent to proper hospitals or just shoved away somewhere out of sight.

At that time, in 1957, I had decided to confine my research for the series of broadcasts to the federal prison for women, at Kingston, and city jails and provincial prisons in the two most populated provinces, Quebec and Ontario. Knowing Duplessis' attitude toward the disenfranchised, I had not been surprised when I was unable to get into the Montreal prison for women. On the other hand, I was taken aback when I was given the run-around by Ontario petty bureaucrats who kept saying it would be impossible for me to visit the Mercer Reformatory for Women in Toronto, a Bastille-like building in a factory district of the city. I finally reached the top of the civil service hierarchy and confronted the Deputy Minister of Ontario Reform Institutions, an authoritarian character, with the remarkable name of Hedley Basher.

At first, Colonel Basher refused categorically to give me permission to visit the Mercer. He changed his mind when I suggested he must be trying to hide something and that if he prevented me from writing a story based on personal observation I would write one based on information I had already received from social workers who visited the Mercer regularly, and from other people who knew a great deal about the place. (One of them was Elsie Gregory MacGill who was later a member of the Royal Commission on the Status of Women.)

Before giving me permission to visit the prison, Colonel Basher made me promise to let him see my script before it was scheduled to be broadcast. He waited until the day it was to go on the air and then went in person to the organizer of the program in Toronto, demanding that it be cancelled. He claimed that the broadcast was inaccurate because I had called the superintendent a matron and had said that the prisoners were forbidden to speak during meals. The organizer, a tough-minded Maritimer named Dorothea Cox, did not like to be bullied. She refused to cancel the broadcast and instead telephoned Don Bennett, a senior producer in Ottawa, who called me out of a luncheon party.

By air time, I had changed the offending word "matron" to "superintendent" and inserted, "Colonel Hedley Basher says the prisoners are given permission to talk at meals but the day I was there no word was spoken by the inmates while they were at lunch." Of course, what the Deputy Minister really objected to was my criticism of the lack of a meaningful rehabilitation program in the grim old institution, as well as the way first offenders, alcoholics, drug addicts and women who had been convicted a number of times for theft or other offenses were not segregated from one another. I was also critical of the way several children were kept in the building along with their mothers who had been imprisoned for bigamy.

I found the Mercer Reformatory depressing because so many of the inmates were aged alcoholics who had been sent there again and again. I believed then that it was a waste of public money and a stupid, old-fashioned concept of justice to send sick people to prison; I still thought so years later after reading the research material provided by the secretariat of the Royal Commission on the Status of Women. All the commissioners agreed with me. We felt that there was neither rhyme nor reason for what was being done to female alcoholics who broke the law, and especially to Indian and Métis women in the West who, in 1968, accounted for between 69 and 100 per cent of the population of the prisons for women in Kenora, Ontario, The Pas and Portage la Prairie in Manitoba, Riverside in Saskatchewan, and Fort Saskatchewan in Alberta.

As the Commission said in its report, "Most of these women are clearly not being rehabilitated by jail sentences, and should get more appropriate help from other agencies."

The truth is that we still have an old-fashioned, punitive attitude toward offenders who break the law because they are drunk or under the influence of drugs, or who steal in order to get the money to buy alcohol or drugs.

I was able to visit the federal prison for women at Kingston because General R.W. Gibson, then the Commissioner of Penitentiaries, was a friend and trusted me. In my broadcast I said the huge, gray stone building behind a high stone wall was medieval, and that it was ridiculous to lock up a hundred or so women, most of them drug addicts, in the cell blocks of a maximum security prison. I pointed out that women do not commit crimes of violence to anything like the same extent as men and so are not, as a rule, any great danger to others. Most of their crimes are against themselves in the form of alcoholism, drug addiction, suicide and prostitution. They are usually brought into court for minor offences such as stealing small sums of money, shoplifting, soliciting, and being drunk and creating a public nuisance, and are sentenced to do time in provincial institutions because the federal government is only responsible for offenders who have received sentences of longer than two years.

I said I thought it was unnecessary to keep women, many of whom came from the west coast, Quebec or the Maritimes, so far away from their families that they seldom received visitors. I pointed out that anyone with any human understanding would realize that their being completely cut off from family and friends was bad for their mental health and made it more difficult for them to be rehabilitated into society when they came out of prison. I mentioned an old woman I saw in the Kingston prison infirmary, sent up for the murder of her husband, who had not had a single visitor during the ten years she had been in the penitentiary.

Sixteen years later, the Royal Commission on the Status of Women recommended that the prison for women at Kingston be closed and the inmates sent to provincial institutions in order to be closer to their families and friends. We also recommended that the provinces give the drug addicts medical and psychiatric treatment, and undertake a special training and rehabilitation program for the handful of long-term prisoners put under their care.

In 1973 there were 8,938 men in federal penitentiaries and 150 women (in the federal prison for women at Kingston). The federal government and all the provinces have now agreed, in principle, that as the RCSW recommended, women sentenced to prison for more than two years should become a provincial responsibility and that more cooperation between federal and provincial authorities is needed. It is now a question of finding space for women in provincial institutions and of providing training, psychiatric treatment and other rehabilitation programs. Agreements have been reached with some of the provinces and some women will be moved from Kingston during 1974. However it will take time before the now over-crowded maximum security prison will be closed as the RCSW recommended.

The Elizabeth Fry Society of Kingston, which for many years has given intelligent, constructive help to female prisoners, is now on the alert to make sure that before the transfer takes place the provinces make a definite undertaking to provide rehabilitation programs as good as the ones given at Kingston by the federal government.

I gave the series of four ten-minute broadcasts about women and prisons on *Trans-Canada Matinée*. The reaction was so positive that I was asked to broadcast them a second time at night right after the CBC ten o'clock news. That evening program had a large listening audience and a number of Members of Parliament and Senators heard the broadcasts and discussed them with approval in the Commons and the Senate.

European Assignments

In 1957 there was a great deal of interest in Germany. The papers were full of stories about the "Economic Miracle" of Ludwig Erhard and how, with the help of the Marshall Plan, he had lifted Germany, with her factories destroyed and her great cities flattened by bombs, from the ashes of defeat and had made her once again into a strong trading nation. There was considerable fear in Canada that an economically powerful Germany might become a threat to world peace if the democratically-minded government of Chancellor Konrad Adenauer were to give way to a neo-Nazi regime. I thought there was also a significant story in the thousands of refugees who were pouring across the border from communist East Germany and East Berlin into West Germany and West Berlin. I made up my mind to go to Germany for at least six weeks to see for myself what was happening there.

When Harry Boyle of the CBC heard that I planned to go, he asked me to write a script and record interviews on tape, to produce an hour-long documentary for *Project,* a series of radio programs he had conceived and organized. I was delighted to have the opportunity to work for such an intelligent and creative man. Harry discussed the thrust of the script with me and made many valuable suggestions. And when I went to Germany in the autumn he sent a young producer, Tony Thomas, to help me with all the technical problems involved in making a long show.

During the previous winter and summer, while I was doing my homework on Germany, I took German lessons a couple of times a week. My teacher and I were both astonished to find that there was so much easy recall of the German I had learned from my governess, Kaekey, when I was a child. It had evidently been quick-frozen, as it were, and

248

stored away in the compartments of my brain waiting to be thawed out by the stimulation of talking and hearing the language again.

When I got to Germany, I found that a nine-year-old has a vocabulary that is very useful in acquiring creature comforts such as water, food, and blankets to replace the ubiquitous eiderdowns which, too short for me, roasted my middle, froze my feet, and fell off many times during the night. However, the lessons had increased a vocabulary which did not include the names of inventions unknown when I was a child, such as radio, television, aeroplane tickets and tape recorders.

Tony Thomas and I spent five weeks travelling hard, so that we saw a great deal of Germany and talked to a great many different kinds of people. I also had fun, since I took four days' holiday in Bavaria and went up into the Alps to climb on easy trails all day while Tony worked in Munich. Thanks to the help of the German government we were able to get a number of good interviews with politicians, which enabled us to put together a significant show when we got home.

When I interviewed Franz-Josef Strauss, I was fascinated by his blue, rather mocking, Bavarian eyes and his smooth replies to my questions. For example, when I asked him if he thought West Germany would resort to force in order to reunify the country he said in his guttural English, "Reunification in a common grave is not to the advantage of the German people."

It was a brilliant answer and yet I didn't trust him.

My impression of Willy Brandt, then the mayor of West Berlin, was quite different. A heavy-shouldered bull of a man, he gave me the feeling that he was not only intelligent, but honest and sincere.

I had been given the usual official run-around when I tried to get an interview with the Mayor. When I told my troubles to Escott Reid, the Canadian Ambassador, he invited me to a dinner party he was giving in West Berlin the next week. He said Willy Brandt would be one of the guests and, with luck, I might be able to persuade him to give me an interview.

I had trouble finding a taxi and was late arriving at the dinner, and so did not have time to look at the seating chart. When I found my seat, I was surprised to see that the Mayor was seated at the left of Ruth Reid, the hostess, while a tall, loud-voiced, arrogant-looking man was on her right. After dinner, while the men were in the dining room and the women were having coffee and liqueurs in the parlour, I sat beside Frau Brandt, a slender, pretty Norwegian woman. I told her how much I admired her husband and how much I wanted to interview him. She was sympathetic and promised to help. She said "When the men join us, I will take you over to him."

I had just started to plead my case with Brandt when the man who had been seated on Ruth Reid's right came over to us and began talking excitedly, in an unmistakable American accent, about the Russian occupation forces in West Berlin.

"It's no use trying to reason with them or work with them," he said. "The only way we can settle the mess here in Berlin is to have a preventive war right away before the Russians get any stronger."

Brandt, who was looking worried and tired, did not say anything. I was furious at the American. Fortified by the good food and wine at dinner, I told him emphatically and at some length that he might think a preventive war was a good idea, but no Canadian in his right mind thought so. I said he ought to be ashamed to talk that way in front of the Herr Bürgermeister who, in order to prevent calamitous reprisals, had gone to the Brandenburg Gate, at considerable risk to himself, to stop crowds of West Germans from joining East Germans in a revolt against the Russians. We had quite a heated argument during which Brandt listened, in silence, with a dead-pan expression on his face.

When the party broke up, Brandt said to me, "Telephone my secretary tomorrow morning and tell him I met you here tonight and promised to give you an interview. He will fix the time for you to come to my office."

The Reids gave me the high sign to stay on after the other guests had gone, for a nightcap and a post-mortem on the party. I asked them then who the American was, explaining that I had neither seen the seating chart nor caught his name during the hasty introductions before we went in for dinner.

"He's General Hamlet," Escott Reid said. "He's the commander of the American sector of West Berlin. He was seated on Ruth's right because according to protocol he outranks the Mayor of Berlin."

The next afternoon, after Tony Thomas and I had taped a long interview with Willy Brandt, I asked the Mayor if I could have a word with him in private. We walked to one end of his huge office and I told him I owed him an apology as I had not known who the American was and certainly had no intention of embarrassing him in front of the general. Brandt's face lit up and for a moment a broad grin wiped away the lines of worry and fatigue.

"You didn't know who he was?" he said. "You didn't know? Well, you were wonderful. You said all the things I wanted to say and couldn't say. Thank you."

I am told that for a number of years after that, whenever Canadian newspapermen turned up in Berlin, Brandt would say, "How is Mrs. Bird?"

Some time after, when he came to Ottawa, there was a reception and as I went down the receiving line he said to me, "General Hamlet has gone now, but I'll never forget that night at dinner."

Later, while he was here, I was one of the three broadcasters who interviewed him on television. As before, I was impressed by his strength and sincerity. It is fortunate for West Germany and the peace of Europe that he has become the Chancellor of West Germany.

While Tony Thomas and I were gathering material for the documentary in Germany we discovered that my nose for news had been sound; there were not only many human interest stories concerning the refugees coming from East Germany, but also an important political story, as was proved five years later when the East Germans built the wall between the East and West sectors of Berlin.

We went to a couple of refugee camps outside Hamburg where East German families were being housed until better living quarters could be found for them. At that time there was a serious housing shortage in West Germany, since many houses had been destroyed by area bombing during the war. Although housing units were being built, there was not yet a sufficient number to accommodate the existing population and its normal growth, let alone the thousands of destitute refugees. I was particularly touched by an interview with a woman from East Prussia who had walked ahead of the Russian troops in 1945, holding her child by one hand and a suitcase in the other. She had just moved into a small apartment after waiting in a camp for eleven years.

"You will never know what it means to have privacy at last," she said. "It seems like a miracle to have a key so I can lock my own front door and be alone."

The camps were clean but there was certainly no privacy. Often two families slept in one small room on three-decker tiers of bunks. The men were quickly absorbed into the work force and left the camps by day, unless of course they were on night shifts and had to get what sleep they could amidst the noise of children playing and women talking. The mothers stayed in the camp, cooking in communal kitchens and complaining about the accommodation, but when I asked some of them if they regretted having left the East they all said, "No, no. It is better here."

It seemed to me, after talking to businessmen and politicians, that Germany's "Economic Miracle" was due not only to the genius of Ludwig Erhard and the assistance of the Marshall Plan, but also to the industry of the German people. An additional contributing factor was the docility of the unions which, remembering the horrors of inflation that followed the First World War, co-operated with the captains of industry to keep wages and prices down and so be competitive in world markets.

As we travelled around the country, Tony and I were astonished by the variety and the high quality of the merchandise displayed in stores in West Berlin and Duesseldorf and by the enormous, delicious meals served to us in the expensive restaurants where we were taken by German officials. We decided that the system of private enterprise and the democratic regime in Germany were safe from either communists or neo-Nazis as long as the booming prosperity continued.

Because of my interest in women offenders, I took a day off to visit a federal prison for women in Frankfurt. The building was even more medieval than the Kingston Prison for Women. As in Canada, the prisoners were doing the usual sort of laundry work and sewing. As in Canada, there was no segregation of prisoners: first offenders lived in cells side by side with confirmed repeaters and with psychopaths who were habitual criminals because they lacked a conscience or a sense of right and wrong. However, the superintendent, a young and intelligent woman with a doctorate in criminology, had enlightened ideas about prison reform and rehabilitation. She was proud of the way some of the women were using the good library and was enthusiastic about the new quarters being built within the wall where some prisoners on parole were to live when they first began to work in the community.

Then in his early thirties, Tony Thomas was an experienced producer and a quick worker. He loved music and knew a great deal about it, but his abiding interest was show business. He and I were a good team: our experience and interests were so different that between us we planned a balanced show, which was what Harry Boyle had thought would happen when he sent us off together.

I found Tony a thoughtful, helpful, travelling companion and enjoyed his sense of humour and gift of mimicry. However, I am a day-person who does her best work in the morning hours, while Tony is a night-person whose day begins when day is done. It suited me well that the Germans are early risers like myself and often gave us appointments at hours when Tony was accustomed to be in deep sleep. I used to telephone his room at 7:30 in the morning to be greeted by unbelieving groans. And, though he would drag himself out of bed, he would be in a state of coma until lunchtime. However, after dinner he would get his own back by insisting that we walk for hours through the streets of every town, window-shopping, exploring alley-ways, and wandering up and down steps that led to unexpected little squares and old buildings. We would end up around midnight in some small café, discussing the thrust of the interviews I was to make the next day.

The documentary about Germany on *Project '59* was a success—which made Tony and me want to do another show together. Accordingly, the following year I submitted to Harry Boyle the outline of a documentary about the successes and failures involved in a welfare state as it had developed in Denmark. Harry liked the idea, and sent Tony Thomas by plane to Copenhagen ahead of me to set up interviews and "case the joint."

J.B. had an assignment in Poland for the *Toronto Star* and decided to accompany me by boat as far as Copenhagen. We booked passage on a lovely ship, the *Gripsholm*. The voyage was dull as far as company was concerned until we bumped into Ed Murrow on the third day out. We saw a great deal of him and his wife during the following week, since we shared so many of the same interests and were unhappy about the way the power and potential of television were being wasted by the exploitation of violence and cheap sensationalism. Ed was planning to do a documentary about Canada but did not live to carry out the project.

J.B. flew to Warsaw for ten days while Tony Thomas and I were working in Denmark, and then joined us again in Copenhagen in order to write his articles. He felt it was easier to write there in that peaceful, civilized country rather than behind the Iron Curtain where the atmosphere was heavy with suspicion.

It did not take Tony and me long to discover that there is much of interest beside the welfare state in Denmark and we consequently prepared a documentary that we hoped represented a capsule portrait of the country as a whole. The show was strengthened because I had the good fortune to get interviews with Niels Bohr, the Danish physicist who had done so much to split the atom, and with Baroness Karen Blixen, the great woman who wrote *Out of Africa* under her own name and *Seven Gothic Tales* under the *nom-de-plume* of Isak Dinesen.

Interviewing Bohr was a rather terrifying experience. A small, intense man, he walked like a caged animal around the edge of the worn carpet in his office, trying unsuccessfully to light his pipe with a succession of matches and saying over and over again, "We told Stalin. We told

Churchill. We told Eisenhower. If they go on testing, if they use the bomb again, it will be the end of civilization."

Interviewing Baroness Blixen was sheer delight. I had read her books and greatly admired her writing. J.B. and I met her at a luncheon party given by John Watkins, the Canadian Ambassador to Denmark. She made a dramatic entrance, an old *grande dame,* slim as a fashion model, wearing a chic French dress and a fantastic headdress which set off her emaciated face with its fine, aristocratic bone structure. She looked like a character in one of her own *Seven Gothic Tales.*

She agreed to give me an interview only because I was a friend of Watkins, explaining that she was not well and soon became exhausted if she had to answer a great many questions. However she said if we came for tea the next day she would consent to talk to me.

Tony and I felt the interview was so important that we asked Radio Denmark to help us with equipment and a technician. They said they would supply us with a radio truck to take us from Copenhagen to "Rungstedlund," the manor house by the sea where the baroness had been born and to which she had returned after the years spent on a coffee plantation in Kenya. However they warned us that she would probably not open her door to us, since she always refused to give interviews.

When we arrived at the house, about half an hour's drive from Copenhagen, we were greeted by Karen Blixen's niece, who ushered us into a big living room where the Baroness was seated at a table behind a silver tea set. Before getting down to work we ate an enormous tea, which included crêpes Suzette made in a silver chafing dish. Baroness Blixen ate nothing, but watched us gorge ourselves with evident pleasure. After that I interviewed her for an hour with a break in the middle to enable her to rest while her niece took us for a walk in the grounds.

Blixen had made a will leaving her estate as a bird sanctuary. She was not sure whether the royalties from her books would be enough to support it, and so had gone to the people of Denmark for help. In an interview on the radio she had asked for small contributions of a krone, about twenty-five cents, from everybody. She was by that time an almost legendary character. The Danes were proud of her, and the coins poured in. She told J.B., who had sat beside her at the embassy luncheon, that when she stepped into an elevator, the elevator man would often hand her a krone. Occasionally, when she was taken as a guest for lunch in an expensive restaurant, her hosts would be astonished when the waiter would come over and tip her.

A great deal of Karen Blixen's character came through in that long interview. She talked about her experiences as a coffee planter in Kenya and her sympathy and admiration for the Masai with whom she used to go on safaris and lion hunts.

When I asked her if it had been hard to return to the narrow confines of Danish society and the physical restrictions of tiny Denmark, she looked at me with an expression of sharply remembered agony.

"It was terrible," she said. "I cannot tell you how terrible it was. I had to write in order to keep from going mad."

We talked about her books, especially about *Out of Africa,* the beautifully sensitive story of her life in Kenya and her relationship with her lover.

Later she told me that she was in constant pain with her back, could hardly eat anything, and had to spend most of the day in bed. She could no longer write in longhand but had taught herself to typewrite and was working every day on a new book.

Approaching death was written on the Baroness' haggard face. She obviously knew she was dying, but was determined to make the most of the time left to her by writing and by remaining wholly alive in her perception of people and the world around her.

That afternoon I had an extraordinary feeling that the two of us understood each other completely and were very close even though we had never met before or would ever meet again. Although she was a great deal older than I and though we had come from very different backgrounds and had had vastly different experiences in life, we had both reached the same conclusions about fundamental living. We both hated racism, war and cruelty. We both loved to feel earth under our feet and to be physically active out-of-doors. We both needed to be alone a great deal. We both enjoyed good food, well-cut clothes made of good material, and the conversation of intelligent people. We both believed that every minute of life is valuable and must be savoured to the full. And we both believed in our own inner strength, the strength of being a woman, and knew the personal liberation given by that self-knowledge. On the way back to Copenhagen in the sound-truck, the Danish radio technician said he had felt the empathy between us.

One afternoon I left Tony Thomas to cut tape in the superbly equipped modern studios of Radio Denmark and took the train to Elsinore. I did not visit the castle where the tragedy of Hamlet, Prince of Denmark, was supposed to have taken place. Instead I took a taxi to a prison located in the midst of a deep forest. It was a minimum security institution, a series of small buildings surrounded only by a high barbed-wire fence. During the war it had been built by the Germans as a concentration camp for Danish people suspected of being actively unsympathetic to the Nazi regime.

After the German occupation of the small country in 1940, Hitler had planned to make Denmark an example of a model "protectorate" to give the world an illustration of the liberalism and generosity of his regime. It was a shock to the Fuehrer when the seemingly docile Danes turned out to be hiding Jews and taking them by night in small boats to Sweden. What's more, they had organized an efficient corps of underground fighters who had quietly murdered a number of German soldiers and helped prisoners of war to escape. When the Gestapo entered the country to impose Hitler's form of law and order, a great many Danes were sent to the camp at Elsinore which, after the war, was turned into a prison for both men and women.

I found there was nothing medieval about the women's section of the prison. It seemed to me that it was like a pilot project designed from a text-book on modern correctional methods. The first offenders, the "beginners," as the superintendent called them, were in one house segregated from the other offenders. There, under the supervision of a matron, they cooked their own meals. The repeaters were in another house, and the criminal psychopaths were in yet another separate building far away from the others.

There was a good library and a training program tailored to the needs of the individual. I found it significant that only 20 per cent of the prisoners were again sentenced to prison, while in Canada between 75 and 80 per cent of women prisoners were repeaters. In Denmark, elderly alcoholics who broke the law were not sent to an ordinary prison, but were kept in a separate institution where they did mild manual labour and were allowed a glass or two of Danish beer every day.

After that trip to Denmark I made documentaries in Europe every year. Between trips I continued to write and to broadcast about national and international affairs on radio and television. For a couple of years I wrote a weekly column for the *Ottawa Journal* about the status of women, and wrote articles about the scientific preservation of food and improvements in agricultural methods for the *Canadian Food Journal*.

In addition to the scientific articles, I also wrote a column about cooking for the *Canadian Food Journal*. I used a new pen-name for it,

Suzette Oiseau, as I did not want Anne Francis to be identified with recipes and cooking, and the editor did not want the by-line of Anne Francis to appear under two or three articles in the magazine every month.

In the long run it had turned out that I was right when I thought, as a bride, that it would be possible for me to learn to cook by using common sense and a cookbook. What I didn't know was how long it would take me to learn. However, by the time Suzette Oiseau came on the scene, I knew how to cook quite well, and enjoyed making complicated, exotic dishes to please J.B. and our friends (and to please myself too, of course, since I enjoy eating good food). Moreover, travel had given me an interest in the food of different countries, since what people eat, and why, is a reflection of their culture and their environment.

The editor of the *Canadian Food Journal* and I had been successful in keeping the identity of Suzette Oiseau a secret from the public, so I was in a bit of a quandary when a letter addressed to Miss Oiseau arrived from the Canadian Restaurant Association. They were asking me to act as one of the judges of the booths at their annual convention. I couldn't accept and risk having Miss Oiseau appear on television where her marked resemblance to Anne Francis would give the game away. I solved the problem by concocting a letter from Suzette Oiseau to the Restaurant Association saying that Anne Francis was the senior correspondent for the magazine and I was sure they could understand that Miss Francis would not be pleased to have me invited instead of her and that I didn't want to risk making her jealous of me.

After I had sent the letter off, I said to J.B., "You know, I really do think it's a funny thing that they asked Suzette Oiseau instead of me. I think I write a lot better than she does and the scientific articles are much more important than the column."

J.B. laughed so heartily that I realized the implication of what I had just said: I had come to think of myself as Anne Francis but not as Suzette Oiseau.

In 1962 I had an assignment to make CBC radio documentaries in France and Germany.

As a preliminary, I spent a couple of weeks in Paris setting up interviews, and then J.B. and I motored through France and Switzerland on a holiday. France was very much in the news because of the terrorist activities of both the F.L.A. (the Algerian nationalists) and the O.A.S. (the underground army opposed to de Gaulle's policy of giving autonomy to the territory of France in North Africa). Germany was also in the news again because of the great increase in the number of refugees escaping to the west from East Germany.

While J.B. and I were in Annecy, after a leisurely drive through the Vosges and the Jura, we heard on the radio that East Germany had built a wall between East and West Berlin. J.B. was like an old fire-engine horse, rarin' to go at the first sniff of a news story in the wind, and insisted on getting back into harness right away.

We drove at once to Geneva, where he wanted to interview several people about the Common Market for a story he was writing for the *Toronto Star,* and then drove straight to Paris where he left me, since I was to meet Jean Smith (now Jean Bruce), a young CBC producer, there. He flew to Berlin, got his story, returned to Paris for the night in order to give me a briefing about East Berlin, and then flew back to Ottawa next morning.

However, Jean Smith and I had to keep our appointments in Paris before going to Germany. In order to make a balanced, objective show we had to interview people who supported the cause of the F.L.A. as well as those who sympathized with the O.A.S.

One afternoon we went to interview a retired general who, we had learned, was bitterly opposed to General de Gaulle and was suspected of being involved in the organization of the secret army which had tried on a number of occasions to assassinate de Gaulle.

The general lived on the third floor of a shabby apartment block in a shabby part of Paris. When he opened the door to us we could hear a radio and smell a strong whiff of cognac on his breath. We set up the tape recorder on the dining-room table and conducted a strange inter-view; the general had put the radio beside him and kept turning it on for a few seconds at a time. He was surprisingly outspoken, saying that de Gaulle was a traitor and a dictator. He said he himself expected to be imprisoned by the dictator at any moment. He ended the interview by saying, "I am a good Christian, but I don't mind saying that I am glad that soon, very soon, General de Gaulle will be with God."

We left after the general had given us a glass of excellent cognac and invited Jean to stay with him. (Once or twice during the interview Jean had surprised me by showing signs of suppressed laughter, and in the taxi, on the way to the CBC headquarters to pick up some more tape, she told me the general had been giving her playful pinches under the table.) When we arrived at the CBC we found everyone in a state of high excitement because the radio had just announced that an attempt had been made on the life of de Gaulle as he was being driven from Paris to his home at Colombey-des-deux-Églises. He had only been saved by the presence of mind of his chauffeur who had kept on driving at high speed. Jean and I were sure the general we had just interviewed had been expecting the news and was up to his neck in the plot.

From Paris, Jean Smith and I went to Bonn, before going to Berlin, to get the official reaction of the West German government to the Berlin Wall. On the morning we were to fly from the capital down the air corridor to Berlin, we became slightly edgy; Dr. Conant, the former President of Harvard University, who had been head of the American sector during the Berlin blockade, was known to be flying to Berlin that day and the Russians had threatened to buzz all planes in the corridor. We became even more edgy when, on the way to the airport, a German press officer told us that Dag Hammerskjöld had been killed in an air crash in Africa. We found it a bit too symbolic when, as we stepped out of the airport to board the plane, a swallow flew into a plate glass window and fell dead at our feet.

The Berlin Wall was a monstrosity. It was a saddening experience to see women, with children in their arms, climbing on ladders propped against lamp posts in order to wave to members of their family on the other side of the Wall. Later, when it was built higher, it became impossible to see over it.

Jean and I went into East Berlin by way of "Checkpoint Charlie" and did not enjoy it when, on three separate occasions, members of the Volkspolizei asked to look into my purse.

Jean Smith was young, in her early twenties, but she was a good producer, with a sound educational background. She was a good researcher, and knew what she was looking for. I enjoyed working with her and found her youth, irrepressible exuberance and humour a helpful counteraction to the gloomy story we were putting together about what was happening in Berlin.

Both the documentaries turned out so well that we decided to go to Switzerland and Belgium the next year. The province of Quebec, and what was mistakenly called "the quiet revolution," were news at that time, and the Royal Commission on Bilingualism and Biculturalism had just begun its monumental, essential study of the most serious internal problem facing Canadians today. It was obvious that the experience of Switzerland and of Belgium, both countries with proud minority groups speaking different languages, would have significance for Canadian listeners. At the last minute, staff changes made it impossible for Jean to go with me, a great disappointment to us both. However, the CBC made arrangements for the Swiss and Belgian radio corporations to provide me with technical assistance, and I was able to bring home a great many tapes of revealing interviews. Jean did the editing with me and produced an hour-long documentary called *Language: Bridge or Barrier,* which is just as significant today as it was then.

It has taken Switzerland about twelve hundred years to work out a system that is viable in spite of having three "official" languages, French, German, and Italian, and a fourth language, Romansh, which, since 1938, has been legally a "national" language because of its cultural contribution to the country. Each canton carries on the work of government and business in the official language spoken by the majority of the people who live there. There are some bilingual areas, such as the city of Biel (in German) or Bienne (in French), in the German canton of Berne, where more than 30 per cent of the population are French. The work of the federal government is carried on in all three official languages and civil servants are expected to be able to read and write in all three. At committee meetings it is customary for each member to speak his mother tongue.

A member of the Swiss federal cabinet said something to me then that I wish would be taken to heart by Canadians who inveigh against the federal liberal party's policy in regard to the use of French in the federal public service and the bringing of more French Canadians into the structure of government. When I asked him how Switzerland managed to keep her minorities happy, he said, "We spoil them. We pamper them. We give them over-representation on committees and commissions and in government departments. It's the only way."

In contrast with Switzerland, the Belgians have not succeeded in finding a satisfactory way of putting an end to the tensions between the Flemish majority and the French minority. Belgium is a death's head, a grim reminder of what could happen in Canada. The country was created artificially by the map-makers at the Congress of Vienna, after the fall of Napoleon. Although the Flemish are a numerical majority they have been, until recently, an economic, political and psychological minority. The Walloons, the French-speaking Belgians, who were rich because of the coal mines in the southern part of Belgium, were the social and political elite who ran the country. They look down on the Flemish who speak what they regard as an inferior language used by only a few people in the world.

Belgium is divided by a linguistic line that goes back to the Roman conquest. In the Flemish territory, to the north of it, only Flemish is used. In Wallonia, only French is used. However, Brussels, the capital, is a bilingual city and the public servants work in both languages. What upset me was the extent of the bitterness and intolerance of the two ethnic groups toward each other. At that time, in Antwerp, French-speaking Catholics on their way to church every Sunday were subjected to insults and sometimes assaults by mobs of Flemish people. The great bilingual University of Louvain was being turned into a Flemish university because it is in Flemish territory.

Like French Canadians, the Flemish have cause for bitterness because of having been relegated in the past to the role of hewers of wood and drawers of water by the Walloons who controlled the power structure, but this bitterness is destroying human rights and freedoms on both sides of the linguistic line. After having seen what is happening in Belgium, I feel that all Canadians must support efforts to keep Canada a united country even if it means that English-speaking Canadians in general, and Westerners in particular, have to go a long, long way toward "spoiling" French Canadians.

The year after making the documentary on Switzerland and Belgium I went to the Netherlands to do a documentary about a school system very unlike Canada's, in another multicultural society. The next year I went to Denmark again, to do a show on housing for the aged and the enlightened geriatric treatment available to old people. Then I went to the United States to do a documentary on the Franco-Americans in New England. And in 1966 I went to Hungary to find out what had happened to the country during the ten years following the revolution.

The travel years were adventurous and they were fun. But in February 1967, just after I had received a telegram from a CBC program organizer giving me the green light to make two new documentaries—one about the prison system in Sweden and the other about attitudes in the U.S. toward the war in Vietnam—Prime Minister Pearson asked me to be chairman of the Royal Commission on the Status of Women.

Initial Stages of the RCSW

I, Florence Bird, do solemnly and sincerely swear that I will truly and faithfully, and to the best of my skill and knowledge, execute and perform the duties that devolve upon me as chairman of the Royal Commission on the Status of Women in Canada, including the duty not to disclose or make known, without due authority on that behalf, any matter that comes to my knowledge by reason of my holding that office. So help me God.

I had thought that being sworn in would be a dramatic initiation into the work ahead. As it turned out, the Assistant Clerk of the Privy Council did not appear until several months after we had been at work, to deliver the oath of office to me, the other commissioners and senior members of the secretariat.

The ceremony took place during a coffee break at a Commission meeting. In turn we raised our right hands, put our left on the Bible, and repeated the oath, while the other members sat around, cup in hand, looking rather embarrassed, or self-consciously studied the pile of documents in front of them.

It was all over in about fifteen minutes. Nevertheless it was an important occasion. It reminded us that our work was confidential. None of the private information obtained for the use of the Commission could be revealed. None of the opinions expressed by members of the Commission and the secretariat could be aired until a consensus of opinion had been reached. And nothing could be made public until the completed, printed report and recommendations had been delivered to the Prime Minister. It was up to the government to decide when the report would

262

be tabled in the House of Commons. Until then we had to be careful that there were no leaks and that the press received no advance notice of our conclusions.

We had, of course, been warned in advance of this, and by the time we took the oath we were already used to keeping our counsel. A good deal had been accomplished by that time and it seemed a century since Prime Minister Pearson had made that momentous phone call.

The Monday following the announcement was my first day on the job. That was a strange morning. I felt like the captain of a ship without a vessel, officers or crew. I had no office and no secretariat. I didn't know who my fellow commissioners were going to be, and could make no decisions without them. I *did* have a chart, though: the terms of reference of the Commission.

In the Order in Council setting up the RCSW we were instructed by the government "to inquire and report upon the status of women in Canada, and to recommend what steps might be taken by the federal government to ensure for women equal opportunities with men in every aspect of Canadian society." There were nine specific areas into which we were to inquire:

1. Laws and practices under federal jurisdiction concerning the political rights of women,
2. The present and potential role of women in the Canadian labour force,
3. Measures that might be taken under federal jurisdiction to permit the better use of the skills and education of women, including the special retraining requirements of married women who wish to re-enter professional or skilled employment,
4. Federal labour laws and regulations in their application to women,
5. Laws and practices and policies concerning the employment and promotion of women in the federal civil service, by federal Crown Corporations and federal agencies,
6. Federal taxation pertaining to women,
7. Marriage and divorce,
8. The position of women under the criminal law,
9. Immigration and citizenship laws, policies and practices with respect to women.

In addition we were to enquire into such other matters in relation to the status of women in Canada as might appear to the commissioners to be relevant.

I had been told to go to see Leo Lafrance, the supervisor of commissions in the Privy Council office. He turned out to be a courteous, correct and patient public servant who did much to guide me through the labyrinth of official procedures.

Mr. Lafrance explained to me that since the RCSW was a surprise move by the government, there was no suitable accommodation.

"It will take time for me to find office space," he said. "Until then you'll have to use the office of the Chairman of the Royal Commission on Farm Machinery."

"I'll need a secretary," I said. "A bilingual secretary."

"It will take time to find you the right person," he replied. "In the meanwhile, some of the girls with Farm Machinery will help you."

He then led me from the East Block on Parliament Hill to a dark and dirty building on Rideau Street. For months afterwards, when people came to call on me they were surprised to see *Royal Commission on Farm Machinery* on the door to my office. (Fortunately Professor Clarence Barbour, the Chairman and the only commissioner for Farm Machinery, was usually away, either on public hearings or travelling abroad, but even so it was rather like the Gilbert and Sullivan light opera *Box and Cox*.) One western reporter remarked to me that the name on the door had a certain validity because for many years farm women had been used as machinery when they went into the fields to work. I topped that by saying there were many days when I felt as though I had been run over by a tractor.

Already, that first morning, there were about two hundred letters for me neatly piled on Mr. Barbour's desk. A polite little secretary brought me a dictaphone, and I went to work.

There were letters of congratulations from my friends, from fans who had been listening to me for years on radio and television, and from women who had long been fighting for equal opportunities. There were also a few insulting ones from strangers and one or two of the usual screwball communications from women who hated men, from men who hated women, and from cranks who wrote pages and pages to prove that God had created women different from men and we had better watch out if we dared to interfere with the work of the Almighty. I answered all of them politely and set up a "screwball file" that soon became potbellied with entries.

When the government announced the names of the other six commissioners ten days later, I invited them immediately to a meeting to discuss
the terms of reference. The commissioners were:

Lola Lange, a tall, handsome, down-to-earth person, a rancher's wife
and farm union woman, mother of three daughters,
Jeanne Lapointe, intellectual, sensitive, professor of French literature at
Laval University, an experienced commissioner who had spent five
years on the famous Parent Commission which revolutionized education
in Quebec,
Doris Ogilvie, a lawyer, judge of the Juvenile Court in Fredericton, New
Brunswick, dependable, thoughtful, with a quiet sense of humour,
mother of four daughters,
Jacques Henripin, head of the Department of Demography at the University of Montreal, always helpful, invaluable in directing research,
father of three daughters.
Elsie MacGill, my right hand until our work was done, tough, tiny and
determined, an indefatigable worker with an exact mind, a long-time
feminist, the first woman in Canada to become an aeronautical engineer,
Donald Gordon, the well-known broadcaster, writer and professor of
political science. (Donald Gordon resigned from the RCSW after eight
months and the government appointed *John Humphrey,* a professor of
law and former secretary-general of the Human Rights Commission of
the United Nations, to take his place.)

It took far more time than I had ever anticipated to build up an
efficient secretariat. By the first week in March, when the Commission
held its first meeting, university people were already signed up for the
academic year. In any case, there is always reluctance on the part of
highly qualified professors and public servants to take on a temporary
job, even though royal commissions are allowed to pay high salaries to
compensate them for moving out of the mainstream and consequently
risking the loss of promotions. I think, too, that in the case of the RCSW
some potential employees were chary of a commission of five women
and only two men dealing with such an explosive subject. Probably
some of them doubted the ability of a female chairman to carry out
such a difficult assignment successfully, and did not want to be associ-
ated with a project they suspected to be doomed to failure. Also, as our
research brought out, many people believe that women are harder to
work for than men.
Another problem was that some of the positions on the Commission

would inevitably be of short duration because people with different qualifications would be required at each stage of its work. Our secretariat was like an accordion: it expanded to about fifty people when we needed a great many researchers to dig out the facts we required; later it shrank to a small working group of senior researchers engaged in preparing draft reports and background papers for the commissioners to discuss. At a final stage we needed writers and editors to complete the detailed, professional work required to reduce the masses of material to a clear, concise, 488-page book. (The opinions and recommendations expressed in the report of the RCSW are, of course, those of the commissioners and no one else, but the research directors were the people who did the hard digging for the facts, who guided the researchers working under them, advised us and gave us their considered opinions, who wrote outline after outline and draft after draft until the report was what we wanted.)

It took months before we moved into high gear with a research management team of four brilliant women. Monique Bégin, a young sociologist from a Montreal business establishment, later a member of Parliament, was our executive secretary, and directed the research on the wide profile of women in our society. Dorothy Cadwell, former secretary of the Public Service Commission, was responsible for the essential areas of economics and labour. (Later, on her retirement, she was made an Officer of the Order of Canada in recognition of her many years of public service.) Monique Coupal, a young lawyer from a Montreal law firm (later secretary of the Canadian Radio and Television Commission), was our assistant secretary, responsible also for the difficult chapters on law and politics. Dr. Grace Maynard, a professor from the University of Manitoba and a member of the Board of Governors of Carleton University, did the groundwork on the chapters on education and poverty. There were, of course, other able researchers in various disciplines who helped to assemble and analyze the material.

Jean Fenton, my executive assistant, was the auxiliary to my mind. She gave up her lunch hours, worked overtime, never mislaid a file, did the research I needed, and no matter how heavy the pressure, she always made my life easier by her sense of humour and her unshakable good nature. Our writers and editors were hard-working, patient, painstaking and long-suffering during the last months when the report was being put into final shape to go to the printers. All in all, the members of our administrative staff, who were supplied by Leo Lafrance, were a god-send; they had worked together on other commissions, knew the ropes, and gave us invaluable and cheerful assistance at every stage of our work. The report would not have been readable without the dedicated

help of Helen Wilson, our senior editor, and Doris Shackleton who re-
wrote many chapters.

During the first six months having to share our quarters with the
Royal Commission on Farm Machinery made working difficult, but it
became even harder when, on a cold and blustery April morning, reno-
vations were started on the building and the heat was turned off. The
following day the women of the secretariat came to work wearing slacks
and carrying electric heaters. Until a late spring brought warmth in
through the open windows we all wore heavy sweaters and sometimes
overcoats.

During that trying period dictation was a problem: the stenographers
often could not hear what I said because of the hammering by carpenters,
the bellowing of bulldozers, and the machine-gunlike volleys from drills
under my office window where a last-minute blitz was taking place to
pretty-up the capital for the Centennial celebrations in the summer.

After a while Leo Lafrance found office space for us in a building
that was in the process of being made over, and during a July heat wave
we moved. So did the Royal Commission on Farm Machinery which had
accommodation down the hall. Socially that turned out to be a good
thing, since most of the members of our secretariat were women and
most of the people doing research into the price of farm machinery were
men. We shared our hilarious Christmas parties, and I gather there was
considerable cheerful co-existence in the cafeteria during coffee breaks
and at the lunch hour.

The new building was cleaner but not quieter than the old one. For
years we were besieged by bulldozers and drills under our windows
while new sewer pipes were laid and excavations were made for a high-
rise building across the street. It was, however, a relief to have an office
of my own. It was a big bright room with lots of windows. The walls
were covered with artificial panelling painted dark brown—a status symbol, I was told to my amusement, like the thermos jug the government
supplied for me but not for the other commissioners or the secretariat.
Although there was a name plate on the door, I did not rate a rug upon
the floor which was covered with a grey plastic material. I was instructed
not to put nails in the panelling, so I used Scotch tape to hang a huge
map of Canada and some large photographs of poor women and their
children photographed in rural or urban slums. I wanted to have them
there as a constant reminder that many women in Canada are poor and
without the education and skills needed to better themselves. I wanted
to be sure that we did not take a middle-class approach to our work and

think chiefly about education at the university level and the problems of working women. I feared that we might pay too little attention to the needs of the two-thirds of the married women in the country who are housewives in the home, of the poor women who are (for the most part) old, or of the sole-support mothers with young children—women who have been widowed, divorced or deserted by their husbands.

As it turned out, my fears were quite unfounded. Our research and the public hearings made us all equally aware of the problems of those three groups of women. And the poverty of women thrust itself upon us and could not be ignored, even though it was not mentioned specifically in our terms of reference.

Before long it also became obvious to us that we would have to study the education of women and the effects on them of the way they have been conditioned by parents, school, mass media and society in general. (Education and conditioning were also not mentioned specifically in our terms of reference, but there was no doubt in our minds about their relevance.)

Over a period of nearly four years we met for 178 days, over and above thirty-seven days and evenings of public hearings. The meetings were mind-expanding, exciting, always exhausting. All seven of us were opinionated, articulate people, and our discussions were often heated. But we frequently changed our opinions after listening to one another and after studying new information provided by research or by the public hearings.

There were days when, after we had argued for hours, I used to think how simple and easy, how much more efficient it would be if, like the Royal Commission on Farm Machinery, there were only one commissioner responsible for making recommendations based on the findings of his research staff and the advice of his research director. However, as time went on, I no longer felt that way, even after meetings when final agreement seemed only a doubtful possibility. Each of us had experience and knowledge that the others lacked, a factor that makes a royal commission effective as a means of studying broad social problems. The wisdom of the group, the synthesis of what we all contributed, was immeasurably better and wiser than the conclusions of any one person. At every meeting some of my ideas were either changed or modified for the better. And that was, I think, true of the six of us who signed the majority report.

One of the first things we did after our research directors and secretariat had been hired was to call for briefs from individuals and organizations. Advertisements were put in newspapers right across the country. I made a personal appeal on audio-tape and on film, to be used by French and English radio and TV stations. This is the usual procedure followed by the royal commissions.

However, unlike the other commissions, we prepared a folder which contained our terms of reference (so that women would know the kind of things we wanted them to tell us about), as well as a description of the way to prepare a brief, where to send it, and the final date for delivery. We distributed the folders in supermarkets and libraries, and sent them to women's associations. We hoped in that way not only to help women prepare briefs and write us letters of opinion but also to stimulate men and women to think seriously about the status of women in Canada. We believed in participatory democracy and were determined to hear the opinions of people in all income groups and with all levels of education, not just those of large organizations that had the resources to prepare well-researched submissions.

We allowed people plenty of time to write their briefs because of the valuable educational process involved in the necessary research, thought and discussion. I am convinced that this preparation, followed by the public hearings, did so much to educate the public and governments that the Commission would have been worthwhile even if we had never made a report.

We worked hard during the months while we were waiting for briefs. We read the standard works on the history of women. These included the great essay "The Subjection of Women" by John Stuart Mill (which Aunt Fol had given me as a wedding present), *The Second Sex* by Simone de Beauvoir, *The Feminine Mystique* by Betty Friedan, and the relevant writings of Margaret Mead, Viola Klein, Alva Myrdal and Alice Rossi. (At that time the influential books by Kate Millett and Germaine Greer had not yet been published.) One of the commissioners read fifty books in four months.

We also studied a massive amount of research material already published in Canada and other countries, in order to avoid an expensive duplication of effort when we set up our research program. We were all strongly aware of the responsibility involved in spending public monies, and managed to stay within our budgets throughout the life of the Commission.

After digesting the available material, we had a good general understanding of what had happened to women in Canada and other parts of the world, but we realized that we needed much more detailed, specific information about Canadian women. At that juncture we were in the inquiry stage of our work. We had to know not only the facts about women in every aspect of our society, but also the reasons for those facts. Only after that could we decide upon the changes we thought necessary, and the best ways to bring about those changes.

In outlining our research program we asked ourselves a multitude of questions:

> What are the cultural and historical reasons for the status of women in Canada today?
>
> What are the vital statistics concerning fertility, infant mortality, the maternal death rate, the life expectancy of women over the past century?
>
> How have the advances of medical science affected the health and lives of women?
>
> What is happening to the family?
>
> What changes, if any, have taken place in recent years in attitudes toward family planning and abortion?
>
> How do women feel about their role in society? Are their ideas about themselves changing?
>
> Are women receiving the kind of education and conditioning they need to fit them for life in an urbanized, industrialized society?
>
> What is the image of women that is projected by the mass media?

In the areas of economics and labour there were a great many questions to answer:

> What economic contribution are women making when they work in the home—in the labour force—as volunteers?
>
> Are they receiving equal pay for equal work?
>
> Are they receiving the promotions for which they are qualified by their ability and experience?
>
> What kind of work are they doing?
>
> Are they satisfied with their jobs?
>
> What sort of training do they need?
>
> How are women progressing in the professions?
>
> Are labour laws, both provincial and federal, adequate to protect women from discrimination if it exists?
>
> What is the financial position of women?
>
> How much influence have women in the fields of finance and business?

Do laws in regard to property discriminate against married women?

We needed to study the Criminal Code, as well as the Quebec Code and the laws of the nine Common Law provinces, to find out if they discriminated against women. We had to find out what happens to women when they come in contact with the law. How are they treated by the police? What happens to them when they go to prison or are put on probation?

We wanted to know why women have played such a small part in politics after having received the vote and the right to hold public office. And we wanted to discover if women were realizing their full potential as individuals.

There were also many other questions:

Do citizenship and immigration laws discriminate against women?
What is happening to immigrant women?
Are native women being discriminated against?
Does the tax structure prevent women from having equal opportunities with men?

After many weeks of work by the research directors and long discussions at Commission meetings, the commissioners approved the research program. Much of the work involved could be done in the office by our own research staff, but a great deal required special studies conducted by experts in the various disciplines, such as sociology, economics, criminal law, civil law, education, labour laws and practices, welfare, taxation, and so on.

While we were setting up the research program, our research directors were working with their assistants to prepare background papers for us to discuss. Papers on economics, pension plans, child care, psychology and sociology were drafted and circulated. One young lawyer on our staff prepared an excellent long thesis on the history of contraception and abortion. (These research papers and the unpublished studies are now available on microfilm in the Public Archives of Canada.)

Then the briefs began to arrive. There were 468 of them. Some were long and detailed; the brief from the Manitoba Volunteer Committee on the Status of Women was a printed book running to over 200 pages, and there were 70 pages in the brief from the Corrections Asociation of Canada. The briefs came from a wide variety of people and organizations: big national women's associations, the Family Planning Association, Indians, church groups, sole-support mothers, nuns, groups of students, groups of women young and old, university professors and deans, unions, lawyers, groups in favour of abortion and groups against it, mental health associations, political associations, the governments of Saskatchewan, and the Council of the Yukon. There were many others —too many to list here. Suffice it to say that the submissions gave us the ideas of a large cross-section of thoughtful women and men in the country.

There were hours and hours of reading in those briefs. Somehow the commissioners managed to read them all, and to prepare questions to ask at the public hearings. This meant working late into the night, on weekends, and when travelling.

Looking after the briefs was the responsibility of John Stewart, his assistant, Jennifer McQueen, and their staff. They prepared an analysis and evaluation of every submission, and arranged for their translation from English into French, or vice versa. They wrote to all of the people and organizations who had sent us briefs to find out if they wanted to appear before us, and later made appointments by letter or telephone for those who had declared their intention of coming to the hearings. And when the hearings were started they travelled ahead of the Commission to make sure that the appointments were kept.

The Hearings

It was in the spring of 1968 that we started the series of public hearings that brought the seven commissioners, the research directors, the support staff and a simultaneous translation team to every province of Canada over a period of nine weeks, with breaks of several weeks in between. We went to the places where the number of briefs justified holding a hearing, which meant that we set up shop in seventeen cities—the capitals of every province and the two territories, as well as Vancouver, Calgary, Saskatoon, Montreal and Ottawa.

At the beginning of each hearing I explained in both English and French that a royal commission is completely outside of politics, and that since a federal election campaign was going on we refused to provide a platform for political speeches of any kind. Nevertheless, on two occasions people appearing before us began to lambaste the government. Each time I brought my gavel down with a bang and said firmly that we would not listen to political speeches. The first time it happened, Doris Ogilvie looked at me quizzically when the hearing was over and said, "What would you have done if they hadn't stopped?"

I replied truthfully that I had taken it for granted that they would respect the authority of the chair, but also confessed that my heartbeat had speeded up considerably.

The commissioners felt that everyone had a right to be heard and be treated with equal courtesy during the hearings. After the formal presentations were completed we gave the floor to people in the audience who wanted to tell us what was on their minds. All of this took time, so that we had to sit from ten in the morning until four, often five, in the afternoon, and again from eight to ten-thirty or eleven in the evening.

In the big cities there were so many briefs that we sat right through the lunch hour, one or two of us taking our turn to slip out for a few minutes for a cup of coffee and a sandwich.

While we were in the West, Lola Lange and Elsie MacGill provided a hot line telephone service from eight to ten in the mornings, so that women who were unable to get to the hearings could talk personally to a commissioner. But we had to drop this service when the pressure or the hours of the hearings became so long and demanding.

We also had to fit in a press conference and a number of radio and TV interviews in each city, since local stations gave us good coverage. I was glad of the years of experience in front of microphones and cameras, since it kept me from being unduly nervous. I actually enjoyed fielding questions, having so often, as an interviewer, been on the asking end.

Our information officer, Angela Burke, was indefatigable and efficient. She made sure that there were plenty of briefs available in both Canada's official languages so that the press, radio and TV reporters would have the documents they needed. She distributed press kits containing photographs and biographies of the commissioners and the research directors. She made appointments for us to be interviewed, and saw that we kept our appointments.

Sometimes the Commission hearings took place in the auditorium of a shopping centre or in a gymnasium, sometimes in hotels, so that we could reach people living in different parts of a city. Usually there was an audience of from two to five hundred people, most of them women. On a number of occasions women travelled as far as three hundred miles by automobile from small towns which we could not visit, in order to bring us their opinions. We kept hoping more men would come to listen; we felt it was important that men be made to understand the needs and aspirations of women, since they still hold the power to administer the policies and the laws in both the public and private sectors of our society.

There was a significant sameness about the kind of people who came to the hearings day by day, in city after city. Most of them were women in their forties and fifties. Many of them spoke from harsh experience, having come up against discrimination and prejudice at work, where they found that equal pay legislation did not give them the same pay as men even when they did work of comparative value and responsibility. Many were housewives who found themselves bored, dissatisfied and depressed, sitting in mechanized homes, no longer needed by their children, with thirty-five years of potentially active and useful life ahead of them.

Many were young and poor, or old and poor. Some were women

without men—widows, divorcées, deserted wives—usually with children to support. Others were married women yearning for more education and training to enable them to use the ability and intelligence they knew they had but had never been able to develop fully. Too many were insecure, dependent women, lacking confidence in themselves, who had until then patiently accepted the passive role that most women have accepted since time immemorial.

Though the majority of women who appeared were past their first youth, a number of young people also came. And some of these conveyed poignant and significant messages. In Vancouver a young woman stood up in the audience and said she had come 500 miles, all the way from Prince George, to say only one thing to us. She implored us to make people understand that it is wrong to make a girl of thirteen get married just because she is pregnant. She said it is wrong for the girl, for the baby, and for the husband. She did not look more than sixteen herself as she stood there, nervous, young and vulnerable, saying, "Pregnancy is not a sufficient reason for marriage. A girl of thirteen is too immature to marry."

In the same city three seventeen-year-old girls presented a brief prepared by high school students representing thirty-six different ethnic groups. The brief spoke on behalf of the students' mothers who had come to Canada as immigrants and had never learned to write or speak English.

During the question period one of the girls explained that immigrant women are like birds who have been kept in a cage all their lives; when they are set free in Canada they don't know how to survive. She said, "Many of our mothers are scared to go out and look for jobs. They feel other people will laugh at them. They don't want to go out of their homes to work because all their lives they have been used to quietly following and obeying their husbands."

In the brief *the mothers* said they thought a woman should stay at home until her youngest child was sixteen and then go out to work if she wanted to. In the question period the girls said *they* thought a mother should stay at home when her children were small but that sixteen was too old; a woman should begin to find outside interests and begin to earn money of her own as soon as her youngest child went to school. Obviously there was a typical generation gap between those immigrant women and their Canadian-born daughters.

In Edmonton, four young and beautiful women appeared before us. They were obviously well-educated and intelligent. All four were divorcées, supporting their children. They explained that it was impossible for them to buy a house because mortgage companies did not regard women without husbands as a good risk. They said they always lived with the fear that if they got sick or lost their jobs they would have to resort to public assistance because they were the sole support of their families. Two of them had been on public assistance and knew what it meant. They pointed out that the welfare payments were insufficient for them to give their children the sort of living conditions they ought to have.

A seventeen-year-old Indian girl who was in Grade 12 came from a reserve to present a brief on behalf of her mother who was ill. She was almost speechless with nervousness until I said to her very quietly, "Don't think about the lights and all the people, just think that you are talking to one person who is a friend, a friend who is very much interested in what you want to tell her."

After that she looked straight at me while she talked, and it was as if we two were alone in the room. She talked about the Indian women who had too many children born in cold shacks without running water, about their destitution and their feeling of hopelessness. I felt ashamed for my own people as I listened to her.

Later I asked her what dreams she had for herself and she said, "I want education. Go back to reserve. Teach Indian children."

When I asked her what her friends were doing she said, "Shack up with man; have baby."

We heard later from a remarkably beautiful young woman who might have been the prototype of the heroine in the play/ballet "The Ecstasy of Rita Joe." She told us how, as an uneducated, ignorant girl without money, she had come to the city from the reserve in search of a job. She had had no friends in the city, only three dollars in her pocket, and no idea about how to go about getting a job. She had drifted into a beer parlour, been befriended by a man, shacked up with him, been taught to drink and take drugs, and been thrown out by him when she had been pregnant for several months. She said that she had managed to work her way up from that period of degradation, had married and now led a good, respectable life. She said she and girls like her could do more than white social workers or government officials to help Indian girls.

From time to time strange things occurred during the public hearings of the Commission which seem funny now though they were not particularly amusing at the time. In Vancouver a woman arrived with a candle which she lighted before she began to read the summary of her brief, as an offering to the "Great God Television" who looked after her children so much of the time. None of the commissioners took notice of the candle, by word, sign or look, but a few reporters treated it is a hilarious episode which illustrated the silliness of having a commission.

In Winnipeg a huge man in a black suit, sitting in the front row, suddenly jumped to his feet and shouted, "Any woman who smokes a cigarette ought to be burned alive."

I told him quietly that he was out of order, but I would be glad to talk to him privately about a matter of such importance. He sat down at once and after the hearing was over we had a quiet chat which left him quite happy.

In Edmonton a young mother, wearing a frilly dress, obviously hoped to shock us. She shouted that no commission could possibly give women what men have inside the crotch of their pants. Seven poker faces greeted this announcement, so that she lowered her voice and began to look embarrassed herself, having failed to embarrass us.

In Toronto we managed to keep our cool and not laugh when a group of young women and men told us we should all resign because we were too old. We maintained our usual, courteous calm, and it was interesting to see how their defiance and antagonism decreased when they realized they were being treated as reasonable adults by reasonable adults. There was nothing in their brief that was surprising, shocking or much different from what we later recommended.

During July, between hearings, we were studying the briefs from the Maritimes and from the national organizations which would appear before us in Ottawa when Mr. Justice Murrow, Judge of the Supreme Court of the Northwest Territories, invited me to accompany him on one of his periodic adoption court circuits in the Keewatin District of the huge area in which he is the arbiter of law, order and justice. I accepted with enthusiasm as it was a wonderful opportunity to see for myself a little of what is happening to native and other women in the far North.

We had scheduled hearings in Whitehorse and Yellowknife, which, because of the expense involved in such a long trip, were to be conducted by Commissioner Lola Lange, the executive secretary, Monique Bégin, and me. When it turned out that there would be room for another commissioner in Judge Murrow's plane it was agreed that Lola Lange would go on north with me from Yellowknife.

William Murrow is big, physically and mentally. He stands at least six-foot-four, a broad-shouldered, muscular man. He has great vitality, a love of the North and its people, and an almost mystical dedication to his job. It was fortunate that we were able to travel with him and have time for long, relaxed discussions about the problems of Eskimo women.

The trip to the Territories turned out to be strenuous but also the most fascinating leg of our hearings. We flew from Edmonton to Whitehorse where we were met at the airport by a group of women who gave us a taste of northern hospitality. They had arranged a party for us that night where we had a chance to talk informally with a number of white and Indian women who, unlike the majority of Canadian women, seemed to have no doubts about their own ability to do anything they wanted to do. It was quite evident that the pioneer spirit was still strong in the land.

During the hearings in Whitehorse some of the women who appeared before us hankered for the good old days when men were men. They wanted modern men to be more aggressive and to exercise their authority in the home. We were surprised when other women told us they felt white women were being discriminated against because the Department of Indian Affairs was providing day care centres for some of the children of native women while no such facilities were available for white mothers.

I had received a confidential letter from an Indian woman in Yellow-knife telling me about the misery of her people. It was so moving that I wanted it to be given as much publicity as possible but could not, of course, reveal its contents without her permission. I hoped I might be able to persuade her to come to the hearings the next evening, but I did not know how to find her. When we arrived in Yellowknife, I went around to the headquarters of the RCMP to inquire if they knew of her whereabouts. They sent me off in a car driven by a Mountie to lower town, the wrong side of the tracks as far as the capital city of the Northwest Territories is concerned.

I told the chauffeur to wait for me a few blocks away from where the Indian woman lived, as I thought the police car might give a wrong impression of the reason for my visit. I had to knock on a few doors until I was directed to her house. When I found her she invited me into a cold, bare room, empty except for a chair and a single burner electric stove on the floor, with a saucepan of what looked like stew on it. My hostess offered me the chair with the gracious gesture of a queen and then seated herself on the floor. We sat close to the stove to get what warmth we could from it.

At first she refused to come to the hearings but changed her mind and promised to appear when I told her that she might be able to help her people if she came. She kept her word. She gave me permission to read her letter for her and then answered questions hesitantly but with dignity. Her submission received good coverage by press and radio as I had hoped it would.

During the next two days a number of people came to see me at the motel because they wanted to talk off the record. Among them were two young men from British Columbia, university students who had been working in a mine during the summer. They were shocked by the way some Indian and Eskimo women were being treated by a number of men—by miners, construction workers and other men from the South who regarded native women as inferior people fit only to be treated as sex objects. It was the sort of situation that often arises in places where there are many men without wives and families, living in a part of the world where they have no social ties or obligations, or when one race of people regards itself as superior to another.

The students told me of cases in which Indian or Eskimo girls were made drunk, taken into a bunk-house, sexually abused by a dozen men and then thrown out, naked, to wander around or lie in the cold. Their solution to the problem was to have licensed brothels where the women would be protected by the police. They were concerned about the high incidence of venereal disease in the North and thought the men would be less likely to contract VD because prostitutes, being professionals, would presumably know how to look after their health. I protested that prostitution is a degrading, miserable way for a woman to earn a living, but they replied that what was happening to many women was even more degrading and miserable.

I heard similar stories from reliable sources about the treatment of native women by white men in other parts of the North, such as Frobisher Bay. Personally I don't doubt that they were true. However, a royal commission cannot rely on hearsay evidence: court action would have been needed to establish proof of what I had been told, so the commissioners felt that the matter was outside our terms of reference or, at least, outside of the capacity of the inquiry. It seems to me this matter should be the subject of another inquiry. Legal means must be found to protect native women from sexual exploitation of this kind.

I have also been told that many Indian and Eskimo women agree to sexual intercourse with white men because they hope to marry them eventually and thus better themselves, unaware that some of those men will abuse them even if they do legalize the relationship.

The terrible truth is that the "fatal impact" of the white man's civilization has gone a long way toward destroying the Indian people and shows every sign of doing the same to the Eskimos. Recently changes for the better have begun to take place as Indians become better educated, insist on their worth as a people and become more militant about their rights, but it will take more than the courts to restore the ethos of native Canadians.

We held the public hearings in the court house in Yellowknife. We did not sit on the bench, since we did not want to look as if we were a tribunal, but on hard, hard undertaker's chairs at a table below the row of large, padded leather armchairs provided for the judges. The occasion was regarded as having high entertainment value and the room was packed with standing room only. I kept finding it hard to concentrate because of the antics of two young men who had seated themselves in the dock. It was evidently an uncomfortable place and hardly big enough for two people because they put their feet into the air, wriggled, hung over the edge, emitted low groans, and altogether achieved the most remarkable contortions. Any minute I expected them to stand on their heads.

We learned a great deal about life in the North that night. Indian women, the wife of an RCMP officer, members of the women's institutes and a number of individuals gave us opinions which helped us greatly when the time came to make our recommendations.

It was a beautiful day in late August when Lola Lange and I joined forces with Judge Murrow and boarded the plane which was to carry us to Coral Harbour, Rankin Inlet, Eskimo Cove and Baker Lake.

During the eight hours it took us to fly to Coral Harbour, we passed over endless wastes of tundra pockmarked by hundreds of shallow, stagnant lakes. Hudson Bay was a surprise; the colour of the water that day was deep blue, azure and green, very like that of the Caribbean. We could see white whales under the surface, and occasionally, along the shoreline, we spied polar bears lumbering across the brown land, frightened by the sound of the engines. I kept wondering if I might see the ghost of my uncle, Elisha Kent Kane, the explorer who went into the Arctic in a tiny sailing ship in 1853 and was caught in the ice for two long years.

When we came down on the airstrip at Coral Harbour it was the first time that either the Adoption Court or, so they told us, the chairman of a royal commission, had ever come to the settlement. The purpose of the court was to establish the legal adoption of Eskimo children so that family allowances and public assistance would be paid to the parents responsible for the children under Canadian law as well as Eskimo custom. Eskimos often hand their children over for adoption, if they have more of them than they want, to couples who want children.

The morning after we arrived at Coral Harbour, a Mountie stuck the end of a tall flag-standard into the ground in front of the small, wooden community hall. The Canadian flag spread out in the cold Arctic wind and the hall became a court house.

Mr. Justice Murrow, his attorney and the law clerk took their gowns and white ties out of a suitcase and dressed in one corner of the single, cold room. Then the judge and an Eskimo interpreter sat down at a kitchen table in the centre of the room, while the other two men sat at a table to one side. About twenty women sat in front of "the bench." Since the adopting fathers had gone fishing there were no men in the court room except for the officials. Lola Lange and I sat at the back of the hall and could only see the backs of the women's heads as they leaned back and forth toward one another whispering apprehensively until the room was filled with a sound like the gentle twittering of birds at dusk. The women were obviously worried: they feared the judge was going to take their children from them.

When called by name by the judge, a woman advanced, took the oath on the Bible, sat facing him at the table and answered his questions through the interpreter. After about fifteen minutes, Mr. Justice Murrow said he was satisfied that the child had been legally adopted. He said, "The court will sit again after the evening meal and I will be here. When your husband comes home from fishing you and he will come here and put your mark on the paper and that will make you the parents of the child according to the law of Canada."

The mother stood up and faced the now silent women in the room. Her face was beautiful with relief and joy as she looked at them. She stretched wide her arms, her hands open-palmed, in a spontaneous, embracing gesture of happiness. I found that I was weeping. I was poignantly aware of the deep kinship between all women everywhere and in all ages.

In all cases Judge Murrow accepted native custom as valid when he had determined that it had been complied with by all parties concerned.

Bob Williamson, an anthropologist on the staff of the University of Saskatchewan, and at that time a member of the Northwest Territorial Council, was living in Rankin Inlet. He flew with us to Eskimo Point and acted as our interpreter during the most interesting of a series of informal meetings with Eskimo women. We all sat in a circle. On my right there were several dignified old women—toothless, with shrivelled brown skins like the outside of an old potato. Old people are respected in the North because it requires exceptional mental and physical stamina to live to any great age in that cruel climate. Old women are particularly respected because traditionally they are the guardians of the history of the people passed on by word of mouth from generation to generation.

Many of the younger women had tiny babies in the hoods of their parkas. If a baby started to cry the mother would lean forward with her head down, catch the infant as it came rocketing over the top of her head, open her dress and feed it at her breast. When one of the babies continued to cry vigorously, its mother kept looking at me apologetically, while I glanced at her from time to time, trying to convey sympathy and encouragement. After a while she got up and, moving away from the circle, performed a little rocking dance—one, two, three, tiny steps forward, one, two, three, back—a dance that must have been as old as time. Soon the baby was rocked to sleep and she resumed her seat while the women near her nodded approval.

Bob Williamson had told me that I should open the hearing by saying that the important men in Ottawa had sent me to find out what they wanted and needed the government to do for them, and that I promised to take their words back to Ottawa. I said what he suggested, but added, looking at the row of old women, "I know what it is like to be old because I am old."

They nodded and said, "Iee, iee" when Bob translated.

I then turned to the younger women and said, "I know what it is to be young because I have been young." And they nodded and said, "Iee, iee."

It did not take the women long to overcome their natural shyness, and they spoke freely about their need for more knowledge about how to feed their children and how best to run the new houses the government was giving them. At times they sounded very much like suburban housewives in the South concerned about consumer affairs. Some of them wanted sewing machines so they could make clothes for the family more easily. Others wanted clothes dryers in the community wash-house since it takes so long for anything to dry in the winter. They wanted more education so they could read the labels on cans and the written words in mail-order catalogues. They wanted educational radio programs in their own language conducted by Eskimos rather than by white people.

Before I went North I had tripped over a hole in the street in Ottawa and strained a ligament below my knee which improved after a few days of rest. Walking on the rough terrain in the northern settlements I strained it again, however, and I was in great pain.

Bob Williamson and his wife, Jean, did not think I should stay in the guest house at Rankin Inlet and invited me to stay with them. At that time the Williamsons had two children of their own and an adopted Eskimo boy. Since then they have adopted an Indian child. It was an intellectually exciting household because Jean is a social worker with an objective understanding of the needs of Northern women and Bob is a warm human being with much more than an academic appreciation of Eskimos. During the three days I was with them, all sorts of people kept arriving for meals, or to spread their sleeping bags for the night on the floor of the living room: professors engaged in anthropological research, geologists, public servants, historians, people writing books about the North. I learned a great deal from them.

While I rested my leg at the Williamsons', a number of women from the South came to see me. They were teachers, nurses, social workers, or were married to members of the RCMP, to employees of the Hudson Bay Company, or to public servants in the Department of Indian Affairs and Northern Development. They sat on the end of my bed and talked very openly, off the record, in a way they would not have done in more formal surroundings.

I saw a nurse in action at the health station. She was a young Pakistani who was carrying on alone as the other nurse was away sick. She examined my knee after she had finished calming a mentally ill woman. She diagnosed my trouble correctly, bandaged my leg and gave me pain-killing pills so I could get some sleep.

At that time, out of twenty-two nursing stations in that area, twenty of the nurses came from countries other than Canada. They were Pakistani, Chinese, British and Australian women, all trained in Britain. It was explained to me that few Canadian nurses were being trained in midwifery, a discipline that is required in Britain, and so are not qualified to deliver babies. I understand that that situation is now changing.

I was impressed by the courage, resourcefulness and stamina of the nurses I met in several of the small communities. They are paramedical people who prescribe drugs, deliver babies, and do many of the things registered nurses in the South are not allowed to do without orders from a physician. The nurses in the North have radio contact with doctors and, in case of an emergency, can order a plane to carry seriously ill people to hospitals in the South. But it is up to them to make the decisions and to carry the burden of responsibility. Often, when the weather is bad, a plane cannot land to bring a doctor or pick up a patient, and then the nurse must carry on alone.

When I saw those nurses in action I was reminded of what I had learned about women in Winnipeg during the war: that they are able to do anything they are trained to do and want to do, provided it does not require great muscular strength. The nurses I met in the Arctic were neither dependent, passive nor lacking in self-confidence, as so many women are. They were proof of what happens when the abilities of women are developed.

I returned from the North to Ottawa at the end of August and spent a few hectic days in the office writing my report on the trip to the Arctic and dealing with accumulated correspondence and administrative problems. Then, early in September, the Commission flew to Fredericton to begin the hearings in the Atlantic provinces.

For me, the smell of the sea and soft sea air are a tonic like no other, and my love for Rhode Island makes me feel at home in the part of Canada which is so much like it. It was also a nostalgic return to the past for me because as we travelled I kept being reminded of J.B.'s Canadian Club tour in 1930. I had never been to Newfoundland but I found the land beautiful and romantic, and I liked the down-to-earth people who appeared before us.

In October we held a week of hearings in Quebec City and Montreal, and it became apparent that the needs and aspirations of French-Canadian women are the same as those of women in other parts of Canada. Radio and television, which has done so much to precipitate "the quiet revolution" in Quebec, has also greatly affected the thinking of women in the province. The voice from the outside world and the TV window looking out from their homes has made many women discontented with their lot and raised their expectations. (It is a sign of the dynamic change taking place in Quebec that the province, once the most backward about giving women their civil and political rights, now has the most enlightened law in regard to the property rights of married women—the "partnership of acquests." And it is interesting that three of the five women elected to the House of Commons in 1972 were from Quebec.)

Late in October we held public hearings in Ottawa for a week. At that time the national associations appeared before us. Long, carefully documented, very useful briefs were presented by associations such as The Canadian Corrections Association, The Canadian Teachers' Federation, The Canadian Nurses' Association, The National Council of Women and the Canadian Federation of Business and Professional Women's Clubs.

When the Canadian Labour Congress presented its brief, Huguette Plamondon, at that time the only female among the CLC's thirty-seven vice-presidents, stole the show. She looked spectacular in a black velvet dress and an Empress Eugénie hat, with diamonds sparkling in her ears and on her fingers. At one point she burst into a torrent of words, saying angrily and at length that although it is true that unions have done a great deal to help working women, they haven't done nearly enough, and they know it. Donald S. MacDonald, the president of the CLC who led the delegation, hastily put on a poker face while she talked but not before his jaw had dropped and he had looked stunned for a second.

There was a dramatic and moving evening during the Ottawa hearings when a delegation of Indian women arrived from the Caughnawaga Indian Reserve near Montreal. They were bitter, and like the majority of Indian women who appeared before us, they were dramatic and compelling in the way they made us feel that bitterness. The Caughnawaga women told us that the Indian Act discriminates against women, something which we had already heard in briefs presented to us from all parts of Canada. The Act provides that an Indian man who marries a non-Indian retains his Indian status and confers it on his wife and children. An Indian woman who marries a non-Indian or a non-registered Indian, not only cannot confer on him the status of an Indian, but loses all the rights and privileges of an Indian, as do the issue of that marriage. She is automatically enfranchised, meaning that she is not considered to be an Indian within the meaning of the Act. On enfranchisement, she is no longer qualified to receive a share of the capital and revenue held by the Crown on behalf of the band, nor is she qualified to receive any other annuities, interest, moneys or rents for which she was formerly qualified. However there will be some compensation for this loss. Within thirty days of her marriage to a non-Indian, an Indian woman is obliged to dispose of her interest in lands and improvements on the reserve. Between 1958 and 1968, 4,605 Indian women had their names automatically removed from the Indian registry following marriage to non-Indians.

That night in Ottawa the delegation of Indian women told us that they would be beaten up by their men for daring to appear before us. We heard later that that is exactly what happened.

The hearings in Ottawa brought to an end the public part of our work during which 890 witnesses appeared before us. In private we interviewed a number of people while we were on hearings and others came before us at our meetings in Ottawa to give us their opinions. In addition, our research directors conducted seminars and off-the-record interviews.

Looking back on those fascinating, often moving, sometimes shocking, occasionally funny public hearings, I keep seeing again the faces of women looking at me from across the table or from the audience. I feel again my admiration of the way most of them presented their briefs with dignity and sincerity, determinedly overcoming their fear of the TV lights, the searching eye of the camera, the demanding snout of the microphone, and the coming and going of the audience. It must have been hard for many of them to understand the extent to which the commissioners were involved, and how sympathetic we were. As one woman put it, "You represent a dream world to poor people who have no polish. Many of us can't go to the Commission hearings because we can't afford to pay for a sitter."

The Report

The final phase of our work was the most difficult. We had to discuss what we had learned at the hearings, read and discuss the special studies, decide what would go into the report and, finally, draft the recommendations. It was a monumental task. From time to time we found we needed more information which required other special studies, such as the excellent one on the status of women working in banks, or long background papers requiring considerable research by the secretariat.

It was essential to agree on the principles upon which we based our recommendations, since otherwise they would be without either a philosophical or a practical justification. After much thought and many "skull knocking" sessions, all of us, with the exception of John Humphrey who wrote a minority report, agreed on the following general principles:

> Everyone is entitled to the rights and freedoms proclaimed in the Universal Declaration of Human Rights unanimously adopted by the UN General Assembly in 1948.
>
> There should be equality of opportunity to share the responsibilities to society as well as its privileges and prerogatives.
>
> Women should be free to choose whether or not to take employment outside their homes.
>
> The care of children is a responsibility to be shared by the mother, the father and society.
>
> Society has a responsibility for women because of pregnancy and childbirth, and special treatment related to maternity will always be necessary.
>
> In certain areas women will, for an interim period, require special treatment to overcome the adverse effects of discriminatory practices.

The writing of the report is always a major headache for a commission as there must be agreement on every word of it as well as on the style in which it is written. In our case it was a long-drawn-out problem to decide what should go into the report and what should be left out. There was enough material to fill two volumes, but the commissioners felt the report would be more effective and more widely read if it were boiled down to one. Although it would have to be used as a blueprint for action by the public servants responsible for implementing the recommendations, we wanted it to be read also by as many people as possible, since we hoped it would be a serious sociological study involving our whole society. Furthermore, it would have to stand up for a long time and be read by people in other countries. All of this made us determined that it should be written in clear, simple language, neither in "civil service gobbledegook" nor in the breezy journalistic style that is the mode of the moment, since nothing dates more rapidly than the smart cracks and clichés of the day.

It was exceedingly difficult to put the chapters on criminal law, family law and taxation into simple language and to escape the sticky bog of sociological jargon. Our writers and editors, as well as the commissioners, spent hours simplifying every paragraph and every sentence so that the sense was absolutely clear. During the summer before the final draft was ready for the printer, we met three times a week for at least six weeks in succession because a strike by post-office workers made it impossible for us to send revised drafts back and forth.

The report of the RCSW is a reasonable, pragmatic document. The fact that it makes 167 recommendations indicates to what extent changes in laws, practices and attitudes are needed. The findings of the Commission are in the report and it would be redundant for me to repeat here at any length what has already been so carefully documented, thanks to our researchers, the special studies, the briefs and the great help given us by Statistics Canada. The irrefutable facts remain the same today as they were when the commissioners presented the report to Prime Minister Trudeau in December 1970, and by now they ought to be common knowledge. Some progress has been made since then, but it is a slow and heart-breaking business to try to get rid of the prejudices and attitudes which the centuries have entrenched in our society.

The facts, quite simply, are as follows:

Canadian women still suffer from discrimination and prejudice. They are outside of the power structure of our society, in business, finance and politics. The most recent statistics make that clear. Although a million women entered the labour force in the ten-year period between 1961 and 1971, the percentage of women in management only rose from 3.7 per cent to 3.9 per cent.

In 1973, there were only five women in the House of Commons with 264 seats. There have been 134 federal and provincial elections between 1917 and June 1970 in which 6,778 men and only 67 women were elected.

Most Canadian women have little money compared with men and many of them are poor, in spite of the often-quoted myth that they control 80 per cent of the wealth of the nation. In fact, according to an analysis of the individual tax returns published by the Department of Internal Revenue in 1967, only about 20 per cent of the total earned income goes to women. Women account for about 50 per cent of the consumer spending but most of the money they spend on food, clothing, and household needs for themselves and their families is earned by men, usually their husbands.

When women marry, if they have no money of their own or do not work for pay, they are totally dependent on their husbands. When they go to work they earn less than men. Most of them are employed in the badly-paid, so-called traditional women's jobs, as waitresses, clerical workers, stenographers, salespeople, nurses. And, although eight out of ten provinces and the federal government have passed equal pay laws, women are still paid less than men even when they do work of comparable value and responsibility. They are paid less even if they have more education. (In 1971, 64 per cent of the women in the labour force compared with 49 per cent of the men had some, or full secondary education, but the average earnings of men with some secondary schooling were 114 per cent higher than those of similar women.

A recent survey made by the Department of Labour in four cities showed that in each of ten occupations, women's average weekly salary rates were less than those of men for similarly described work. For example, in Halifax, the average weekly salary rate for women materiel record clerks were $71 as compared with $106 for men. In Toronto they were $86 as compared with $120 for men.

This inequality in pay rates goes right on up to the top, to the élite of the work world. One would expect universities to give leadership by adopting equal pay for men and women professors. But that is not the case. The Commission found that women professors receive an average of $2,262 a year less than men with the same or lower academic degrees.

Canadian women are poor. In a personal interview survey carried out across Canada in 1970, it was estimated that nearly two-thirds of all welfare recipients were women. There were more than one million women in Canada receiving welfare assistance. Two-thirds of them were widowed, separated, or divorced. More than half of them had children under twenty-one years of age. These do not include the 600,000 women aged sixty-five or older who received the old-age guaranteed income supplement.

The value of the work of the housewife is underestimated and downgraded. In our society it is the tradition for people to give lip-service to motherhood and to extol the virtues of devoted wives. But in a society where material remuneration is the measure of success, the mother at home looking after her children does not actually have a high rating in the social pecking order. Her contribution to the economy in the form of cleaning, cooking, laundry and child care is not included in that widely quoted index of the production of the nation, the Gross National Product. She is, in fact, regarded as a financial liability: a husband is given an exemption on his Federal income tax when his wife does not work for pay even though most wives at home with two or more children work an eleven-hour day and a seven-day week, something which organized labour would not tolerate.

Girls have been brainwashed by their parents, their teachers, their guidance counsellors, their text-books and the mass media, to accept a passive, supportive role in society. As a result, many of them are dependent, unsure of themselves and fail to realize the potential inherent in their brains and ability.

Many girls are ill-prepared for life in an urbanized, industrialized society which has changed greatly in thirty years and is still changing rapidly. For many of them this means that they will be unhappy, unfulfilled when they become middle-aged or old.

Many young girls today are still dreaming about their future as unrealistically as their grandmothers did. They have not yet understood that the life cycle of the majority of modern Canadian women is to enter the labour force after leaving school or university, marry young, leave the labour force when their children are small and go back to work when their youngest child is is in school.

Parents, teachers and school counsellors have not yet taught the majority of girls to be aware of the many options open to them:

> They can marry, raise a family, and then do volunteer work, take a job or pick up the career they had started when they married.

> They can marry, have children, and without taking time out carry on with a career, as more and more women are doing, and as more and more would like to do if there were day-care centres in their neighbourhood where their children could be given a sound nursery school education.

> They can marry and decide not to have children if they feel they are not going to be good mothers and would prefer to concentrate on a professional or other interesting work suited to their ability.

> They can stay single and have a career.

Many women are frustrated. This frustration has led to the rise of several kinds of women's liberation movements in Canada as well as in the United States and Europe. Women's Lib only began to make itself felt during the last year or so that the Commission was at work, but it was brought about by the same hard facts that led to the appointment of the RCSW. The time in history had come when masses of women could no longer endure discrimination, prejudice and alienation. Inevitably the recommendations of the RCSW were bound to be the same as many of the demands of the different kinds of groups concerned with the liberation of women. We had, of course, more information than they, because of the research in depth that would be impossible for women's groups without the powers and money that were at our disposal.

The RCSW found that a network of community day-care centres is greatly needed in Canada. If women are to have a higher status, society as well as fathers and mothers must take on some of the responsibility of looking after young children as it now does for school-age children. Day-care centres are needed not only to help mothers who want to work for pay outside of the home or continue their education, but also for women who decide to stay at home while the children are young, since from time to time, even the most competent mother needs to get away from her children and have some time to herself.

I think that at present more emphasis should also be put on the importance of day-care centres for the healthy development of children as well as for the liberation of women. The research of the RCSW showed that children develop better mentally and physically if they are in the care of more than one cherishing adult.

In the days of the extended family, when three generations often lived in the same house, there was always an aunt, uncle or grandparent around to play with the baby and the young children. But the extended family is now largely a thing of the past except in some rural areas and among a few ethnic groups. Moreover, Canadian women now give birth to only 2.3 children. As a result, there are today many pre-school children who need the companionship not only of more than one cherishing adult but also of other small children, regardless of the income of the family or whether the mother stays at home or not. For many children living in crowded city apartments, a well-run day-care centre can be a place where they are stimulated by toys that develop their reasoning powers and manual skills. There is also always a danger that if a mother and child are constantly in each other's company, the mother may become over-possessive and over-protective of the child, and the child over-dependent on the mother.

The two recommendations on abortion were obviously the most controversial. The majority of the commissioners recommended that "the Criminal Code be amended to permit abortion by a qualified medical practitioner on the sole request of any woman who has been pregnant for twelve weeks or less."

We further recommended that "the Criminal Code be amended to permit abortion by a qualified practitioner at the request of a woman pregnant for more than twelve weeks if the doctor is convinced that the continuation of the pregnancy would endanger the physical or mental health of the woman, or if there is a substantial risk that if the child were born it would be greatly handicapped, either mentally or physically."

Two of the seven commissioners felt that the clause in the Criminal Code in regard to abortion should remain unchanged from the 1968 Amendment. One thought that abortion should be taken out of the Code entirely.

We discussed abortion again and again at intervals for over three years. I wish those debates could have been taped and been made public because they were an inspiring exercise in which seven people strove mightily to find a wise solution to a difficult problem charged with emotion. Each of us respected the point of view of the others and listened with sympathy and understanding even when we were in deep disagreement. Between discussions we read about the history of abortion, the different methods used, the procedures in other countries and the physical dangers involved. We heard many briefs in favour of it, and many against it. At no time did we "fight" over this issue; it was too serious a matter for that.

There is no doubt in my mind that implementation of the two recommendations on abortion would go a long way toward giving women equal opportunities with men. They are moderate, reasonable proposals in line with what should be acceptable at this stage in our history. Unfortunately I see no signs that even these will be implemented in Canada for a long time.

I am convinced that as attitudes continue to change abortion will eventually be removed from the Criminal Code. In the meantime the restriction will mean tragedy for thousands of women and the birth of many unwanted, unloved children. The law will be constantly broken or evaded, as it is now. When unable to obtain a therapeutic abortion from a hospital committee, many poor women turn in fear and desperation to back-alley abortion butchers or commit abortions on themselves, as my poor housekeeper in Winnipeg did, while richer women go to New York State or other places where abortions are legal.

It is my personal opinion, speaking as a private citizen, that it is barbaric for the law to attempt to force a woman to bear a child she does not want to bear. I consider it cruel and puritanical to prevent a woman from having a legal abortion when she has conceived as the result of rape or incest, as the Criminal Law now does. I think the RCSW's recommendations were wise and humane. I personally believe that a woman, after consultation with her physician, should have the right to decide for herself whether or not to have an abortion during the first three months of pregnancy. I believe that for two reasons. First, it is safer to have an abortion during that time than it is to go through with a pregnancy. Second, up to the end of three months the foetus is surely not a human being, since it could not possibly survive outside of the womb. Many people regard it as murder to destroy a foetus at any stage of its embryonic growth, but I do not agree with them.

I respect the attitude of people who object to an abortion on their own moral grounds. A change in the law would not affect their belief or force them to have an abortion. It would merely free others to follow *their* moral beliefs.

I realize that for many people abortion incurs such dreadful sanctions that it is out of the question for them unless they are prepared to sacrifice the solace of their religion. I understand their position, but I think they should respect the position of people who do not share their religious beliefs. Church law should not dictate the criminal law of a country where church and state are separate.

I do not think that any intelligent person in his or her right mind could regard abortion as a desirable form of birth control. It should, however, be legally available as a last resort to prevent an unwanted child from being brought into the world and to give women the right to decide if they do or do not want to go on being pregnant. If the recommendations of the RCSW in regard to family planning were carried out vigorously they would go a long way toward reducing the need for the many abortions, legal and illegal, that are taking place in Canada today. Nevertheless, some abortions will always be necessary for medical reasons, because of accidents, or because unplanned pregnancies occur as a result of drunkenness or the taking of drugs.

In the short term a great deal could be accomplished if, as the RCSW recommended, birth control information and contraceptives were given free of charge to anyone who wants them. At present there are not nearly enough public clinics in the country to provide that service on a large scale. A national education program is also needed, using the mass media to the utmost to give it publicity, in order to make couples aware that family planning can be an advantage to themselves, their children and their society now that the population explosion has become a menace to life on this planet. Advertising at the local level should inform people where to find family planning clinics, provided of course, that there are any to find. Mobile family planning clinics should go to women as the Red Cross mobile blood transfusion units do.

A long-term education program is also needed. Family life courses should be taught in our schools to children of both sexes together by well-balanced teachers who have been given special training for this work. Courses similar to those given the teachers should be made available to the parents. It is the responsibility of both parents and schools not only to teach children the biological process involved in reproduction, but also to try to instil in them an understanding of the power and importance of sex and of the way the sexual drive can affect their future ability to enter into a mature, satisfactory and lasting relationship with a person of the opposite sex. They should also be taught to have a sense of responsibility toward others so that they do not regard the conception of a child lightly.

Sex and family life education are needed because many young women have a phoney idea that preparing for sexual intercourse by using contraceptives shows them to have a contrived, unspontaneous attitude toward love making. Others have no idea how to prevent themselves from becoming pregnant and are afraid to ask for information even if it is readily available. Some are quite simply feckless. Men should, of course, be helped to understand their responsibility toward the women who are their sexual partners because of the children which may be the result of their relationship.

For the last three years, as the RCSW recommended, the federal government has been putting up money for research into new and safer forms of contraception since the pill, the most reliable method, has serious side effects for some women. Money is also being provided to train personnel to work in birth control clinics, and grants have been given to the Family Planning Association, which has done such magnificent pioneer work in this field, and to Serena, an organization which teaches the rhythm method of avoiding conception.

Since the RCSW based its recommendations on the general principle that everyone is entitled to the rights and freedoms proclaimed in the Universal Declaration of Human Rights, the commissioners believed that our recommendations should attempt to establish a measure of equality that is now lacking for men as well as for women. That is why we recommend that the Criminal Code and provincial laws be amended so that a wife who is financially able to do so may be held to support her husband and children in the same way that a husband may now be held to support his wife and children.

I am from time to time surprised to meet women who do not agree with the RCSW's principle that if women are to have equal rights, privileges and opportunities with men they must accept equal responsibilities in every aspect of our society—in other words that they must regard themselves as adults and behave like adults. I think such women have been frightened by the implications of the principle because they find it much less demanding to allow someone else to earn the money, pay the bills and make major decisions for them. For generations women have been trained from infancy for a passive, dependent role in society, so it is not surprising that many of them enjoy that role and resent any suggestion that it should be changed. Such women, unwilling to become mature adults, do great disservice to their daughters by training them to follow the same path as their own. Since the home is the greatest influence in a child's life, mothers of that kind deprive their daughters of the motivation which may enable them to become more mature adults, with the result that they are likely to find themselves frustrated and resentful in middle age.

Since women are so often dependent, lacking in self-confidence and suffering from a feeling of inferiority, the commissioners believed that for a brief interim period they will need special treatment, encouragement, counselling and training to enable them to realize their potential. This point, one of the four specific principles of the RCSW, has been misunderstood and misinterpreted. None of the commissioners wanted women to be promoted to management jobs, put on boards or elected to positions in government for any reason other than for merit. The cause of women's rights would be put back a long way if women of second-rate intelligence, ability and character were asked to do jobs requiring first-rate qualifications; their failures would reflect back on all women.

What we did think necessary was that women be helped to overcome the conditioning due to traditions, myths and attitudes handed down from prehistoric days when physical strength was the main source of power and prestige. Western women have come a long way since they were chattels but many of them still have doubts about their own ability. It is a matter of simple justice that women, for so long passed over in favour of men, should be given the help they need to find their own individual place in our society. Consequently efforts should be made by governments, business and financial organizations to encourage women to take training courses and to give them the promotions they deserve instead of invariably giving the promotions to men. Until a substantial number of women are trained and given a chance to show what they can do in junior and middle management, there will continue to be only a few women in senior management.

We felt that political parties should feel an obligation to encourage more women to enter politics in an active, rather than a supportive, role. They should make a point of nominating women in constituencies where they would have some chance of winning, instead of leaving them to fight a battle doomed to be lost, in constituencies where the party has little or no chance of success.

Public Reaction

The RCSW had a valuable educational effect even before its report was completed.

When Prime Minister Pearson announced that the government was setting up a Royal Commission on the Status of Women in Canada, the leading editorial in the *Ottawa Journal* of February 4th, 1967, ran in part as follows:

> The reaction of Canadian men to news that a royal commission on women's rights has been appointed is what one would expect of a tough, hard-working, straight-talking male: fear. Everyone knows what commissions are like at their worst. Everyone knows what women are like at their worst. Put the two of them together—well we could end up with the longest established permanent royal commission in history. Somebody once said that individually, women are something, but together they're something else. . . .

> What makes these girls think any Canadian man in his right mind would sit on such a commission? . . .

> By all means let the girls gather facts and opinions about women's rights in Canada and see how they can be strengthened where they need it. Bosh! But we suggest to them, for their own good, of course, that they do it in the same way that they have advanced their cause in recent years—quietly, sneakily and with such charming effectiveness as to make men wonder why they feel they need a royal commission. . . .

It all boils down to this, really. Women may make advances on men if they want to, but let 'em do it in their own way, and one at a time.

During the first six weeks of the hearings it was disheartening to read editorials, columns and "letters to the editor," written by people who either could not have attended the hearings, or if they did, had failed to see or hear. The following letter to a columnist, Elizabeth Thompson, in the *Globe and Mail,* is typical of some early reactions to the hearings:

I had some good laughs reading the accounts of the more outspoken submissions. I felt the representations for the poor people and the Indians had good points but as the hearings dragged across the country I have reached the point where I am ashamed of women suffragettes for holding us all up to ridicule as they are doing with their petty grievances. I have never seen a single woman stand up and make a plea for the cause that did not look absolutely idiotic and the only ones who have a shred of dignity are the really poor ones who have a real axe to grind. Not the well-fed stunning-looking types who only come off as whiners.

An editorial in the *Vancouver Sun* showed the same blindness:

Hearings of the Royal Commission are not off to a promising start. We cannot look forward to the sort of self-destruction evident at the opening of the hearings in Victoria. . . Probably the make-up of the Commission and the nature of its terms of reference doom it to be a wailing wall for every scatterbrain, malcontent and frustrated pope in skirts.

To our amusement, the day after that editorial appeared there seems to have been considerable consternation in the *Sun* office when it was discovered that the daughter of the publisher, Stuart Keate, was presenting us with a brief. The telephone kept ringing and *Sun* reporters kept asking when the brief would be heard. That evening there were more male reporters than usual at the press table, when Stuart Keate and his wife came to hear their young, intelligent, very "mod" daughter make a ringing plea to have abortion taken out of the Criminal Code. She was given good coverage in the *Sun* the next day.

The public hearings had a tremendous impact, thanks to the wide coverage they received from the communications media. Hard-working Rosemary Speirs of the Canadian Press, who travelled with us from Victoria to St. John's, was determined to get the Commission off the women's pages and onto the front pages, and frequently she succeeded.

As a rule local newspapers sent women staff reporters, and most of them, even those who were young and inexperienced, did a very good job, presumably because their hearts were in their work. I found it an interesting indication of attitudes toward women that in the entire country a mere handful of male reporters were assigned to cover the hearings. Even in Ottawa, where most of the big national organizations presented their briefs, only one or two male reporters or columnists deigned to attend our hearings.

The CBC was more enlightened. Ed Reid, a sensitive and intelligent broadcaster and producer, travelled with us the whole way, accompanied by a camera crew. The young men on the crew went through an interesting metamorphosis: At the beginning they were disgusted with their assignment to cover the Commission; they thought it would be dull, dreary work and they had no sympathy with our aims. But after a couple of weeks of listening to the hearings and to Ed Reid's interviews with some of the women who appeared before us, they began to find new understanding of the problems of women. They were surprised to find that the commissioners were not fanatical battle-axes as they had feared, but hard-working, sensible people making an immense effort to improve Canadian society by bringing justice to half its population. They were so stimulated by what they had heard that they asked permission to present us with a confidential brief. We gave them a buffet supper in our hotel sitting room in Saskatoon the night before they left us. They presented the brief and we discussed it with them as friends, comfortably, in a relaxed way. It was a very outspoken, personal brief that gave us a useful slant on the point of view of intelligent young men.

Gradually a change began to take place in the attitudes of both the public and the press, as a result of the public hearings and the wide coverage given to them by the mass media. The briefs by large organizations pointed out clearly the areas of discrimination and the hardships experienced by many women because they were women. There was strong emotional appeal in some of the submissions by Indian women, by sole-support mothers and elderly widows, most of them poor. As time went on the majority of responsible editorial writers ceased to jeer at the Commission, and began to take it seriously.

As a result, the report was treated thoughtfully by the responsible press, by the spokesmen of the three major parties in the House of Commons, and by men and women on both sides of the Senate. As was to be expected, there was considerable criticism of some of the recommendations, such as the ones on abortion, but it was serious criticism, devoid of the silly coyness with which the Commission had, at first, been greeted by many otherwise intelligent people.

During the public hearings in Ottawa, the leading editorial in the *Ottawa Journal* of October 3rd, 1968, ran in part as follows:

> Though the Royal Commission has two of its seven members who are mere males, it is a women's show. All its visible supporting staff appear to be women (what is wrong with male secretaries?). But it seems to be going about its work so intelligently that the commission itself may prove to be one of the strongest arguments that there is nothing to hold back any woman from taking her full place in society. . . .
>
> A dozen Royal Commissions probably wouldn't be enough to illuminate all the dark corners of male prejudice. There is something ingrained in our culture that has made the struggle of women for full equality under the law slow and unfinished business. Men, it seems like it that way. . . .
>
> This commission as the French say, is *formidable*.

The day after the Report was tabled in the House of Commons, the leading editorial in the *Ottawa Journal* of December 8th, 1970, ran in part as follows:

> There is much to approve in the content, in the calm, deliberate tone and lucid exposition of facts and opinion in the Report of the Royal Commission on the Status of Women. The report is a masterpiece of condensation, so crammed with information and so sweeping in scope that the length of time required to bring it forth is now almost understandable. Moreover, women's lib and all, it has not been overtaken by events: the report is almost agonizingly relevant.
>
> The commission's work should be approached with some humility, especially by males. The report is too complex to be either uncritically praised or damned. Its recommendations, after all,

number 167, putting Heinz in its place.It would be a weak-kneed, bland Royal Commission if some of those recommendations did not cause profound disagreement. This report is so far from being bland that four of the seven commissioners found reasons to record their dissent from some majority recommendations.

The systematic and thorough searching-out of inequities experienced by women in the work force, in education, under the law and, yes, in the family, is the most useful part of the commission's work. The documentation of discrimination is irrefutable, whether deliberate or an unthinking perpetuation of male prejudices in the line of Lord Chesterfield's comment: "Women are to be talked to as below men, and above children." The commission has supplied enough material for amendments to legislation to keep MPs and MLAs busy thinking about women for a dozen sessions.

Some editorial writers were surprised to find the Commission's report was moderate, while others regarded it as a bomb.

On Tuesday, December 8th, 1970, the leading editorial of the *Montreal Star* ran in part as follows:

A moderate plea for women's rights

The most significant thing about the report of the Royal Commission on the Status of Women is the extent to which social attitudes in Canada have changed during the three-and-a-half years in which the report was in preparation. The appointment of the royal commission by the Pearson government in 1967 was regarded by many commentators as a form of mild eccentricity whose chief value would be as a harmless outlet for the energies of the handful of club-women who really cared about such things. Now, only a few years later, women's liberation is one of the hot issues of the day, spurred on by a whole new army of feminists ranging from the moderate to the revolutionary.

It would seem, then, that at least in the general thrust of their recommendations, Mrs. John Bird and her fellow commissioners are putting forward an idea whose time has come. The idea is simply that no Canadian should be denied self-fulfilment by the biological fact of being a woman or by the prejudice and barriers which have been built up in our society over the years.

The royal commission attacks these barriers with a mass of detailed recommendations which deal with almost every aspect of social and economic policy which affects the way women live in Canada today. Not all of them will be accepted, at least immediately. . . .

Above all, the evidence of inequity and discrimination uncovered in the report's 418 pages leaves no doubt that the inferior status of women constitutes a serious social problem which must be tackled by governments at all levels.

On February 8th, 1970, a greatly respected syndicated columnist of the *Toronto Star,* Anthony Westell, wrote:

At 2.11 p.m. in the House of Commons Monday, the Prime Minister rose, bowed politely to the Speaker, and tabled a bomb, already primed and ticking.

The bomb is called the Report of the Royal Commission on the Status of Women in Canada, and it is packed with more explosive potential than any device manufactured by terrorists.

As a call to revolution, hopefully a quiet one, it is more persuasive than any FLQ manifesto.

And as a political blockbuster, it is more powerful than that famous report of the controversial commission on bilingualism and biculturalism.

This 488-page book, in its discreet green, white and blue cover, demands radical change not just in Quebec, but in every community across Canada. It is concerned not merely with relations between French and English, but between man and woman.

The history of the problem it describes and seeks to solve is not 100 years of Confederation but the story of mankind.

First attention focuses naturally on the commission's 167 proposals for practical action, from reform of the law to provide abortion on demand to rewriting of schoolbooks which teach sexual discrimination to our children.

But controversial as some of these proposals may seem now, they will quickly be accepted in substance, if not in every detail. They are reasonable answers to real problems which can no longer be ignored, and governments and public opinion are ready for reform.

Implementation

I was interviewed dozens of times during the years that the Commission was at work and, invariably, I was asked the same question: "Do you think the report will be pigeonholed and forgotten like so many others?" Even Prince Philip asked me that during a reception at Government House when the Queen came to Ottawa during Centennial Year.

Always I replied, "No. This report won't be pigeonholed."

And I was right about that.

(Incidentally, Prince Philip was concerned about what is happening to women with higher education. He said, "What are you going to do about the brilliant scholar who marries and has children? Usually her Ph.D. goes down the drain with the baby's bath-water.")

Today, in Canada, men make the laws and administer government departments. It is, therefore, a significant and hopeful sign of a change in the attitudes of some men that many of the Commission's recommendations have been implemented by both the federal government and Parliament.

The recommendations directed specifically at the federal Public Service have been carried out or are in the process of being implemented. John Carson, Chairman of the Public Service Commission, and Commissioner Irene Johnson have put their minds to changing conditions and attitudes, and are making a real effort to upgrade women professionally when they work for the government. Since the federal government is the largest employer of women in the country, its example should help not only its own female employees but those working for provincial and municipal governments and those employed in the private sector of our economy.

303

The Public Service has opened an Equal Employment Opportunities Office to recruit and train women. It has prepared a brochure about the many interesting careers open to women in the hope that provincial departments of education will distribute copies to guidance counsellors in schools and universities. Sex typing in recruitment literature has been done away with. A guidance counsellor, a woman experienced in personnel work, has been hired by the Public Service to help applicants to find jobs other than the traditional supportive occupations. Training courses for secretaries have been set up to enable them to develop their potential and to prepare them to move into management. A special effort has been made to include women in the prestigious Career Assignments Programme in order to train them for top management positions.

It is going to take time for women to make any sizable dent in the hitherto cast-iron power structure of the Public Service because a substantial number of them will have to be given training and experience in introductory and middle management before they will be qualified for top management jobs. Some progress has been made: During an eleven-month period in 1972, the number of women between the ages of thirty and forty earning between $14,000 and $20,000 a year increased from 120 to 240. However, since there were 1,400 men in the same age and salary bracket, women still have a long way to go.

As we recommended, Prime Minister Trudeau has issued a directive to government departments to make a special effort to give women a fair break. In some departments this order is being carried out by committees set up for the purpose. In others little is being done. Encouraging and promoting women still depends to a great extent on the attitudes of many men in senior positions, who still harbour unsubstantiated beliefs that all women are "until" workers, more prone to illness and absenteeism than men, harder to work for, and given to tears when they can't get their own way. Statistics about the record of career women in management refute these theories but they still linger on.

Amendments to the Fair Wages and Hours of Labour Regulations and Fair Wages Policy Order add age, sex and marital status to the prohibited reasons for discrimination in hiring by a contractor working on a federal government contract.

A long-awaited and often promised amendment to the Canada Labour Code (Fair Employment Practices) has not yet been introduced to Parliament by the Minister of Labour. The Commission recommended that sex and marital status be prohibited as reasons for discrimination in employment and union membership in those areas that fall under federal jurisdiction. This is a very important amendment which could, if well enforced, go much farther than the present equal pay legislation toward putting an end to the present discrimination against many working women.

As we recommended, recent amendments to the Adult Occupational Training Act enable a person to qualify for training allowances after being out of school for one year. Between July and December 1972, the number of women entering courses under the new eligibility rules increased by 35 per cent over the same period in 1971.

The RCSW's principle that society has a responsibility for women because of pregnancy and childbirth, and that special treatment related to maternity will always be necessary, has been accepted by the men in Parliament. Women working in industries under federal jurisdiction such as transport, banks and communications, have been granted seventeen weeks maternity leave, and it is now illegal for them to be fired because of pregnancy. All but two provinces have passed somewhat similar legislation. An amendment to the Unemployment Insurance Act now makes it possible for women in every part of Canada to use their benefits for fifteen weeks, after an initial waiting period of two weeks, during maternity leave.

The need of low-income women for help with their children was recognized by the federal government when it introduced its Family Income Security Plan, a bill to provide taxable family allowances to the mother amounting to an average of $20 a month for each child.

As the RCSW recommended, in order to help poor women, the income tax for people in the lower income brackets has been substantially lowered, the Old Age Security benefit has been increased and adjusted to the cost of living index, and the Guaranteed Old Age Security Supplement has been increased. As we recommended, serious thought and study is being given to the feasibility of providing a guaranteed annual income for all Canadians who have fallen below the poverty level: if this can be worked out it should go a long way toward restoring the dignity and ambition of many people on public assistance as well as people who work hard all their lives and still remain poor. We recommended that as a second step (the first step has already been taken by giving old people a guaranteed annual income), a guaranteed annual income should be given to sole-support parents.

Women can now serve on juries in every province in Canada although in some they can still plead off on the grounds that they are women, a privilege the commissioners found out of line with the principle that women must accept the responsibilities as well as the rights and privileges of equality. Women should, of course, be able to be excused from jury duty, as men are, if business or family responsibilities make it impossible for them to serve.

Prime Minister Trudeau kept the promise, made in a speech in Toronto the night before his surprise wedding, to encourage women to run for Parliament and to put a large number of women on government boards and committees. In the 1972 election, three women, Monique Bégin, Albanie Morin and Jeanne Sauvé, were given strong Cabinet support in their successful efforts to win the nominations and to be elected in Liberal ridings in Quebec. In that election, Quebec was the only province where the Liberals had a hope of providing any candidate with a safe seat. Fortunately for the party, all three women are intelligent, able and hard-working and need only experience to be able to hold their own with any male politician. Sauvé was made a Cabinet minister, a token appointment perhaps, but one which also puts an intelligent, able woman in a position where she can prove her worth.

Women in the Opposition parties do not seem to have been given much support. The NDP's indefatigable, intelligent Grace McInnes, for many years the only woman in the Commons, did not need extra help, while brainy, energetic Flora MacDonald won Kingston and the Islands for the Conservatives because she knew more about the great game of politics than most men in the country.

After the election, Prime Minister Trudeau asked Senator Muriel Fergusson to become the first woman Speaker of the Senate. Senator Fergusson is one of the old guard who has fought for the rights of women for many long years. She has been one of the most intelligent and hard-working of senators, never forgetting the needs of women, as successful career women frequently do, in order to be accepted as "one of the boys."

Five judges, three of them to Superior Courts, and two to County Courts, have been appointed since the report was published. Sylvia Ostry, a brilliant economist, has been made head of Statistics Canada, with the rank of deputy minister since she is responsible for the administration of a department with over 4,000 employees. Beryl Plumptre, an economist, the first president of the Consumers Association of Canada and the dynamo behind the organization in its early days, has been made Chairman of the Prices Review Board—as difficult a job as can possibly be imagined. Anne Carver has become the first woman to sit on the Canadian Transport Commission. And Jean Edmonds has been appointed Assistant Deputy Minister of the Department of Manpower and Immigration.

Recently two breakthrough appointments were made when Pauline McGibbon was named Lieutenant-Governor of Ontario to succeed W. Ross Macdonald, and when Dorothea Crittenden was made Deputy Minister of the Department of Community and Social Services—the first woman to hold such an office.

Federal money (in 1972 about $8-million) and, in some provinces, provincial money has been found for day-care centres, but nothing resembling the network of centres recommended by the Commission has been put into operation. There are not yet nearly enough centres of different kinds for the children of working mothers, let alone for the children of mothers who decide to stay at home while their children are young. We recommended that the cost of keeping a child in a day-care centre be paid for on a sliding scale based on family income, as is now being done in many places. The new $20-a-month taxable family allowance for each child should help many working women to pay for day care and enable more stay-at-home mothers to send their children to day-care centres for at least part of the time—provided, of course, that centres are available. There are not enough centres to meet the demand in any western country, including enlightened Sweden, or for that matter the Soviet Union and Hungary, but Canada lags *far* behind most of them.

In May 1973, the federal government set up an Advisory Council on the Status of Women that reports to the Minister of Labour, the Cabinet minister who, at the time I am writing, is responsible for seeing that the Commission's recommendations are implemented. That is not what the RCSW recommended. We recommended specifically that a council with a small secretariat of highly qualified, innovative men and women should be established under the authority of an independent board of both women and men appointed by the federal government. It would require initial funds adequate for at least a five-year period and would make an annual report through a minister. Our recommendation read, in part:

> Specifically [the Council] would inform and advise governments and the private sector. It would not confine itself solely to research but would be concerned with action. It would continually assess changing public attitudes toward the status of women and would be concerned with identifying new needs and formulating new proposals. It would be empowered to set up pilot projects. It would

maintain a permanent liaison with the numerous voluntary organizations concerned with the status of women.

I have some misgivings about the ability of the Advisory Council on the Status of Women, as now constituted, to accomplish very much. It is large—twenty-six women and two men—which may limit discussion and make it difficult to reach decisions. Inevitably it will lack the independence the RCSW wanted for the sort of council it proposed, since it is an arm of the government that will report to a Cabinet minister instead of to Parliament *through* a Cabinet minister. There is a consequent danger that it will be less critical of the government in power, whether Liberal, Conservative or NDP, than it should be to get the action needed to help women at this time and in the future. However, I have some hope for its ultimate usefulness. It has a strong executive; some of its members are intelligent people with varied experience; and the Chairman, Dr. Katherine Cooke, is a respected public servant, a sociologist with understanding of the problems of women.

The Minister of Labour has undertaken to review the Council in a couple of years' time, in which case, if it proves to be ineffective, there is still hope the Commission's recommendation will be reconsidered. In the meantime, if the Advisory Council is given an adequate budget, it may be able to help change some of the attitudes which act as invisible barriers against the progress of women. It has begun well by advising the government to implement a number of important recommendations about which nothing has yet been done.

They are demanding the change, recommended by the RCSW, that the Canada Pension Plan allow the widower of a female contributor to receive the same benefits on the same terms as the widow and children of a male contributor. Women pay exactly the same premiums as men but when they die their husbands and children do not receive benefits automatically, the way the wives and children of male contributors do, unless they have been wholly or largely supported by the wife or mother. This is an obvious injustice against men and relegates women to a second-class position.

Nothing has yet been done to allow a wife who has contributed her share by working in the home to have a share of a husband's Canada Pension Plan benefits if the marriage has been broken by separation or divorce. Nor has there been any mention of allowing married women working in the home to make a voluntary contribution to the Canada Pension Plan.

These are all matters requiring agreement between the provinces and the federal government and at present other matters have a higher priority on their agenda. The Advisory Council and women's action groups should go on demanding that attention be given to further changes in the Canada Pension Plan since in old age so many women are poor, having outlived their husbands and having been able to put little aside even if they have worked, because of being employed in badly paid jobs.

The government has declined to change the Indian Act, as the RCSW recommended, to allow an Indian woman to retain her Indian status upon marriage to a non-Indian and to transmit that status to her children.

In 1973, a test case was taken to the Supreme Court of Canada on behalf of an Indian woman, Jeannette Lavell, who had lost her Indian status because she had married a non-Indian, to see if this constituted a violation of the Bill of Rights. The precarious situation of women's rights in particular and human rights in general in Canada was revealed when the Court brought down a five-to-four judgment that the Indian Act, a Statute of Parliament, overruled the Canadian Bill of Rights. Dismaying as it certainly was, this decision should not have been a surprise. When in 1960 the Diefenbaker government brought in the Bill of Rights, many constitutional authorities insisted that it was not an adequate safeguard to fundamental rights and liberties because it can, at any time, be overruled by Parliament. Prime Minister Trudeau was aware of this and in 1968 made a considerable effort to have a Charter of Human Rights entrenched in the constitution, where it could only be abrogated by amendment to the constitution itself. He met with no success because the provinces and the federal government failed to reach agreement on a method of amending the constitution.

Until the Bill of Rights is an integral part of the constitution, the only way to provide for equal treatment for Indian women and men is for Parliament to amend the Indian Act. The minority Liberal government elected in 1972 has made it clear that it has no intention of changing the Indian Act as it now stands in regard to women, and it is doubtful that any other government would do anything about it in the foreseeable future. Canada's Indians, as a result of the long years when they were discriminated against and exploited, have now become vocal and aggressive. They are a worrisome political problem, and no government is likely to interfere with the status quo which reflects the wishes of the majority of Indian men and also of some Indian women who, like many women in other areas of our society, do not want to offend the dominant males or endanger their long-established submissive status.

The attitude of the Department of Indian Affairs was made pretty clear when it paid the expenses of Indian men—but not of Indian women—who wanted to attend the Supreme Court proceedings. A few women earned the money to come to Ottawa by selling beaded moccasins and other handicrafts. Many Canadians like myself regret the women's bitterness about this injustice but, at the same time, share it.

Whether Indians keep or lose their rights when they marry non-Indians is a separate question. What is important is that Indian men and women be treated in the same way under the law. It is the principle involved that makes the Indian Act as it now stands a serious threat to human rights in Canada.

There is an ironic coincidence about the constitutional situation leading to the Supreme Court's ruling which is so destructive to the rights of women. The Lavell case is, in fact, a reminder of that other historic judgment, made in 1928, when the same court decreed that Section 24 of the British North America Act, the written part of Canada's constitution, does not include female persons and therefore women are not eligible to sit in the Senate.

It was after this judgment that five embattled, undaunted women from Alberta appealed the case to the Imperial Privy Council, then the final court of appeal. In 1929 Lord Sankey announced that the Supreme Court's decision had been overruled. ". . . Their Lordships have come to the conclusion that the word persons includes members of the male and female sex, and that therefore . . . women are eligible to be summoned and become members of the Senate of Canada."

As a result of this decision, in 1930 Prime Minister Mackenzie King made Cairine Wilson the first woman senator and in 1935 Prime Minister R.B. Bennett summoned Iva Fallis to the Upper House. When the bill to make the Supreme Court of Canada, instead of the Imperial Privy Council, the final court of appeal was brought before the Senate in 1949, Senator Fallis, long of memory, refused to vote for it. She told me she would never trust the Supreme Court to uphold the rights of women and had more confidence in British justice. At the time I disagreed with her and we argued through a long lunch in the parliamentary restaurant. I still disagree (although she seems to have had the gift of prophecy) because I think it is essential for our national dignity and our maturing as a people that we should not have to go to Britain for our final legal decisions.

The RCSW thought that a federal human rights commission could do a great deal to help women. It is clear, however, that its ability to do that will depend upon the dedication and intellectual integrity of its directors and to the way they interpret its terms of reference. Laws are, of course, made by Parliament and legislatures, but a human rights commission should act not only as a watchdog but also as a goad to the conscience of the elected representatives of the people. It should also be responsible for making the public aware of the need for change.

The need for changes in provincial laws has been driven home by the recent Supreme Court decision in the case of Murdoch versus Murdoch. An Alberta rancher's wife, legally separated from her husband, sued him for a share of the property after having been granted $200 a month maintenance by a lower court. She based her claim on the contribution made by her own work during the twenty-eight years they had been married. When asked by the court what sort of work she had been doing, she replied, "Haying, raking, driving trucks, tractors and teams, quieting horses, taking cattle back and forth to the reserve, de-horning, vaccinating, handling—everything that was to be done." When asked if she had ever been alone on the ranch, she said she had been alone for five months every year while her husband was away working for the Forestry Service. In spite of these very active contributions, however, the court ruled against Mrs. Murdoch.

Obviously the Alberta law in regard to married women's property, as well as similar laws in the Common Law Provinces, should be changed, as the RCSW recommended, to conform with the Quebec Act Respecting Matrimonial Regimes which came into force in 1970. This system of "partnership of acquests" respects the equality, autonomy and independence of both the husband and the wife during marriage by establishing separation of property between them. Each administers his own assets and is responsible for his own debts. However, at the dissolution of the marriage by death, divorce or judicially pronounced separation each participates in the gains achieved by the other during marriage. Each is therefore given a claim to one half of the other's acquests, that is to say to all the property acquired after marriage otherwise than by gift, will or legal succession. This new regime in Quebec accepts the idea that marriage is an equal partnership, assuring to each partner an equal share in the property derived from their joint efforts and savings during marriage.

The case of Murdoch versus Murdoch should make women in all the provinces and territories, other than Quebec, aware of the way the law discriminates against them when they marry. Under the system of separate property now in force in nine of the ten provinces, a husband's earnings and savings are his exclusive property. When the marriage ends by death, his widow has no automatic legal right to share in the assets he may have accumulated. Even the belongings in the home are considered to be the property of the husband. If the marriage ends by divorce or judicial separation, the wife is entitled only to maintenance.

The Supreme Court's judgment should now make even the most complacent housewife aware that her pew is not as comfortable as she imagined when she stayed in the home and did not work for pay in order to build up assets exclusively her own. I am told that it has come as a shock to many women that all their hard work as wife, housekeeper and mother is held in such low esteem that under law it has no cash value.

Women's action groups should not give provincial governments a minute's peace until the married women's property laws are changed in the Common Law provinces. Until that is done, women bent on matrimony should insist upon having a marriage contract giving them a "partnership of acquests" before they go to the altar or to the City Hall. Parents and teachers of family life courses should make it quite clear to girls why they ought to have a marriage contract.

No doubt many women will not hold out for a contract for fear of offending the men they hope to marry or because of the phoney romantic concept of marriage that prevails in our society today in spite of the growing incidence of divorce and marriage breakdown. I can sympathize with that attitude because I had it myself. J.B. insisted on our having an ante-nuptial contract because he had lived on the island of Guernsey where it is customary to have contracts to protect the financial position of the wife. I felt I was being materialistic, somehow unloving and showing lack of confidence in him when he finally persuaded me to sign it.

No doubt many men will object to a marriage contract because a "partnership of acquests" accepts a principle that denies the concept of the dependence of the wife on the husband, dependence so destructive to the ego of the wife and so inflating to the ego of the husband.

I find it a significant social phenomenon that Quebec, the province that lagged so long behind the others before giving women the vote and married women the right to enter into contract, has now brought in new, enlightened legislation into Canada in regard to married women's property. There are now in Quebec three matrimonial regimes to choose from: community of property, separate as to property, and "partnership of acquests." At the public hearings of the RCSW Quebec women showed themselves so determined to make up for past indignities that I think many knowledgeable couples will opt for the "partnership of acquests."

Since the publication of the report of the RCSW the private sector of our society as well as governments has become more sensitive to changing public opinion in a rapidly changing society. Corporations and unions have begun to give the rights of women more attention than in the past. But progress is deplorably slow and the advancement of a few token women has not made a dent in the depressing statistics about the proportion of women in management.

Considerable changes are taking place in colleges and universities, where several courses in the history of women have been introduced into the curricula. They are well attended by women, but by few men, which is a pity since the commissioners considered it essential that men, who hold the power in our society, should try to understand what has happened to women and why. A number of universities are now making it possible for people to spread their work for a B.A. over a period. Increasingly, classes are being arranged at hours convenient for married women. At some universities, day-care centres for the children of students have been provided. As a result, every year more older women are continuing their education on a part-time basis. Unfortunately, the federal government has not yet made part-time students eligible to receive loans, as we recommended.

An *ad hoc* committee of the Canadian Association of Universities and Colleges is keeping after our schools of higher learning to implement the RCSW's recommendations in regard to equal pay and promotions in faculties.

In order to give women a positive influence on our society, women's organizations should bring pressure to bear on provincial and municipal governments as well as on Ottawa. And in provincial and municipal elections they should support candidates who are concerned about the rights of women.

There are encouraging signs that an increasing number of women are becoming aware of the power of the vote, and are willing to cross party lines to cast their ballots for candidates who stand for the things women want and need. I feel it is essential that we elect to public office women and men who show a sympathetic awareness of what has happened to women over the centuries, who are willing to try to stop wasting the potential of women and to work toward giving them equal rights and opportunities.

I see nothing to be gained by women running as independent "women's candidates," as two did unsuccessfully in Toronto during the 1972 election. In doing so they split a potential women's vote and so help to elect candidates who may be unsympathetic to women. They are also helping to take women out of the power structure instead of concentrating on getting as many competent, qualified women as possible into the established parties at a policy-making level and doing everything possible to see that more women are nominated in constituencies where they have a chance of being elected.

In my opinion, the goal of women should be to break down, not to build up, the artificial division between women and men in politics as well as in every other aspect of our society. First-class human beings are needed to make our laws and to see they are carried out, not just women's candidates or men's candidates.

Recently, while I was in Sweden, I asked Alva Myrdal, a cabinet minister and long-time feminist, and several women members of Parliament what they thought about the idea of women running as independents or members of a "women's party." They said that years ago they had considered such an idea and rejected it as being retrograde and impractical. They pointed out that in order to have any impact at all, it is essential for an M.P. to have a party organization behind her and to be able to raise her voice in caucus and be accepted as an equal by the male majority. The validity of that decision is proved by the fact that in 1973 there was a ratio of one women to seven men in the unicameral Parliament of Sweden, while in the same year the radio in the Canadian House of Commons was one woman to fifty-two men.

For a married woman, experience in municipal and provincial government can be a stepping-stone for federal politics. While her children are young it is often easier for her to start her political career close to home and later aim for the House of Commons when her children are older. In any case, in the fields of labour and civil rights, the provinces are of greater importance than the federal government and they reign supreme in education which is why a substantial number of the RCSW's recommendations were aimed at them.

Changes in education can do a great deal to change the status of women in a surprisingly short time. For example, provincial departments of education should get rid of text books that sex-type children and adults, and should insist that guidance counsellors be trained to understand the modern life cycle of women.

Obviously big city governments are becoming more and more powerful and co-operation with the federal government and the provinces is needed in order to provide day-care centres. School boards can, as the RCSW recommended, help women teachers to get the promotions they deserve; provide family life courses from kindergarten on through high school; provide school lunches; and make school facilities available for the care, after school, of children whose parents are still at work. Women can be effectively involved in all these areas.

Although a great deal of progress has been made, women still have a long way to go. But they are on their way. The Royal Commission's report has not been shelved. Women will not *allow* it to be, of that I am certain. It is still being read and studied by new readers. The English report has run through three printings. A fourth printing has now been made and copies are available after a wait of several months. The French translation has had three printings and copies are still available.

By this time—spring of 1974—three years and three months after the report of the RCSW was tabled in the House of Commons, the federal government has implemented a third of the 122 recommendations which fall under its jurisdiction. Another third have been partly implemented. Nothing has been done about the rest. Understandably, the easiest and least controversial were the first to be carried out.

It is evident that the RCSW's work was worth the time, money and effort put into it: not only has it led already to changes in a number of laws and practices, but it has fostered a growth of awareness that is beginning to change attitudes. Its impact has justified the seemingly unending hours of reading and writing of memoranda, the long discussions during meetings, and the sneers and jeers which the commissioners had to endure.

I am optimistic about the future of the Commission's recommendations because I am convinced that the timing of the report was right. Its thrust will not lose momentum. The women's liberation movement, expressed by a great variety of groups with different aims and interests, has given new consciousness to an increasing number of women in their twenties and thirties. For years, older women in established organizations have been patient feminists asking for equal pay, fair taxation and representation by qualified women at the policy-making level in business, government and political parties. They accomplished a great deal and we owe them much. But rapid changes in our society have now turned many young women into impatient feminists, aware of other, equally important, immediate needs such as family planning, abortion, day-care centres, equal conditions for part-time and full-time employment, and improved social services. All of these have been pointed out in the report.

As a result, it is not only a blue-print for governmental action but also for the women's action committees that have sprung up in many parts of Canada. Hardly a day goes by without some mention of the RCSW in media accounts of meetings concerned with some aspect of the rights of women. Today, the long-established organizations and the new organizations are on the same beam and could gain much by close co-operation; women of all ages must work together to change attitudes as old as history.

As time goes on I have become increasingly happy about the report because of the obvious impact it is having on our society. It has turned out to be an effective instrument for social change. It is a report not only on the status of women but also on the status of men. It shows that we live in a male-dominated society in which all laws governing our lives are made by men; that, compared with women, men are rich, independent, and in control both in government and in business. It also shows, however, that some laws which reflect old-fashioned attitudes about the ability and responsibility of women, actually discriminate against men, and we recommended that these be changed.

It seems to me now, with hindsight, that we did not sufficiently emphasize the way in which our recommendations can help men, as well as women, to have less frustrated, fuller lives, and so improve the quality of our society.

Many men feel that their dominant position is being threatened by the principle that women should be given equal opportunities as well as responsibilities. And the men are right about that. If jobs, pay and promotions are based on the worth of the individual, regardless of sex, a great many women will participate in the management of business and government. This may lead to hardship for some men but I am convinced that in the final analysis it will be better for all concerned because then the abilities of *everyone* in the community can be utilized. If laws are changed to give women equal property rights in marriage, a husband will no longer be as likely to act as dictator in the home, but he will also be less likely to have a resentful, nagging wife or a broken marriage.

I am convinced that men will benefit greatly if they are no longer forced by tradition into the role of sole breadwinner, as two-thirds of married men are now. I think they will have happier, more rewarding lives and will live longer if they are not so exposed to the pressures of the competitive work world or so driven by the necessity to earn money to provide for their families. The number of women in the labour force has risen astronomically in the last decade, largely because two pay has risen astronomically in the last decade, largely because two pay cheques are now needed in many families, to keep pace with the soaring cost of living and rising aspirations. For the sake of men as well as women, this trend should be encouraged.

The increase in the divorce rate and in the number of deserted wives and husbands convinces me that we must teach young people to have a new concept of marriage. Today marriage for many women and men is a straitjacket that binds them until they learn to hate each other. Some married men feel that they have been sentenced to a lifetime of hard labour outside of the home. And some married women feel the same about work inside the home.

To change this destructive pattern of unhappiness we must try to make boys and girls understand that marriage can be an enriching, sustaining experience if it is a partnership between equals who share in running the home, bringing up the children, earning the family income, and taking part in public life. My husband and I have had that kind of marriage, and I know that it can bring lasting happiness.

It is, I believe, important that boys be trained by parents and teachers to understand what it means to be a father. Young couples should be prepared for marriage by being made aware that their children will have a better chance of growing up to be integrated, secure and loving human beings if they receive a father's interest, respect and love as well as a mother's. My own father taught me the value of the father as a cherishing adult by the way he treated me when I was a child and an adolescent.

I believe that parents, teachers and schools must make a great effort to enable boys to understand that male domination in the home or at work is wrong, since it denies women the right to think and act as adults.

It is, of course, equally important for girls to be made to realize that passivity and dependency are destructive to their being. They must be made to believe in themselves, to have confidence in themselves. They must be made to feel that they are glad to be women. Like the unnamed woman (who is all of us) in Margaret Atwood's *Surfacing,* each must search for her own identity. Each must find and follow her own path.

We all need courage for the journey. It is a long, slow passage that is often discouraging—and sometimes frightening. There are many invisible barriers, forged by tradition and deeply ingrained attitudes, that stand in our way. For some women poverty is a seemingly insurmountable road-block—and yet many manage to climb over it. For others the restricting moulds into which they have been cast by parents or husbands are obstacles—yet many succeed in breaking out of those moulds. Society still offers most women little but dependency and a supportive role, a sort of perpetual childhood—yet many women grow into mature adults who have developed their potential to the full.

I deplore what has happened to women and is still happening to them because of customs, attitudes and laws which go back into the beginnings of history. But I am not despondent about the future because I know what women can do when they are given the opportunity and have the courage to seize it. I have been inspired by this knowledge and by my belief that women are now beginning to come into their own.

Personally I have been extraordinarily fortunate because of the love and sense of worth my parents gave me, and because of the way my husband has always encouraged me to grow. But I was born with a silver spoon in my mouth and it almost choked me. It is in the hope of helping other women to find themselves that I have written these reminiscences of my slow growth from a pampered, conceited girl to a woman with some self-knowledge, whose eyes and heart have been turned outward by experience toward other people.

My life has been interesting and happy. I have had a lot of fun and I have been fortunate in that I have received and given much love and friendship. Yet it took me a long time to find myself, to be able to surface for a time and know what I should do at each stage of my life. Today I am still searching, because the search never ends.